Goethe's Social Philosophy

UNC | COLLEGE OF ARTS AND SCIENCES
Germanic and Slavic Languages and Literatures

From 1949 to 2004, UNC Press and the UNC Department of Germanic & Slavic Languages and Literatures published the UNC Studies in the Germanic Languages and Literatures series. Monographs, anthologies, and critical editions in the series covered an array of topics including medieval and modern literature, theater, linguistics, philology, onomastics, and the history of ideas. Through the generous support of the National Endowment for the Humanities and the Andrew W. Mellon Foundation, books in the series have been reissued in new paperback and open access digital editions. For a complete list of books visit www.uncpress.org.

Goethe's Social Philosophy
As Revealed in *Campagne in Frankreich* and *Belagerung von Mainz*

ALFRED G. STEER JR.

UNC Studies in the Germanic Languages and Literatures
Number 15

Copyright © 1955

This work is licensed under a Creative Commons CC BY-NC-ND license. To view a copy of the license, visit http://creativecommons.org/licenses.

Suggested citation: Steer Jr., Alfred G. *Goethe's Social Philosophy: As Revealed in Campagne in Frankreich and Belagerung von Mainz*. Chapel Hill: University of North Carolina Press, 1955. DOI: https://doi.org/10.5149/9781469658445_Steer

Library of Congress Cataloging-in-Publication Data
Names: Steer Jr., Alfred G.
Title: Goethe's social philosophy : As revealed in Campagne in Frankreich and Belagerung von Mainz / by Alfred G. Steer Jr.
Other titles: University of North Carolina Studies in the Germanic Languages and Literatures ; no. 15.
Description: Chapel Hill : University of North Carolina Press, [1955] Series: University of North Carolina Studies in the Germanic Languages and Literatures. | Includes bibliographical references.
Identifiers: LCCN 55062599 | ISBN 978-0-8078-8015-9 (pbk: alk. paper) | ISBN 978-1-4696-5844-5 (ebook)
Subjects: Goethe, Johann Wolfgang von, 1749-1832. | Campagne in Frankreich. | Goethe, Johann Wolfgang von, 1749-1832. | Belagerung von Mainz.
Classification: LCC PD25 .N6 NO. 15 | DCC 928/ .3

TO JEAN
AND OUR FAMILY

TABLE OF CONTENTS

	PAGE
Preface	xi

Plates I, II, III

A. Introduction 1
    I. Problems of Interpretation Posed by *Campagne-Belagerung* 1
    II. The Family Concept an Outgrowth of Goethe's Scientific Studies 9

B. *Campagne in Frankreich* 21
    I. The Writing of *Campagne-Belagerung;* 1792-93; 1819-20; 1821-22 21
    II. Goethe's Journey to Overtake the Army 30
    III. The Roman Monument at Igel 42
    IV. Invasion 58
        a) Inefficiency of Command 58
        b) Émigrés 66
        c) French "Volk" 69
    V. Valmy 72
    VI. Retreat 76
        a) Inefficiency of Command 76
        b) Émigrés 80
        c) French "Volk" 83
    VII. Interludes at Luxembourg-Trier-Coblenz 88
        a) Goethe's Personal Role 88
        b) Families in Trier and Coblenz 90
    VIII. *Zwischenrede* 95
    IX. Pempelfort 103
    X. Duisburg. "Schreckbild Plessing" 113
    XI. Münster. Princess Gallitzin 119
    XII. The Winter in Weimar 125

TABLE OF CONTENTS

	PAGE
C. *Belagerung von Mainz*	146
I. Military Operations	146
a) Inefficiency of Command	147
b) Anti-War Comment	152
c) *Lücke*	152
II. The Conquered City	156
III. Mannheim and Heidelberg	160
D. Conclusion	165
Annotations	169
Bibliography	172
Index	176

PREFACE

Grateful acknowledgement is due to Professor Ernst Jockers of the University of Pennsylvania who, in connection with *Wilhelm Meister*, first drew the author's attention to the importance of the family concept in Goethe's classical works. This inspiring scholar and teacher presented the vital role of Goethe's morphological thinking in his classical period as a challenge to a reexamination of that period.

It is a pleasure to acknowledge indebtedness to Professor Howard Comfort of Haverford College for assistance with the inscription of the Igel monument, to Professors John A. Kelly and Harry W. Pfund for valuable suggestions, and to Marguerite Wolff, M. A. *cantab.*, of London for assistance with the manuscript. Grateful appreciation, finally, is due to the Carl Schurz Memorial Foundation of Philadelphia for generous financial support.

A. G. STEER, JR.

University of Pennsylvania,
Philadelphia, Pa.
February, 1955.

Plate I

Plate II

Plate III

A. INTRODUCTION

I. PROBLEMS OF INTERPRETATION POSED BY THE CAMPAGNE-BELAGERUNG

In commencing an investigation of this kind it is well to look first at the questions and problems inherent in the material, questions with which the various biographers and critics have had to deal. The first of these should doubtless be: to what extent is one justified in subjecting these neglected works, the *Campagne* and the *Belagerung,* both of which are of course autobiographical, to an interpretation? For are not the two works in question biographical, that is to say, largely factual or historical, and is not interpretation or criticism a method to be applied primarily to literary material?

The answer is naturally that the two works comprise both autobiography and literature or "fiction," and that the latter element is of very much greater importance than has often been assumed. There are many evidences of this, the first of which is to be found on the title page of the first edition, where the sub-title reads: *Aus meinem Leben. Zweiter Abtheilung fünfter Theil,* which thus establishes its position as a continuation of *Dichtung und Wahrheit.* In the latter title, of course, the position of the word *Dichtung* is no accident. Thus interpretation is justified, although its extent depends on two further problems, first that of the way in which the works were written, and secondly the problem of source material.

In the first place the events described occurred in the late summer and fall of 1792 and in the summer of 1793, although the experiences had to wait twenty-eight years, until 1820, before Goethe began to cast them into literary form, and 1822, when he finished. As a result, the work represents two Goethes, the older man of the eighteen-twenties telling about, and also sitting in judgement on, the forty-three year old Goethe who actually experienced the events described. The editors then have to indicate where the Goethe of the seventeen-nineties is speaking directly, and where he is being edited by his older self.

Furthermore, what Goethe wrote twenty-eight years later differs in many details from the actual events, insofar as they can now be ascertained. This has made neccessary considerable research into just what actually did happen and here the critic is deeply indebted to Chuquet,[1] Roethe,[2] and others. The critic must present these discrepancies and, if possible, explain them. In addition, there are places where Goethe has changed the emphasis. Many things, as for instance the retreat from Valmy, are presented in a light so different from the actual incidents that the naive reader gets a false impression.

Lastly, the commentators are confronted with the difficult problem of source material. It was originally assumed that Goethe wrote the account from a detailed diary that has since been destroyed or lost. But as more and more research has been devoted to this problem of sources, it has become evident that a very considerable portion of the *Campagne* and the *Belagerung* was based by Goethe on the writings and reports of contemporaries. The question thus arises as to how much goes back to Goethe's personal experiences and how much he "owes" to others.

The next great problem that must be considered is this: is it justifiable to treat the *Campagne in Frankreich* and the *Belagerung von Mainz* together? Do the two form one organic whole? In fact, the question may well be asked as to whether it is justifiable to consider even the *Campagne* alone as a unified whole, for both Dove[3] and Roethe (158) have denied it. The literary composition of the *Campagne* is puzzling. The first third of the volume contains, in fast-moving diary form, an account of the military events of the campaign; the last two-thirds, however, are broad and leisurely sketches of Goethe's visits to the Jacobis in Pempelfort, to Plessing in Duisburg and to Princess Gallitzin in Münster, concluding with a lengthy account of his life in Weimar during the winter between the campaigns. How is this apparent lack of unity, both in form and in content, to be explained?

This question of the unity of the two works is one of the basic concerns of the entire ensuing examination, and hence, to anticipate, the conclusion must be stated here—namely that not only does the *Campagne* not split into two intrinsically unrelated parts, as Roethe felt, but that it, together with the *Belagerung*, forms one organically united whole around the central and basic Goethean conception of the family as "Urform" and "Metamorphose" of all forms of human society. This key concept opens up a whole series of fascinating insights into this unappreciated masterpiece as the following chapters will show.

The third great problem that must be answered in connection with these works, namely what precisely Goethe means by the family as "Urform" and "Metamorphose" of human society, and what justification may be adduced for applying this idea to the *Campagne* and the *Belagerung*. This problem is traced in detail in the following chapter; but first it is necessary to outline the answers advanced by earlier commentators to the first two problems cited above, together with an evaluation of their results.

The first great commentator on the two works was **Alfred Dove** in volume twenty-eight of the *Jubiläumsausgabe*. Although it appeared as early as 1902-1907 and contains some faults, it has not been surpassed since. Therefore, in citing from the *Campagne* or the *Belagerung*, the page and line numbers from this edition will be used. In the following discussion of the works it will be frequently necessary to analyze Dove's view at some length. Here it must suffice to outline the valuable contributions he made to a better understanding of the material.

He was the first to recognize the vital importance of the stimulus of the events of the year 1819 in leading Goethe to write an account of the *Campagne* twenty-eight years after the expedition had taken place. Dove summarized the political events of the post-Napoleonic Europe of 1819; characterized the spirit of the times as the revolution and the struggle against it, and showed how the *Campagne* is Goethe's reaction to those political events (Dove vii-x). He explained how, during Goethe's first period of occupation with the work (January 8 - March 23, 1820), additional political events on the European scene strengthened Goethe's reaction (Dove xii). And he went on to indicate how the second period of work (7 November, 1821 - April, 1822) found Goethe in a similar frame of mind (Dove xiv).

He saw Goethe's purposes in writing the two works as twofold; first, to throw light on his own development, and second, to demonstrate the shattering effect of the French Revolution on himself and his contemporaries. This dual purpose he said, forges the two works together in a unit (Dove xvi).

It is in the troublesome second part of the *Campagne* that

Dove became uncertain, and with his statements on the winter in Weimar, his explanatory ingenuity finally began to run dry. At Goethe's account of the color experiments and the gem collection, Dove figuratively threw up his hands:

> Mit Betrübnis sehen wir ein Goethesches Meisterwerk, das sich an ein grosses historisches Interesse der Mit- und Nachwelt wendet, hier plötzlich entstellt durch den greisenhaften Zug verfallender künstlerischer Selbstbeherrschung (Dove xxviii).

The *Belagerung* he saw as a " . . . leicht behandeltes Finale des ganzen Buches . . . (Dove xxxvii)."

Finally, Dove treated rather gingerly the problem of Goethe's source material. No lengthy diaries or other extensive material which might serve as a basis for the *Campagne* have survived. It is known that Goethe leaned heavily on the memories and works of others. How much is then his own and how much is from secondary sources? Dove concluded:

> . . . die für die Darstellung gewählte Kunstform darf uns nicht darüber täuschen: eine im engeren Sinne sogenannte Geschichtsquelle, wie sie dem Boden der Wirklichkeit unmittelbar entspringt, haben wir in den historischen Partien unseres Bandes nicht vor Augen (Dove xxviii).

The question of the diaries is a crucial one. Goethe reported from Pempelfort (158:14-28)[4] that he reviewed his papers from the campaign, only to burn "das ganze Heft," out of the realization of his own errors. If nothing did survive to 1820-22, this would imply that the writing, except for the few short items which will be discussed later, was done from memory and the reports of others, oral as well as written. Dove at least admitted that this was a possibility:

> Vollständige Fiktion eines eigenen Tagebuches wäre angesichts der klaren Erdichtung von gleichzeitigen Aufzeichnungen aus Pempelfort und Münster immerhin möglich (Dove 268).

Although Dove has failed to come to a clear-cut conclusion on this matter, he has at least outlined the problem and its alternatives. In conclusion he assessed the works thus: "*Eine Poesie der Geschichte* in dieses bestimmten Dichters reifster Art (Dove xxxviii, italics added)."

In 1919 there appeared the only monograph to date on the *Campagne-Belagerung*, written during the first World War by Gustav Roethe, an official of the German occupying forces in

Northern France, who served in the same areas that Goethe had traversed on his unhappy military adventure a century and a quarter previously.

In considering the important source problems, Roethe dealt first with the detailed journal of the Weimar "Kämmerier" J. C. Wagner, *Meine Erfahrungen in den Jahren 1792. 1793. 1794. in den gegenwärtigen Kriegen*.[5] To this diary Roethe correctly assigned special importance:

> Dieses Tagebuch hat, wie ich zeigen werde, nicht nur im Excerpt, sondern auch im Original für Goethes Werk eine entscheidende Rolle gespielt, so gross, dass die Annahme eines *eigenen* fortlaufenden, ausführlichen Tagebuchs ... entbehrlich erscheint (Roethe 21).

Following this, there is a detailed consideration of the other sources that Goethe used in writing the *Campagne* (Roethe 158 ff.), from which the reader can only conclude that Goethe depended on the work of others for a very considerable portion of the military parts of the *Campagne*. Roethe did not attempt to show any meaning for or purpose in this.

Next he proceeded to a discussion of the works as works of art, without, like all his predecessors, being able to arrive at any satisfying explanation. In discussing the apparent break between the two parts of the *Campagne*, Roethe saw the influence of romantic ideas on form:

> Der zweite Teil der 'Campagne' unterscheidet sich so wesentlich von dem ersten, dass nur eine äussere Einheit besteht. Den ganz anderen Aufbau ... begründet Goethe selbst in einer 'Zwischenrede,' deren abgeklärter Altersstil ebenso wie ihr Inhalt die späte Entstehung sichert. Eine solche Einlage, die den Zusammenhang mehr schädigt als fördert, schmeckt von vornherein nach dem Alter: die 'Lücke' der 'Belagerung von Mainz,' die 'Zwischenrede' der 'Wanderjahre' atmen dieselbe Sorglosigkeit, die, den Romantikern immer geläufig, bei Goethe erst in seinen späteren Jahren auftritt (Roethe 246).

This external break, according to Roethe, is reflected internally as well, in that the first, military, portion of the *Campagne* has as its real subject the French Revolution, while the second part, from the *Zwischenrede* on, deals with a different central problem, namely the gifted individual versus the demands of society. Both of these viewpoints are, of course, true in a sense, though no one realized more clearly than Roethe that they are not sufficient to forge the works into an organic whole.

With the winter in Weimar Roethe also could make little headway. He noted that it will not fit the theme of the gifted individual *vs.* society, but rather comes closer to the main idea of the first part—the revolution.

The latest edition of the works by Kunz, in the *Gedenkausgabe*,[6] has a short introduction which is in some respects the best yet written on the cryptic *Campagne*. Kunz's outstanding contribution consisted in the fact that he viewed the works biographically against the larger canvas of Goethe's inner development, with careful accounting for the importance of Goethe's scientific studies. This sympathetic understanding for the morphological point of view caused him to come tantalizingly close to a full understanding of the works as a whole, without ever completely doing so.

The Pempelfort and Münster visits he analyzed correctly in attributing the misunderstanding between Goethe and his hosts to their different views on antiquity. Jacobi could not understand Goethe's view of nature, which Kunz defined as the balance of freedom and necessity, and "das Ineinander von Urform und Metamorphose" and the limit to boundless striving, the area of mutual limitation (Kunz 791 ff.). In this sense, then, if nature is necessity and human life is freedom, antiquity is of importance as the only era in which human life attained complete harmony with natural necessity.

Furthermore, Kunz correctly noted the importance of Italy for Goethe in another respect, namely in the question of how Goethe came to understand there that art was not an elevated realm, but a natural expression of the common people. This insight is important for the *Campagne*, as we shall see, for, among other things, it enabled the author to understand the Igel monument as "Mass in der Masslosigkeit des Geschehens," and also to see the family as "die Urzelle, die Urspannung." In this connection it is amazing how close Kunz came to seeing the family as the central factor in the *Campagne*, without ever using the word. It almost seems as if he were consciously avoiding it by using every imaginable synonym—"die organische Mitte," "Urzelle," "Urspannung," "Zusammensein von Eltern und Kindern," etc., etc. Only once did he use it as a part of a compound, "Familienkreis."

From Italy then Goethe returned home conscious of the need to organize life in accordance with nature: "Bindung der auseinanderstrebenden Kräfte in der Organischen Mitte . . . (Kunz 793)." This was the task that had to be done to counteract war and revolution, Goethe felt. With what forces could this be accomplished? With ". . . die Naturformen des Daseins . . . (Kunz 798)," in which connection Kunz specifically mentioned the Igel Monument.

Kunz closed with the following comment on the unity of the different parts of the *Campagne*:

> Die bisher gegebenen Hinweise genügen, um den Grund aufzuweisen, der Goethe bestimmt hat, diese beiden Teile, den Bericht über die Kampagne und den über die Besuche, in einer Schrift zu verbinden. Beide sind Auseinandersetzungen mit den Mächten der Zeit: eben der Vorgang der gesellschaftlichen, geistigen, sittlichen Entwurzelung, den man bei diesen Besuchen beobachten kann, hat auch zu den geschichtlichen Ereignissen geführt, deren Folgen Goethe gerade am eigenen Leibe zu spüren bekommen hatte (Kunz 803).

From the brevity of the foregoing it should not be assumed that these were the only men to have said anything worth while on the *Campagne* and the *Belagerung*. Bergemann's work, for instance[7] is the most convenient one volume edition of the works although, with the exception of some excerpts from Wagner's diary not available elsewhere, it adds little new material. And in his perceptive book Buchwald also recognizes how large the amount of "Dichtung" is by characterizing the *Campagne* thus:

> . . . ein biographisches Kunstwerk in Gestalt eines Tagebuchs, das nachträglich aus dem Studium vielfältiger Quellen: eigener und fremder Aufzeichnungen sowie literarischer Dokumente, hergestellt worden ist.[8]

Buchwald's work also represents a notable advance in that it clearly shows the importance of the morphological approach in assessing Goethe's political and social thinking. The crucial importance of these morphological conceptions leads directly to the subject of the next chapter.

The aim of the investigation will be then to apply Goethe's concept of the family to the puzzling challenge of the *Campagne-Belagerung* for what light the results may shed on the troublesome discrepancies between the events as described in the two works and the events as they actually occurred. If it can be shown that a considerable proportion of such discrepancies were purposeful, then an interpretation of the whole is justified. In this connection the methodology must be made clear. In many instances it is impossible to say precisely what the historical event was, and hence to what extent, if any, Goethe's account is at variance with it. Even where it is possible to be fairly certain, the fact that Goethe's account differed may be explained by a number of different factors, for instance faulty memory. Such discrepancies assume significance only if it can be demonstrated that the mass of them show a specifically definable common tendency. Thus a considerable amount of detail in the ensuing discussions will be unavoidable, for a general conclusion must rest upon an accumulated body of carefully evaluated individual items.

Furthermore the role of the family idea as it affects the form and the content of the works must be examined. Are the *Campagne* and the *Belagerung*, as has been generally assumed up to now, merely a fascinating series of rather inaccurate autobiographical sketches, or do they form a unified entity with significant meaning? But before this can be done, the use of the family idea must be justified, its origin traced and its meaning for Goethe demonstrated.

II. THE FAMILY CONCEPT AN OUTGROWTH OF GOETHE'S SCIENTIFIC STUDIES

In the preceding pages the opinions of important commentators on the *Campagne-Belagerung* have been summarized. It was found that each commentator fell short of a complete or satisfactory evaluation, due to his failure to see the functional importance of the family concept in the two works. Before going any farther it is therefore necessary to justify the use of this conception—the family—in the interpretation of these works. In what way and for what reason has the family idea been advanced by Goethe here? Are these two works subject to special treatment, different from that applied to his other works, or do they all represent and exemplify a philosophy that is typical of Goethe?

The answers to such questions must be sought in Goethe's state of mind at the time he experienced the events described as well as twenty-eight years later when he gave them their final literary form. For determining this, the diaries, letters, conversations and autobiographical works, with a few exceptions to be treated later, offer very little information indeed. It is to be noted here that Gräf's great work treats neither the *Campagne* nor the *Belagerung*. The real answer, in fact the real key to understanding Goethe's classic works, must be sought in his scientific interests and occupations. For with advancing years these latter became ever more methodical as Goethe searched for the spiritual links which held the manifestations of life together in one unity of effectiveness, subject to identical laws. This being so, the relationship of his scientific work to his literary work, which is in essence his expression of poetic truth, must be of central importance and must be so recognized.

The *Campagne* and the *Belagerung* both give abundant indications that scientific endeavors and interests were uppermost in Goethe's mind at the time. He spent hours contemplating colors of a bit of pottery at the bottom of a pool; in long conversations he defended his scientific interests to Prince Reuss, and later to Wyttenbach in Trier, to the Jacobis in Pempelfort, to the Gallitizin circle in Münster. He made it a point to visit friends with whom he had maintained contact on scientific subjects, for instance Sömmering and Forster in Mainz and

Merrem in Düsseldorf. He observed the mineralogy of the regions through which he passed. The only book to accompany him to France was a physics dictionary. Before Mainz he risked his life more than once in the search for pathological bones in an old, abandoned graveyard. Finally, during the winter in Weimar, studies and experiments in color absorbed him and accompanied him to Mainz, where he wrote an essay on the subject, an essay which was later to become the bone of contention in the argument with Schlosser in Heidelberg.

The course of Goethe's scientific studies, his varied and deep scientific interests, has been traced repeatedly, but none-the-less it must be reviewed briefly for our purposes.[9]

For Goethe, science had a deeply ethical and even religious character. As a student of Spinoza, Goethe also saw nature as a manifestation of God; nature was God, God nature: *deus sive natura*. Thus the study of nature was a matter of greatest seriousness to him, almost a rite. It filled him with reverence and had the effect of an urgent imperative to recreate nature in poetic symbols. The highly spiritual nature of these scientific pursuits is further reflected in Goethe's methods of study. He felt that the merely quantitative methods of mechanical and mathematical interpretation were insufficient. To him science was more than just a matter of measuring. One must learn with the whole being, he felt, qualitatively as well as quantitatively. This demanded of the scientist inner purification, moral control, concentration, service and "Ehrfurcht." Thus the scientist fulfills a priest-like function. In his own restrained words:

> Der Geist übte sich an dem würdigsten Gegenstande, indem er das Lebendige nach seinem inneren Werte zu erkennen und zu zergliedern suchte; aber wie sollte ein solches Streben einen glücklichen firfolg haben, wenn man ihm nicht seine ganze Tätigkeit hingäbe (J. A. v. 39, 194).

The same mood of almost religious dedication speaks from a reflection written years later:

> Alles, was wir Erfinden, Entdecken im höherem Sinne nennen, ist die bedeutende Ausübung, Betätigung eines originalen Wahrheitsgefühles das, im stillen längst ausgebildet, unversehens mit Blitzesschnelle zu einer fruchtbaren Erkenntnis führt. Es ist eine aus dem Innern am Äussern sich entwickelnde Offenbarung, die den Menschen seine Gottähnlichkeit vorahnen lässt. Es ist

eine Synthese von Welt and Geist, welche von der ewigen Harmonie des Daseins die seligste Versicherung gibt (J. A. v. 39, 70).

These scientific interests and studies developed early, as is well known. In Strassburg Goethe attended anatomical lectures and witnessed dissections. Later he wrote a short and rhapsodic contribution to Lavater's physiognomy, showing how the skull and bones of the face control the fundamental outlines of the features (J. A. v. 39, 117). Thus his earliest interests were clearly in anatomy and osteology.

From 1782 on Goethe continued with Professor Loder of Jena his work on osteology, which reaped its first fruit in his "discovery" of the intermaxillary bone in man, for the view had long prevailed that man had no intermaxillary bone, which fact distinguished him from the lower orders of the animal kingdom. Goethe's joy at making this discovery was extreme, as seen from his letter to Herder of 27 March, 1784:

> Nach Anleitung des Evangelii muss ich dich auf das eiligste mit einem Glücke bekannt machen, das mir zugestossen ist. Ich habe gefunden—weder Gold noch Silber, aber was mir eine unsägliche Freude macht—das *os intermaxillare* am Menschen!
> Ich verglich mit Lodern Menschen- und Tierschädel, kam auf die Spur, und siehe da ist es! . . . Es soll dich auch recht herzlich freuen, denn es ist wie der Schlusstein zum Menschen, fehlt nicht, ist auch da! Aber wie! (W. A. IV, v. 6, 258).

The beginner's joy at making a discovery, even when it refutes an old established conception, is not sufficient to explain this exultation. Instead, Goethe's intense satisfaction here stems clearly from the realization that this discovery was concrete evidence that his manner of thinking, his comparative-synthetic approach to the phenomena, was fruitful and productive. In this connection one must note that for present purposes it is not so much what Goethe's scientific results were that is important, but rather the method by which he obtained them.

What was this method of observation? From the account, first published in 1820 (J. A. v. 39, 179), it is obvious that Goethe's thought ran along the following lines. In his anatomical studies he had come intuitively to a concept of the osteological type, that is the realization that the same bones fulfill similar functions in various animals. Nature, he devined, operates in accordance with certain archetypes, which, like Platonic ideas, are models from which individual forms are derived in a constant process of metamorphosis. In contrast to its individual modifications, this archetype is not destroyed. Thus when Goethe heard the traditional view that all animals except man had an intermaxillary bone, it aroused his disbèlief; man had to have such a bone also. For man to be an exception was an unacceptable flaw in nature's processes, as he understood them. Thus he was led to look carefully for the bone in man, which then he soon found, almost completely grown together with adjacent bones.

The method he used here was to examine the skulls of animals from the turtle to the elephant and arrange them in an orderly series, proceeding from the simplest to the most complex by the smallest possible steps. This arrangement permitted him to see clearly the various metamorphoses that nature uses to accomplish her varying purposes, still without departing from the basic type.

In the following years the approaching French Revolution forced the reluctant Goethe to turn his attention to political maters, to problems of human association. Since it must be assumed that Goethe applied this morphological method of thought, derived from his scientific preoccupations, to the social sphere, it is evident that the family must have occurred to him, either as the type or archetype of human association, or as one of the simpler elements in the series of phenomena that his method would have required him to set up for careful analysis. However, by proceeding more deeply into Goethe's scientific thought and method it will be possible to replace this "assumption" with demonstrable proof that the family formed a vital element in Goethe's social thinking.

The year 1790 witnessed the writing of an important essay on the subject, *Versuch über die Gestalt der Tiere* (J. A. v. 39, 188 ff.), though it was not published until after his death. But from this fragmentary essay, as from the following one of 1792, *Versuch einer allgemeinen Vergleichungslehre* (J. A. v. 39, 127 ff.), it is evident that Goethe had run into difficulties. The osteological type in all details had thus far eluded him. The conviction that it really existed was even stronger in his mind than before, but Goethe was unable as yet to work it out satisfactorily in all of its implications.

So Goethe found it necessary to interrupt the osteological inquiries and concentrate more on his botanical studies, where, it developed, success was easier to obtain. Early in the 1780's he had been intensely pre-occupied with botanical matters and the more luxuriant flora of Italy afforded him many additional insights into botanical growth. The fan-leafed palm in the horticultural garden at Padua impressed him deeply, for instance, and it was in Sicily that the concept of the long-sought "Urpflanze" finally dawned on him, expressed in the words "Alles ist Blatt."

The results of these studies are contained in his *Versuch, die Metamorphose der Pflanzen zu erklären* (J. A. v. 39, 249 ff.), published in 1790. It is highly instructive to trace Goethe's thoughts here. First he established the concept of metamorphosis, or change in form, and classified it in three ways: the "regelmässige oder fortschreitende Metamorphose," secondly the "unregelmässige oder rückschreitende Metamorphose," and lastly the "zufällige." To these concepts he added those of "Steigerung" and polarity — namely, "Ausdehnung" and "Zusammenziehung" — and with these conceptual tools he traced the development of the typical annual from seed to plant, to flower, and then back to seed again.

The germination of the seed and the appearance of the first primitive leaves, the "Kotyledonen," represented the first "Ausdehnung." Then followed the stem, which, after the "Kotyledonen," represented contraction. The stem grew to the first node, from the eyes of which emanated the first real leaves. This was, of course, expansion. Alternate expansion and contraction continued until the plant was ready to blossom. At this point there came a mighty expansion in the "Kelch" or calyx, which sprang from a node with, instead of the usual one or two leaves, a whole series of leaves or sepals, which then grew together into the calyx. After another contraction another great expansion followed in the "Krone" or corolla, the petals proper. Still another contraction and expansion resulted in the stamens and pistils ("Staubwerkzeuge"), and a final similar process brought forth the seed. In these processes Goethe saw a progressive transformation, "fortschreitende Metamorphose." One basic organ, the leaf, was transformed successively to perform a number of different functions. Furthermore the principle of "Steigerung" was at work here also. The first leaves, the "Kotyledonen," were large, rough and shapeless, but as the plant grew the new leaves became progressively more refined in structure, texture and outline. This process of intensification was, of course, crowned by the formation of the various parts of the flower, and it climaxed in the development of the seed. Thus what Goethe meant when he said that "Alles ist Blatt" becomes evident. From the point of view of this inquiry, the idea of the family is close at hand, for here Goethe saw a number of individual units (leaves), basically similar, but varying according to their purpose, united by the same laws of growth and co-existing in the same natural environment.

The thought of the family came even closer when Goethe went on to examine the node-to-node rhythm of plant growth. The area along the stem from one node to the next contained eyes from which the leaves develop. Inasmuch as the leaves, potentially, can turn into flower and seed, one sees each area from node to node then as a potentially independent plant (J. A. v. 39, 284-285). This Goethe found borne out by experiments on a number of plants, cuttings from which will grow into independent individuals. Thus a complete adult annual then appears to be a "family" of potentially independent plants. In his discussion of compound fruits and flowers, the family idea is again immanent. "Alle Blumen, welche aus den Augen entstehen, sind als ganze Pflanzen anzusehen, welche auf der Mutterpflanze ebenso wie diese auf der Erde stehen (J. A. v. 39, 286)." The family concept came closer yet when Goethe considered two types of plants, first the types in which the flowers appear at intervals along the stem, and secondly the flowering shrubs, where each twig develops flowers. Here Goethe saw a development of the simple plant, for each blossom represented a potentially independent plant growing from the basic one, *i.e.* a "family" of child plants, so to speak, arranged on the parent plant. To be sure, he did not use the word "Familie," but it is important to note that he did use the term "Mutterpflanze (J. A. v. 39, 284-285)."

One more point in this essay deserves comment, namely the fact that Goethe carefully considered abnormal growths as well as normal ones. First he described a rose, then a carnation, both of which had suffered from a similar malformation. After the calyx and corolla had been formed, the following expansion, instead of producing pistils and stamens, resulted in a continuation of the stem, from the upper end of which the plant then attempted, unsuccessfully, to form a new flower. In his discussion of the "durchgewachsene Rose und Nelke" it becomes evident that he valued such "rückschreitende Metamorphose" for the light that it threw on normal development. In other words, abnormality is often of value in that it illuminates processes that are difficult or impossible to observe in normal growth.

In his botanical studies, Goethe had then by 1790 succeeded in finding the type or archetype in the leaf. He now turned to osteology again, and a number of writings followed at relatively short intervals. The story of this study is fascinating in itself, but for present purposes it will be sufficient to mention the salient points.

Versuch einer Allgemeinen Vergleichungslehre was written in 1792 (J. A. v. 39, p. 128). This essay is marked first by a clear perception of the vital influence of environment on living beings. Environment is one of the prime causes of metamorphosis. A part of this environment is of course the interrelationship of various animals to each other in the animal kingdom, "... wo ein Geschlecht auf dem andern und durch das andere, wo nicht entsteht, doch sich erhält." He continued this thought in the next essay (*Erster Entwurf einer allgemeinen Einleitung in die vergleichende Anatomie, ausgehend von der Osteologie.* J. A. v. 39, 137), observing that animals are developed "... durch Umstände zu Umständen." It is in this essay that Goethe finally succeeded in enunciating the general animal type. He conceived of it as consisting in three main parts, first the head which contains the sense organs and the mouth; next the upper body which contains the heart and lungs; and lastly the afterbody which contains the organs of digestion, excretion and sex. Goethe noted furthermore that the auxiliary organs of locomotion, the arms, legs, or fins, are always attached to one or both of the last two, never to the first.

To use this type for osteological purposes, Goethe believed that one should first examine any one bone, and compare it with the equivalent bone in all other animals, then arrange the various phenomena in a series, proceeding with the smallest possible steps from the simplest to the most complex. Here again we see Goethe's concept of the series as a most important element of his scientific method. The family concept is of course close to the Goethean series, for each individual member is surrounded by closely related forms, all derived by metamorphosis from a common archetype.

In 1795, at the instigation of the von Humboldts, Goethe worked out a number of lectures on his osteological concepts. The first of these, *Von den Vorteilen der vergleichenden Anatomie* (J. A. v. 39, 161 ff.), pictured each animal as "eine kleine Welt" in which the internal organs mutually influence each other. So here Goethe saw a family of internal organs in an internal environment, an inner milieu analogous to the external environment. Although it may seem self-contradictory to speak of an internal environment, or tautological to speak of an external environment, it is well to note Goethe's distinction here, for the contrasted types of environment will appear frequently in the *Campagne* and the *Belagerung*.

The second lecture is notable for the enunciation of two main ideas, the first concerning the relationship of the individual to the law, about which Goethe wrote: "Die Klassen, Arten, Gattungen und Individuen verhalten sich wie die Fälle zum Gesetz; sie sind darin enthalten, aber sie enthalten und geben es nicht (J. A. v. 39, p. 168)."

The second point for which this lecture is notable is the way in which Goethe sought evidence of metamorphosis, namely through comparison. In man, for instance, he postulated the importance of comparing all the various races and tribes with each other in turn, then comparing the sexes with each other, then the organs one against another, as for instance equivalent formations of the upper and lower extremities, or the individual vertebrae. His method emphasizes related forms, or a "family" of forms.

The third lecture contains a statement that is vital for the present inquiry (*Über die Gesetze der Organisation überhaupt*, J. A. v. 39, 171 f). In attempting to formulate a principle that applied to organic life in general, Goethe returned momentarily to the botanical world.

> Die Pflanze erscheint fast nur einen Augenblick als Individuum, und zwar da, wenn sie sich als Samenkorn von der *Mutterpflanze* loslöst. In dem Verfolge des Keimens erscheint sie schon als ein *Vielfaches*, an welchem nicht allein ein identischer Teil aus identischen Teilen entspringt, sondern auch diese Teile durch Succession verschieden ausgebildet werden, so dass ein *Mannigfaltiges, scheinbar verbundenes Ganze* zuletzt vor unseren Augen dasteht (J. A. v. 39, 174; italics added).

To be noted carefully are the words "Mutterpflanze," "Vielfaches," "Mannigfaltiges," "scheinbar verbundenes Ganze," for any one of which the word "Familie" could be substituted without doing violence to the sense of the passage. The really crucial point, however, is that the statement is meant to illustrate a basic principle of all organic growth, for the title of the lecture is *Über die Gesetze der Organisation überhaupt*.

There are, of course, other writings on Goethe's scientific interests, but they bring little additional new material. The basic outlines have already been indicated above. The writings on mineralogy and meteorology, for instance, are of minor importance for this investigation. Furthermore, the color theories, on which Goethe spent so much time and effort, show but another instance of the central method that Goethe used in his scientific thinking. He examined the phenomena of color carefully, and then he proceeded to induce a central "Typus" or archetype, which, he reports, dawned on him during his Silesian campaign in 1791, and which consisted in the recognition that " . . . Hell und Dunkel Farben erzeuge."

For present purposes the indispensable Goethe pronouncement is to be found in the *Verfolg* (J. A. v. 39, 317) to his *Geschichte meines botanischen Studiums* (J. A. v. 39, 296). He began this account by reviewing his lonely and hopeless state of mind after his return from Italy. He reviewed the points that had attracted his principal attention during his Italian stay. First, on the subject of art he felt that he had learned to understand how the Greeks had come to develop the highest art " . . . im eigenen Nationalkreise." To be noted here is the word "Nationalkreis," which could be replaced by "Volk." In the second place came his interest in nature, *i.e.* science, in which connection he reported that he was convinced that he had learned how nature proceeded to bring forth her works according to laws.

On the third interest that had occupied him in Italy, he reported in these words:

> Das Dritte, was mich beschäftigte, waren die Sitten der Völker. An ihnen zu lernen, wie aus dem Zusammentreffen von Notwendigkeit und Willkür, von Antrieb und Wollen, von Bewegung und Widerstand, ein Drittes hervorgeht, was weder Kunst noch Natur, sondern beides zugleich ist, notwendig und zufällig, absichtlich und blind. *Ich verstehe die menschliche Gesellschaft* (J. A. v. 39, p. 318; italics added).

With this crucially important statement Goethe ranked art,

science, and human society in a group as the three great areas of his concern. It is this trinity which is at the basis of his classicism. In his own words then Goethe reported that "die menschliche Gesellschaft" formed one of the three main areas of his concern, and this statement not only entitles the Goethe student to seek evidences of this social concern in Goethe's works, it also obligates him to do so.

He went on to state that he undertook to give written form to each of these areas of thought. Concerning his interest in art he wrote the essay *Einfache Nachahmung der Natur, Manier, Stil* in 1789. In this essay the arrangement is to be carefully noted, proceeding namely from simple to more complex phenomena; in other words, an evidence of his application to aesthetic matters of a method which he derived from his scientific studies. The second and more important matter to be noted here is the difference that Goethe saw between the simplest element of the series, the simple imitation of nature, and the most complex at the other end, style. The artist who is capable of the highest level, style, he says, does far more than copy nature. He shows through his work that he has comprehended nature to its depths in the sense of Goethe's morphological thinking. Thus mere external observation of nature is in Goethe's view not enough. The highest art is produced only by the artist who is capable of the penetrating and understanding appreciation of nature's secrets that Goethe had developed in his writings on morphology. This is a thorough-going application of scientific or morphological thought to the realms of art.

The second of the three mentioned essays was the *Metamorphose der Pflanzen* which has been examined above. It is largely on this foundation that his morphological method of scientific thought had been developed.

The third product of those dark days on returning from Italy was *Das Römische Karneval*, which resulted from his concern with the "Sitten der Völker," behind which he sensed the same laws that determine the phenomena of nature and art.

The account of this Roman holiday is broken up into sections with subtitles, from which it gradually becomes evident that we have here a rough and approximate Goethean series. For one of Goethe's first steps in scientific analysis, as has been shown, was to construct a careful series of the phenomena, proceeding from simple to complex by the smallest possible steps, as he did for instance with the mammalian skulls in searching for the intermaxillary bone. But *Das Römische Karneval* is a report of actual events, not of scientific results or of imagined actions, so that the author is more limited in constructing his series, and, consequently, the latter is not so easily recognizable. Nevertheless an observing eye can see here not one but three series in rough outline. First Goethe proceeded, in space, from the geographical through the architectural to the human; secondly he proceeded in accordance with a chronological series, and lastly in accordance with a rough social series, introducing first individuals, then smaller groups, then the "Volk" itself. Of this work Jockers says:

> Das Volk als natürliche, alles umfassende Einheit entdeckt er (Goethe) erst in Italien. Der Römische Karneval erscheint ihm wie ein grosser Menschengarten, in dem alles scheinbar zügellos zugeht, bei näherm Zusehen aber sich in ryhthmischen Gruppen bewegt, die von bestimmten Menschentypen ausfluten und wieder zu ihnen zurückzufluten scheinen, so dass der Eindruck eines gesetzlich bewegten Ganzen entsteht.[10]

From the preceding considerations it should now be clear that, due to Goethe's serious occupation with scientific studies (which, by the way, he considered more important than all his poetic endeavors), morphological concepts underlie his sociological thinking. In both areas of thought he established typical forms as models, original and guiding principles in the process of development, and in both these areas of thought it was the natural sphere of activity, the family, in which such organic development is alone possible. Thus the family, like any other type, appears in a three-fold capacity: it is the maternal, life-producing force, the impulse from which all striving for individual form originates; secondly it is the goal toward which this striving aims in self-fulfillment; and finally it is a corrective principle which either holds violent actions in check or strengthens weaker elements so that they can resist attack successfully.

The campaign of 1792 was conducted by representatives of the *ancien régime* in Europe against the hated French Revolution. Goethe, as a responsible minister of state, was reluctant to participate for a number of reasons, not the least of which was the fact he had no wish to interfere in the internal affairs of another state. In addition he had no sympathy for the political goals of either side in the impending conflict—rather it was an active antipathy. Goethe was opposed on principle to a military adventure, and in addition his sense of responsibility to the government he served led him to urge strongly against risking any of the duchy's slender resources in such a campaign, with such allies. Only when he realized that the revolutionary spirit unleashed in France might do harm to his own country and to the cultural structure which he had helped to erect there, did he exchange his passive attitude for a more active one— but not without deep-seated doubts and reservations.

But he remained an active defender of that natural, stable element of society which was one of the first to be threatened by the onrush of the revolutionary storm—the family. It is easy to recognize the growing sense of responsibility for the family in Goethe's poetic works after his return from Italy. The idea of the family is supreme in the "Revolutionsdichtungen," *Wilhelm Meister, Die Wahlverwandtschaften, Hermann und Dorothea,* and the *Natürliche Tochter.* That these family ideas should also be in the *Campagne-Belagerung* is not surprising; it is necessary. And by applying this key idea of the family to these works we shall see what an important role they play in Goethe's thought, a role which, up to now, has been almost completely overlooked.

B. CAMPAGNE IN FRANKREICH

I. THE WRITING OF THE CAMPAGNE-BELAGERUNG; 1792-93; 1819-20; 1821-22

The *Campagne-Belagerung* is somewhat unusual among Goethe's works. First of all it is based to a large extent on the work of others, even to the point of containing verbatim excerpts from them. Also it is the uneasy synthesis of two widely separated periods in Goethe's life; the years of the military adventures themselves, 1792-1793, when Goethe was in his early forties and sorely troubled by the problems posed by the French Revolution, and the later years 1820-1822, when the two works were written, twenty-eight years later, at a time when Goethe was in his early seventies. The synthesis between these two periods is not complete. There are "lapses of memory," "errors," many of which, as will become evident, were conscious and purposeful, and, as will be shown, conscious distortions and suppressions of events, as well as inventions of whole cloth. As a result predominance is given to the aged Goethe and the middle-aged man is disguised or veiled. Thus Goethe in his seventies is "editing" the Goethe of his forties. The essential question throughout will be, however, to note the tendency or purpose, if any, of each change, suppression or invention, and, most important, to determine whether any over-all significant pattern can be discerned in his handling of events.

The two levels of time that are involved in this work are of particular importance for this investigation. Goethe's ideas on the family of 1792-1793 have been heavily overlaid with the more or less final opinions of the Goethe of 1822 on the subject. And the places that show a difference in the actual events of 1792 and Goethe's 1822 account of them will be of prime importance in determining, by finding Goethe's reasons for the changes, what his real thinking was on the subject of the family. So it is clear that three things will have to engage our close attention; first the process of the actual writing, second the contributions of the various sources, and lastly the differences between the actual historical events and Goethe's account.

Why did Goethe wait until 1820 to begin writing the account of his military experiences? The fact that he had not done so before about 1815 can be explained by two considerations. First, Goethe was very critical of many things in the political and military organization of the German states of the time, particularly of Austria and Prussia; but as a responsible minister of one of the smaller of those states, he was very reluctant to speak frankly. He was afraid he might harm the position of Sachsen-Weimar as well as hurt his friends and benefactors, and perhaps also undermine his own position. Secondly, between 1789 and 1815, event had followed event with such dizzying rapidity that it was psychologically difficult for the author to achieve the necessary detachment for a final word on the subject. After all, the problems of the age, still being fought out, in part under Goethe's very nose, were sore thorns in the flesh of all Europe.

But this is still not a complete answer. Why didn't Goethe wait until later, or indeed why did he write down the experiences at all? He never did give full biographical treatment to other important incidents in his life, why then to these? One reason may be seen in the fact that the rapid succession of revolutionary events had ceased and a calm consideration of the past was for the first time possible. But, though calm prevailed externally, the great events and ideas of the Revolutionary and Napoleonic eras were still occupying the minds of the people. The air was full of political discussion, and although liberalism was being suppressed in Germany, the debate on the reform of constitutions and democratic institutions was continuing at passionate heat. Karl August had given Sachsen-Weimar its first constitution in 1816. Prussia was still strengthening itself through internal reform, while in contrast the Austrian Metternich was using his mighty influence to repress liberal elements everywhere.

A summary of the events of the time and Goethe's connection with them is illuminating. The Wartburg student festival had occurred in October of 1817, when a group of Jena students had met to celebrate the anniversary of the Reformation and the Battle of Leipzig. During the affair a student group led by Massmann had burned symbols of reaction, militarism, and French fashions. This gave rise to outraged cries of revolt and conspiracy on the part of the reactionaries. Goethe, was, of course, keenly concerned, for as curator of the University of Jena, responsible minister and supporter of civic order, he could not tolerate disturbances of the public peace, although in his heart he probably sympathized with the rebels, who doubtless reminded him of his own student days.

Student life elsewhere gave cause for concern. A "Geheimbund" had been discovered in Giessen, and a supposed conspiracy in Berlin. Then in March, 1819, the Jena student Carl Sand stabbed to death the sentimental poetaster Kotzebue, who was roundly hated by the liberals, not only as a publisher of a reactionary weekly, but also because he was accused of being a spy for the Russians and was blamed by many for causing the "conversion" of Tsar Alexander from liberalism to reaction. The murder caused a great stir throughout Europe; and Metternich used it as an excuse for a new wave of suppression of liberalism and academic freedom. Goethe was naturally keenly aware of this danger, for, although he considered order to be the first virtue for the middle class, he did not want to see it achieved at the expense of individual dignity and the right of self-determination.

The *Annalen* for 1819 are full of evidence of Goethe's political concern. Literally dozens of royal and diplomatic personages are named. He praised the luck of a friend who, "angegriffen von den unaufhaltsam wirkenden revolutionären Potenzen (der Zeit) (J. A. v. 30, 324 ff)," died in time to miss the murder of Kotzebue. And Goethe tells of his meeting in Karlsbad with Metternich, though without giving date or subject of the conversations.

In September of the same year there followed then the ill-famed "Karlsbader Beschlüsse," which represented the Prussian surrender to Metternich, for according to the terms, Prussia agreed to suppress freedom of the press, of academic teaching and learning, and to create a special judicial body to investigate the "conspiracies" against the governments. Now the time had come for Goethe to intervene, and, insofar as he could, to protect his beloved Jena from the danger of intellectual emasculation. For this reason he went to Karlsbad shortly before the agreements were announced to plead that no restrictions should be placed on Jena. He was not successful. Later, of course, he discussed the agreements with the duke. From his *Tagebücher* we know that at this time a number of political discussions took place with Meyer and others. To Kanzler v. Müller he said that: "Die Mächte hätten in Kohlen geschlagen, die nun an Orte hingesprungen, wo man sie nicht haben wollte."[11]

The months of 1820 in which Goethe started working on the *Campagne-Belagerung* were accompanied by other, similar political events. There was a revolution in Spain, which, as we know, Goethe followed with keen interest. In Paris occurred the political murder of the Duc de Berry, and in Vienna conferences were conducted on the further suppression of liberalism, as Goethe learned from his duke. Of particular importance to Goethe was the appearance of the memoirs of Mme. Roland, a remarkable French woman, liberal but reasonable, who had written the memoirs while waiting to be guillotined in 1791. And in May of 1820 Goethe had written Zelter in Berlin, asking him to use care that the manuscript of his youthful rebellious poem *Prometheus* should not be allowed to circulate, for fear of inflaming the youth of the day (W. A. IV 33, 28).

Against this political background, then, Goethe's renewed interest in the campaign of 1792 appears to be more than an effort to fill in a gap in his autobiography. It represented also his veiled political judgment of an era, which judgment, to be sure, was disguised and restrained out of consideration for the personalities involved. And at the same time, the works constitute a warning to the German people to adhere, in the midst of the general turmoil, to the natural, sociological fundamentals upon which their own national life, as indeed that of all other peoples, was based, namely the family. To prove the last statement will be the burden of this investigation.

For reasons already outlined, the detailed account of the writing of the *Campagne-Belagerung* is of great importance, because a careful comparison of the source works used with the finished work shows that an astonishingly large part of the latter has been drawn from them. Why the personal recollections should need to be emended in this particular work is a question that will have to be discussed later in more detail.

Late in the year 1819, then, Goethe apparently made up his mind to give his experiences in the campaigns of 1792 and 1793 full literary treatment. As early as 1795 he had come into contact with the memoirs of the French general Dumouriez. In the early days of January, 1820, he again reviewed this work.[12] On the thirteenth of that month he borrowed Lauckhard's *Leben und Schicksale* from the ducal library.[13] On the following day he borrowed a map of France, and on the twenty-seventh, Pockel's *Karl Wilhelm Ferdinand, Herzog zu Braunschweig und Lüneburg*.[14] On the day following, he drew Custine's *Mémoires Posthumes* and on the thirtieth Girtanner's *Historische Nachrichten und politische Betrachtungen über die französische Revolution*. On the first of February he referred to the Weimar Court calendar for 1792 ("Entstehungsgeschichte" follows Roethe 9 ff.) and on the fourteenth of that month he consulted the "Kämmerier" J. C. Wagner's diary, which was to have the greatest influence on the work in preparation. Wagner had been in the retinue of the duke since 1763 and had accompanied him on most of his trips in the capacity of ducal treasurer. Not only did he keep a careful financial account of the duke's expenses but also a day-to-day diary as well. This diary has never been published. It was consulted by Roethe, who gives the only available detailed account of it. When Roethe consulted it during the First World War, it was in the library at Weimar where, presumably, it still is.

The actual dictation of the *Campagne* began on the fourteenth of January, as the diaries record. On the twenty-seventh of that month Goethe borrowed from the ducal library the *Original Briefwechsel der Emigrierten, I. Theil, aus dem Französischen übersetzt*, Frankfurt und Leipzig, 1793. This volume, a strange publication, put out by a "Committee of Security" of the Parisian revolutionary government, contains portions of letters from French émigrés outside of France to friends and relatives in France, letters that fell into the hands of General Kellermann's forces after the French reoccupied Longwy in 1792. It is a propaganda effort, which, by using judiciously selected excerpts, makes the émigrés appear in as poor a light as possible in that it shows their insolence, greed, irresponsibility, arrogance and egoism. Unavoidably it shows many a truly poignant human problem as well. It was used by Goethe not only as a basis for the incident of the post-box at Grevenmachern, but also may well have contributed isolated incidents to document his aversion to the émigrés as a whole.

By the first of February, 1820, Goethe was far enough advanced in the work to be able to read portions aloud to various of his friends, to correct them and to outline the remaining material. Early in that month his interest turned to the siege of Mainz, for on the twelfth he borrowed material on Mainz from the library. Again the *Tagebücher* speak of making outlines, and on the twenty-second of the month follows the note: "Schluss von 1793."

Two characteristics of this phase of the work are worth mentioning. In the first place, it was largely the purely military parts of the works as they now stand that Goethe committed to paper. Roethe estimated that the first part of the *Campagne* up to about page 99 of the "Weimar Ausgabe" was written at this time. The larger part, namely the lengthy account of his round-about trip home via Pempelfort, Duisburg and Münster, was still to come. There are to be sure a few references in the *Tagebücher* to this part of the work, for instance on the twenty-first and twenty-eighth of February and on the third of March. But inasmuch as Goethe was doing other things at the same time, it is most likely that this long and important portion of the finished work could have been attacked only in outline or in isolated spots. And it is just this portion that is of such interest for this investigation. The second important factor in the method in which Goethe wrote is the fact that the *Campagne* and the *Belagerung* were taken up together in January and in February, in roughly chronological order. In the last month, separate items in the first work, then in the second, were considered. Thus the parallelism of form and content existing in the two works must lead to the conclusion that together they form one artistic whole. This conclusion based on externalities will be confirmed conclusively later on the basis of the internal structure.

The second period in which Goethe occupied himself with the two works did not come until a year and half later (the following is from Roethe 15-16). It began on the seventh of November, 1821, and lasted until the middle of April, 1822. During this time the series of external political events that accompanied the first period have no parallel, but it is interesting to note that, halfway through, Goethe stopped long enough to read a lengthy work on the revolution in Spain. As might be expected from the above account of the first period of work, the material at first was sent regularly and rapidly to the press at Jena. Riemer helped with the editing. By the thirteenth of January, 1822, the printer was in possession of the completed manuscript up to the return to Trier, *i.e.* the strictly military part of the *Campagne*. Then things went more slowly. The stay in Trier and the Mosel trip occupied him until late in the month. The visit to the Jacobis in Pempelfort was treated from the thirty-first of January until the fifth of February, and the Plessing portions occupied his attention from the sixth of that month until the twenty-fourth. During this period also there is isolated mention of the *Zwischenrede* and of the winter in Weimar. Goethe then went back to the chronological order, and from the twenty-fifth of February until the fifth of March he worked on the visit to the Gallitzins in Münster, then on the journey home and the winter in Weimar, all of which occupied him off and on until the twenty-third of March, when the last sheets of the manuscript of the *Campagne* went to press.

In commenting on the fact that the strictly military parts of the *Campagne* and the *Belagerung* were completed in the first period of work with little trouble, and that the latter part of the *Campagne*, on the other hand, gave its author considerable difficulty, Roethe contrasts the two types of material. In writing of the military portions, Goethe was dealing, "mit einem leichten, unverbunden kunstlosen Tagebuchstil, der das vorhandene Material schnell und bequem in sich aufnehmen konnte (Roethe 15)." The implication of this is that the final parts of the *Campagne*, from a purely literary point of view, demanded much more attentive composition, because it was to contain the "Tendenz" that Goethe had in mind, namely to show the importance and the implications of the family in a distraught time. Being thus the core of the whole, Goethe's sociology *in nuce*, he had to devote to it his most conscientious concentration.

In considering the form which Goethe has given the *Campagne-Belagerung*, the musical form of the three part song comes to mind. This has an introductory theme *a*, a central theme *b*, then a repetition of theme *a*, frequently in altered form, recalling the introduction and at the same time forming a finale. Incidentally, this is the form of the revolutionary song "Ça ira," which Goethe mentioned twice in the *Belagerung* (219: 31 and 255:23). By this analogy, the introductory theme might be the military part of the *Campagne*, the main theme from the *Zwischenrede* to the end of the *Campagne*, and the repetition of the first theme in final position be the *Belagerung*, recalling as it does the first part and at the same time bringing the whole to a conclusion. That such characterization of the form is justified will become evident as the study progresses, but for the present it is not amiss to call attention to the fact, certainly no accident, that the *Campagne-Belagerung* begins at Mainz and moves as it were through a circle that leads back to Mainz.

That the central portion of the *Campagne-Belagerung* was of particular importance to Goethe was demonstrated by continuing reference in the diaries to problems of organizing the material[15] and the frequent use of the words "Schema" and "Durchsicht," in connection with it.

Roethe was correct when he said:

> Goethe hat auch dieses biographische Werk trotz seiner so anscheinend lockern chronologischen Form keineswegs leicht genommen; zumal der Briefwechsel mit Riemer belehrt uns, wie er wieder und wieder überdachte, revidierte, von Riemer nachprüfen liess, mit Riemer durchsprach, abermals überprüfte und umschrieb (Roethe 16).

And Roethe went on to cite a contrast that Goethe established in a letter to Zelter of the eighth of August, 1822, between his, Goethe's, own effort in re-writing and recasting the material, and the superficial ease with which " . . . du (es) jetzt verschluckst (W.A. IV v. 36, 110)." But Goethe was confident that his friend would know how to read between the lines, for he said later in the same letter: "Für dich ist mir übrigens nicht bange, deine Natur weiss zu *assimilieren*, worauf doch alles ankommt (italics added)." But he realized also that few would read it with such care. Goethe was conscious of writing for two audiences, for the superficial readers who would find in the work nothing more than a relatively innocuous autobiographical series of sketches, and for the "assimilating" audience, for whom the *Campagne* would become a meaningful and important Goethean judgment on the revolutionary era, and on its various political, and, not least, social phenomena.

Of course, Goethe wished to appeal to the assimilating reader who would be able to supplement what he, out of consideration for higher personages or for fear of being misjudged as a political "liberal," did not want to bare to public view, which in the heated partisanship of the day, would be quick to misunderstand and to accuse. His innermost thoughts and convictions he always kept secret, a tendency that contributed much to make him seem to be the stiff, cold, unapproachable "Geheimrat" of which he was and still is accused by those who see only

with the physical eye. He never had any sympathy for the liberal "doctrinaires," although, on the other hand, his wish to avoid the appearance of taking the reactionary side was just as strong. One must never forget that Goethe was a responsible minister of a state closely allied with Prussia; that his friends and benefactors among the Prussians were many, and furthermore, that the most critically treated leader, the Duke of Brunswick, was the brother of Goethe's revered friend and patroness Anna Amalie, and uncle of Karl August. In writing about the expedition, then, Goethe's choices were seemingly three; first to be silent, second to give an emasculated and hence essentially false account, or third to tell the whole truth, thus estranging friends, laying himself open to accusations of ingratitude and possibly even *lèse majesté* ("Majestätsbeleidigung"), as well as undermining his own position. Goethe's solution, was, however, none of these. Instead he told the whole story, in veiled form, softening the critical elements with such skill that the "gulping" reader gets the impression that the account is essentially harmless and matter-of-fact, while only the "assimilating" reader divines the full implication of everything that Goethe had to say. In the *Tages- und Jahreshefte 1821* he described the writing of the *Campagne-Belagerung* thus:
" . . . man wollte durchaus wahr bleiben und und zugleich den gebührenden Euphemismus nicht versäumen (W.A. I. v. 36, 188)." As a result, the *Campagne* must be read almost as if it were a cryptogram, penetrating the seemingly innocuous and carefully contrived surface to lay bare the fundamental substratum of primary significance.

II. GOETHE'S JOURNEY TO OVERTAKE THE ARMY

We now turn to the *Campagne* itself. In the summer of 1792 Goethe was not at all inclined to embark on a military adventure. After his return from Italy he had again entered into the life in Weimar, though with a keen realization of what he was missing after the Italian sojourn. He had again taken up part of his official duties at the little court, but he devoted much more time to his own work, particularly his scientific investigations. Moreover he had formed a liaison with Christiane Vulpius, who had borne him a son. The duke had given him a fine city house, which was in the process of being remodeled. Thus Goethe would have had personal reasons enough to stay at home.

There were other considerations which caused Goethe's reluctance to take part in an invasion of France. He had anticipated the revolution in France, and he watched the early stages of it with a sense of shock and deep uneasiness. In the *Verfolg* to his *Geschichte meines botanischen Studiums*, mentioned above, he related the sense of loss that had accompanied his return to Germany. What he lost in the way of art, aesthetic values, is well understood. But in connection with our political and social pre-occupations, it will be recalled that the third of the great concerns that had occupied him in Italy and after his return was "die menschliche Gesellschaft." The writing of *Das römische Karneval*, he tells us, was the result of this concern, and the Roman "Volk" was the center of that work. And in the essay that embodied his aesthetic concern, *Einfache Nachahmung der Natur, Manier, Stil,* Goethe states that he had come to understand how the Greeks had developed the highest art in their own national circle, "im eigenen Nationalkreise." From these expressions and from others, particularly from the *Venetianische Epigramme*, it is clear that Goethe had discovered the vital role that the "Volk" played not only in the realm of art, but in that of politics as well. And part of the sense of loss, then, that oppressed him after his return from Italy was the fact that he found no German "Volk," no cohesive, self-conscious group with which or from which to work in promoting the establishment of a similar German "Volk." On the other hand, the French people, as witnessed by the revolution, had clearly attained that degree which he called "Volkheit." And so the prospect of participating on the side of monarchial and dynastic interests in an expedition against a "Volk," however intoxicated or misguided, must have been distasteful to Goethe.

There was yet another reason for Goethe's reluctance, a reason that touched on high policy. For some time Karl August, who was related to the Prussian royal house, had been inclined toward a policy of alliance and collaboration with Prussia.[16] He had accepted a generalship in the Prussian army and had made various arrangements to align Sachsen-Weimar militarily with Prussia. All of this had been against Goethe's advice, partly out of a mistrust of Prussian motives and partly out of a hard-headed realization that military adventures were most unsuited to the modest means of the little duchy. After all, as minister in charge of fiscal affairs, he had had only too thorough an insight into the narrowly limited and inflexible resources of the duchy. Thus when Goethe complied with the duke's call to accompany him on the expedition, he did so unwillingly. On the eighth of August with his servant Paul Götze he left Weimar for Frankfurt, where he arrived on the twelfth. There he stayed with his mother until he received further orders on the twenty-first.

Frau Rat Goethe, with true motherly zeal, expressed happiness at her new, though illegitimate, grandson, and a wish to see mother and child. She also packed a number of items as gifts for the little family, about which Goethe duly wrote to Christiane. Through the campaign he wrote her dutifully once a week with husbandly regularity! But the mood of rebellious dissatisfaction and unwillingness to be torn away from his own family shows clearly in the records of those days in Frankfurt, and the mood continues on into the *Campagne* itself. On the eighteenth of August he wrote to his old friend Jacobi:

> Meine alten Freunde und meine zunehmende Vaterstadt habe ich mit Freuden gesehen, nur kann es nicht fehlen dass man nicht in allen Gesellschaften lange Weile habe, denn wo zwey oder drey zusammenkommen, hört man gleich das vierjährige Lied *pro* und *contra* wieder herab orgeln, und nicht einmal mit Variationen, sondern das crude Thema. Desswegen wünschte ich mich wieder zwischen die Thüringer Hügel, wo ich doch Hauss and Garten zuschliessen kann (W. A. IV, v. 10, 6).

Later on, in a letter to Voight referring to those days in Frankfurt, he made clear his dissatisfaction with the city:

> Auch bin ich jetzt da ich meine Vaterstadt besucht habe, aufs

lebhafteste überzeugt, dass dort für mich kein Wohnens und Bleibens ist. Haben Sie die Güte von dieser Sache und diesen Äusserungen niemanden zu sagen (W. A. IV, v. 10, 6).

Thus before the *Campagne* proper even begins, the family, particularly his own, is seen to be in the forefront of his thoughts. It is important to note that Goethe considered his own to be a fine example of a family, even though it existed *de facto* and not *de jure*, for later he will be seen expressing sharp disapproval of superficial, temporary liaisons. He resented being separated from his own little family, and in Frankfurt he re-visited his mother for the first time in many years, thus renewing long neglected ties to the parental family.

The mood of grumbling ill-humor accompanied him on to Mainz, where he arrived on the twenty-first. At noon that day he was a luncheon guest of Freiherr Johann vom Stein, older brother of the famous Prussion minister and reformer. At this point the *Campagne* as such begins. On the very first page there are no less than three evidences of Goethe's critical and disapproving mood. To be sure, they are all disguised and moderated. In the first line he tells of visiting vom Stein, a great friend of Karl August's, by the way, who was the Prussian representative there, " . . . und (der) sich im Hass gegen alles Revolutionäre gewaltsam auszeichnete (3:4-5)." This is surprisingly strong language for the Goethe of the *Campagne*. There will be repeated occasions to note how Goethe's language in this work is remarkably moderated and veiled, particularly when he is dealing with political subjects. So it is clear that passionate opinions on either side of the burning political question of the day would annoy him. For another thing, the good Freiherr was living at that time, and had been for some time previously, in the house of the famous (or infamous) Frau von Coudenhoven,[17] a friend of the mighty, and mistress to many a famous personage and thus an example of the superficial and amoral sex relationships that were so frequent under the *ancien régime*, and which are essentially antithetical to true family life. To be sure, Goethe made no reference to the gentleman's domestic affairs, possibly out of consideration for the brother Karl vom Stein, a friend of Goethe's, who was still living at the time Goethe wrote. At any rate, Goethe could not possibly have been ignorant of the situation.

Interestingly enough, the next paragraph is devoted to two

French ladies whom Goethe met at the Freiherr's table, the mistress of the Duc d'Orleans and the Princess Monaco, mistress of the Prince de Condé. The former was beautiful, dark, and quiet, the latter blond, gay and irresistible. It is of the latter that Goethe said that he was amazed to find Philine here in the flesh (3:24).

This woman presents an interesting puzzle. Goethe described her as a most attractive person:

> . . . die Zierde von Chantilly in besseren Tagen. Anmutiger war nichts zu sehen als diese schlanke Blondine: jung, heiter, possenhaft; kein Mann, auf den sie's anlegte, hätte sich verwahren können (3:22-23).

But the lady's oldest son at this time was thirty-four years of age! Could a Philine in her fifties have presented such an attractive picture? Would not the sight instead have been repugnant? It is to be noted that he came close to calling her irresponsible in the contrast he established between her and the others: "Sie schien weder so gespannt noch aufgeregt als die übrige Gesellschaft, die denn freilich in Hoffnung, Sorgen und Beängstigung lebte (4:14)."

Goethe makes his personal reaction to these luncheon guests quite clear in the closing lines of the section devoted to it:

> Der gepresste Wunsch dieser Personen ward nur noch bänglicher, als sie nicht verbergen konnten, dass sie die schnellste Rückkehr ins Vaterland wünschen mussten, um von den Assignaten, der Erfindung ihrer Feinde, Vorteil ziehen, wohlfeiler und bequemer leben zu können (4:13-18).

This unsecured paper money, printing press currency, Goethe considered to be a crime and a deceit. The *Campagne* marks Goethe's first personal contact with this institution, and it left on him a deep impression of dishonesty, as will be seen further along in the work, and as can be seen from the famous portion of *Faust II*. It is clear what Goethe's attitude was toward people who wanted to profit from such money.

Thus on the first page of the *Campagne* there is evidence not only that Goethe's grumbling mood of Frankfurt was continued, but more important, no less than three "families" were enumerated. Three extra-legal domestic relationships were touched upon, two explicitly, one passed over in silence, but well known to contemporaries. To contrast them with the Goethe-Christiane liaison is illuminating. The former were typical of the loose, amoral relationships of the *ancien régime*, more or less temporary relations for sexual gratification, for material or social advancement, or for any mixture of the three. The Goethe-Christiane union, however, through its intent for permanence and willingness to assume responsibility for the resulting children was "eine Gewissensehe" as Goethe himself termed it, which, although it lacked the legal bond, was in every respect a real marriage, an indissoluble family.

To view these "families" from the point of view of Goethe's scientific method of thought, the three liaisons in Mainz are to be considered as "unregelmässige oder rückschreitende Metamorphosen" of the family, while Goethe's own represents "die regelmässige oder fortschreitende Metamorphose." Magnus has pointed out that Goethe was one of the first to understand the importance of pathological forms in understanding nature at work.[18] In Goethe's own words,

> Weil aber beides, (das Normale und das Abnorme) nah zusammen verwandt und, sowohl das Geregelte als Regellose, von *einem* Geist belebt ist, so entsteht ein Schwanken zwischen Normalem und Abnormen, weil immer Bildung und Umbildung wechselt, so dass das Abnorme normal und das Normale abnorm zu werden scheint (J. A. v. 39, 334).

Thus all forms of "family" association engage Goethe's attention, even, to use a scientific term, the pathological ones.

It is not going too far to refer to these "families" as pathological, for they are not genuine families in the best sense of the word; they are founded on selfishness, individual gratification and materialistic gain, while the true family is based on selflessness, love and readiness to sacrifice for others. To be sure Goethe does not say this explicitly, but his criticism of Philine-Monaco is clear, as well as his displeasure with the selfish materialism of the whole émigré group, as is seen from his reference to the "assignats."

The evening of the same day and the following evening Goethe spent in the circle of old friends and acquaintances, the Sömmerings, Hubers, and Forsters. The contrast between this group and the luncheon group must have been pleasant for Goethe. He dwelt with pleasure on the similarities that his friends found between himself and his mother, whom they all knew and loved. The time passed " . . . in einem natürlichen, *angebornen* und angewöhnten Vertrauen (4:30; italics added)."

But even this gathering was not without its cloud. Goethe ended the account with these words:

> Von politischen Dingen war die Rede nicht, man fühlte, dass man sich gegenseitig zu schonen habe: denn wenn sie republikanische Gesinnungen nicht ganz verleugneten, so eilte ich offenbar, mit einer Armee zu ziehen, die eben diesen Gesinnungen und ihrer Wirkung ein entschiedenes Ende machen sollte (4:32-5:4).

The word "offenbar" deserves particular emphasis here; it can only mean that Goethe failed to declare himself politically and permitted the group to assume that he was in the opposite political camp. For there were strong adherents of the revolution in the group. Forster particularly was enthusiastic. With Adam Lux and Potocki, he had gone to the convention in Paris, to demand that the French annex Mainz. Later he remained in the city as a member of the French administration, and the Prussians, after the recapture of the city, had put a price on his head.[19]

This account is quite important for another reason, for it gives the impression that the harmony between the old friends was not complete, and that politics was one of the main causes. Immediately after the visit, Huber had written to Körner, both praising and criticizing Goethe:

> Die ihn früher kannten, finden, dass seine Physiognomie etwas ausgezeichnet Sinnliches und Erschlafftes bekommen hat. Ich glaube an Begeisterung an ein höheres Ziel in Goethe nicht mehr, sondern an das Studium einer gewissen, weisen Sinnlichkeit, deren Ideal er vorzüglich in Italien zusammen gebaut haben mag, und in welche denn mannigfaltige und, gegen seinen ehemaligen Geist, oberflächliche Beschäftigungen mit wissenschaftlichen und anderen *vorhandenen* Gegenständen mit einschlagen (Dove xxiii.)

Noteworthy here are the words "Sinnliches," "Sinnlichkeit," and the patronizing reference to the scientific endeavors as "oberflächlich," and finally Huber's own derogatory emphasis on *"vorhandenen* Gegenständen." Here speaks a typical philosophical idealist with his slightly superior scorn for the senses and material things. Most noteworthy, however, is the fact that he placed the emphasis on philosophical and psychological matters. The only reference to political things was a passing one, that Goethe "appeared" to have political matters in mind.

In addition to this there are two further reports on the meeting from Goethe's own pen. The first was from 1819, when he was bringing the *Annalen* up to date. Huber's collected works had been published in 1806, and Goethe knew the appraisal contained in the letter just quoted. About this period, then, the *Annalen* say:

> Bei meinem Besuch in Mainz, Düsseldorf und Münster konnte ich bemerken, dass meine alten Freunde mich nicht recht wieder erkennen wollten, wovon uns in Hubers Schriften ein Wahrzeichen übriggeblieben, dessen psychische Entwicklung gegenwärtig nicht schwer fallen sollte (J. A. v. 30, 15-16).

Here Goethe specifically links the uneasiness with former friends not only to Mainz, but also to Düsseldorf (the Jacobis) and Münster (the Gallitzins), a most important trait, for the latter part of the *Campagne* deals at length with visits to former friends and the impossibility of coming to a complete understanding with them.

The paralipomena to the *Campagne* are remarkably few and short, but in this instance there is a fairly detailed outline that mentions this meeting. It probably dates from the first period of work, and is on half a sheet folded lengthwise, as follows:

> Mainz
> Forster u. Frau
> Huber
> Mad. Böhmer, nacherige Schlegel
> Sömmering u. andere. Vergleichende Anatomie angeregt
> Grosse republikanische Spannung der Gemüther
> Mir ward unwohl in der Gesellschaft
> Damalige Reflexion darüber
> Aufgeklärt durch Hubers Lebensbe-
>   schreibung und Briefe.

On the right side of the same sheet appears the following note:

> Schwer zu entziffernde Complication innerer Geistes-Verhältnisse und äusserer zudringenden Umstände. Auf Kunst und Natur drang ich los als auf Objekte, suchte nach Begriffen von beyden. Zerstörte alle Sentimentalität in mir und litt also Schaden am nahverwandten Sittlich-Ideellen. Neigte mich in solcher Hinsicht ganz zu einem strengen Realismus (W. A. I, 33, 363).

Here too Goethe noted that the misunderstanding arose from philosophical and psychological matters as well as political ones. Dove is doubtless at least partly right in saying that Goethe did not go into the full situation in these opening pages of the work, where they would have been out of place artistically.

Most important is the fact that there was a deep lack of understanding between the old friends. In other instances later on we shall see Goethe exaggerating or distorting the accounts of disagreements with old friends, for reasons that we shall have to examine more closely when we treat those instances. In this case however, the disagreement is made to seem less serious than it actually was, for, as will be seen, Goethe is working up, by means of "Steigerung," to a climax, the disagreement with his brother-in-law Schlosser in Heidelberg at the end of the *Belagerung*. One of the main reasons for these painful failures to attain complete understanding was, of course, the great change that occurred in Goethe in Italy and later, with the result that Goethe had grown away from his friends. But how serious Goethe's reaction to the situation was can be seen from the words "Mir ward unwohl in der Gesellschaft."

Such then are the first two pages of the *Campagne*. At this point it is necessary to stop and consider another beginning that Goethe drew up, but which he later suppressed in preference to the present pages. It is to be found among the paralipomena, and is worth quoting verbatim:

> Man darf sich nicht verbergen, dass seit dem Hubertusburger Frieden, wo die Partheyung, welche Deutschland zwischen Preussen und Östreich theilte, aufgelöst ward, die Deutschen etwas anderes suchten und ein gewisser, unbestimmter Sinn, wo nicht zu etwas Besserem, doch zu etwas Anderem sich nach und nach in ihnen entwickelte. Der dritte Stand bildete sich fortschreitend aus, der Adel wollte nicht zurückbleiben und trat mit ihm in Verbindung.
>
> Nach dem Antheil den man an Corsika sodann aber an Nord-Amerika genommen, rückte das Interesse näher; die Franzosen machten einen Versuch ihren Regierungsformen andere Gestalt zu geben; diese Neuheit unterhielt jedermann, und gewiss der grösste Theil von Deutschland war geneigt, sie gewähren zu lassen und allenfalls zu sehen, was aus diesem Experiment herauskommen möchte.
>
> Diese Gesinnungen verbreiteten sich um so eher, als man in dem Betragen der nordischen Monarchen eben keine entschiedene Sittlichkeit gewahr werden konnte. Polen ward getheilt und wieder getheilt, bis endlich nichts mehr davon übrig blieb. Hier sah man Monarchen die einen ihres Gleichen in Pension zu setzen gedachten, dort rührte sich ein Volk um ähnlicher Weise mit seinem König zu verfahren.
>
> Man hätte wie bisher auch der inneren Gährung zugesehen, welche durch mancherley Umwandlung den Zustand von Frankreich nach und nach völlig aufzulösen schien, aber sie hatten in

> Betracht mancher gegen sie vorgenommenen Verbindungen und Rüstungen Östreich den Krieg erklärt. Aber gleich zu Anfang des Feldzugs, da jedermann aufmerksam war wie kräftig sie sich benehmen würden, verloren sie durch schmähliches Beginnen allen Kredit; ihre angreifenden Heere lassen sich durch panische Schrecken zurücktreiben, zerstreuen, nirgends erblickt man Übereinstimmung; Volksrepräsentanten und König, Minister und Generale, nirgends bemerkt man gleichtätigen Sinn nicht einmal gegen den Feind.
>
> Man fängt an, sie gering zu schätzen, die Emigrirten gewinnen erst recht entschiedenen Glauben; der Krieg war diesseits geschlossen (W.A. I, 33, 377).

That there was at one time an even lengthier introduction is to be seen from the present state of the manuscript, for in the opening pages of the work numerous references to a preceding portion have been crossed out in Goethe's hand (W.A. I, 33, 334). The quoted fragment is the only extant portion of that or another similar introduction. On its suppression, it is interesting to note Goethe's comments in the *Tages- und Jahreshefte 1821*:

> In der Mitte November ward an der *Campagne von 1792* angefangen. Die Sonderung und Verknüpfung des Vorliegenden erforderte alle Aufmerksamkeit: man wollte durchaus wahr bleiben und *zugleich den gebührenden Euphemismus nicht versäumen.* (J. A. v. 30, 356; italics added).

The very fact that this introduction was too blunt for Goethe's purposes is interesting. Here attitudes, ideas and reactions are exposed clearly, which, in the finished work, occur only in veiled form, if at all.

The first paragraph of the fragment establishes the viewpoint from which the events are considered, namely the German, even the patriotic point of view, for the statement that the Germans were seeking something else can only refer to nationalistic stirrings. In this first paragraph, the reference to the middle class and the nobility is significant for its social emphasis. The manuscript was later corrected, by Goethe, to the much more explicit version:

> Der dritte Stand bildete sich fortschreitend aus, der bessere Adel, der sich etwas zutraute, wollte nicht zurückbleiben, und trat mit ihm in Verbindung, *der andere, der auf seine Gerechtsame pochte, behandelte den dritten Stand mit Abneigung, mit Verachtung,* besonders die Frauen (W. A. I, 33, 337; italics added).

The second paragraph of the fragment is remarkable in that

it places the French Revolution in the same series as the Corsican and American revolts. Goethe had shown sympathetic interest for the Corsican and American struggles and so, at least by implication, it would seem that his reactions to the French Revolution had been similar for a time. The fact that he stated that most of Germany was willing to preserve a benevolent neutrality would seem to bear this out.

It is also significant that Goethe nowhere used the hated word "Revolution" in referring to the French upheaval. Instead, he says "Versuch, ihren Regierungsformen andere Gestalt zu geben," and "Experiment." He saw it thus as an internal affair of the French, who had every right to proceed as they pleased in putting their own house in order. There is still another element worth noting in this paragraph. When Goethe says "And certainly the greatest part of Germany was inclined to let them have their way and in any case to wait and see what might come of this experiment," he is saying in effect that when the Austro-Prussian invasion of France did occur, it was not a popular, national military operation, but rather a cynical manifestation of dynastic and monarchial policy. This is also borne out by the fact that the sole occurrence of the word "Volk" in this introduction is applied to the French. In contrast to the more or less united national group or "Volk" of the French, united in the justifiable cause of self-defense, the Austro-Prussian forces in their war of aggrandizement acted directly opposite to the popular will, and thus in an unjustifiable cause. Thus also the French national unity or "Volkheit" is underlined, and by implication the German disunity.

The third paragraph of the fragment is also interesting in that it contains Goethe's clear disapproval of the "northern monarchs" on moral grounds, for "keine entschiedene Sittlichkeit" was to be noted in their behavior. For Goethe, this is strong language. Furthermore, though both the French and the northern monarchs were engaged in disenthroning a ruler, Goethe's attitude to the two actions was quite different. Toward the French he was willing to wait and see, but in the case of Poland he expressed sharp disapproval.

The last two paragraphs continue this criticism of the northern monarchs (of Austria and Prussia) in a more obscure form. He said in effect that it was Austria, through alliances and armaments directed against France, that caused the latter to declare war. And then, when the French armies showed panic, the French state disunity and confusion, only then was " . . . der Krieg diesseits (be)schlossen." The "diesseits" can only refer to Prussia, as Austria was already engaged in hostilities. Thus both powers were put in a very bad light. Austria really caused the war, according to Goethe, and Prussia waited cynically until the French state showed signs of disintegration before joining Austria to administer the *coup de grâce* and, of course, share in the spoils.

The above analysis of the first two pages of the final version of the *Campagne* shows a relationship between its underlying tendencies, that is, the attitudes from which the present formulation arose, and the much more bluntly expressed ideas of this suppressed introduction, ideas which, as the study proceeds, will reappear again and again, although always in a far more disguised and veiled form.

On the morning of the twenty-third Goethe left Mainz to overtake the army, and on the road he met a French émigré lady in difficulties with her overburdened carriage (5:5-7:20). On the face of it this was merely a pleasant interlude on the road in which Goethe helped a beautiful lady in distress. But there are less favorable undertones. In the first place the lady's coach was slowing traffic and the postillion was excited to passionate hate, which even Goethe's well-intended reproof failed to moderate. In conversation with the lady Goethe found that she was joining her husband partly out of need to live from the devaluated paper money, the "assignats;" and what paper money meant to Goethe has already been indicated. Thirdly, it became apparent that the baggage stacked on top of the French lady's carriage was as high as a hay wagon, for the carriage would not pass under a mill-race that had been built over the road, with the result that everyone had to stop, help unpack the carriage on one side of the mill-race and repack it on the other. Goethe referred several times later to the impractical, unrealistic side of the émigrés in carrying impossible amounts of baggage. Finally, the lady requested Goethe to help her find her husband in Trier, the next town, in a demanding and impractical manner. She requested Goethe, who would precede her to Trier by several hours, to find her husband's address and leave a note with the guard at the city gate!

Even that is not the end of the matter. It is possible that

JOURNEY TO OVERTAKE THE ARMY

Goethe's servant Paul Götze had an affair with the lady. After his arrival in Trier, Goethe noted that Götze disappeared as early as possible each day and returned as late as possible, and was also reluctant to depart from the city. The puzzle was solved when he found out that Götze had been able to find the French ladies by the pyramid of baggage on top of the carriage, and had been spending his free time with them. It may have been a perfectly innocent affair, but later (194:16-23) Goethe had cause to tease Götze about the French ladies of Trier.

To this point then Goethe's impression of the émigrés can be summarized thus:

1. immoral—the ladies in Mainz, and possibly those on the road; 2. impractical—the baggage of the ladies on the road; 3. irresponsible—Princess of Monaco in her small concern about the outcome of the campaign; 4. demanding—request of the lady on the road for Goethe to find her husband for her; 5. unscrupulous—in profiting from the paper money; 6. beautiful and charming—all described up to this point are women; 7. in sore financial straits. It will be necessary throughout to note carefully what Goethe had to say about the émigrés. With some exceptions, mostly in the latter portion of the *Campagne,* his attitude was quite critical. It must be noted for what he criticizes them and why. So in the opening pages of the *Campagne* the émigrés, formerly the wealthy and privileged noble class of France, have been cast in a leading role, and not a very sympathetic one.

III. THE ROMAN MONUMENT AT IGEL

On the morning of the twenty-sixth of August, Goethe left Trier for Luxembourg, travelling via Igel and Grevenmachern. In the village of Igel, near the confluence of the Mosel and the Saar, stood a monument of Roman antiquity that engaged Goethe's attention. The road of Goethe's time led past the monument; so it is certain that Goethe at least saw the monument in passing. It is quite doubtful that he took time to examine it closely or reflect upon it, for as Roethe pointed out, on the twenty-sixth and the morning of the twenty-seventh Goethe covered about seventy-five kilometers of mountainous terrain in very bad weather, including a lengthy stop at Grevenmachern. There could have been little leisure. Furthermore none of the extant letters of the twenty-sixth or the twenty-seventh of August make any reference to the monument, while the letters subsequent to his return trip on the twenty-second of October do. Wagner's diary for the latter date makes a specific reference to the monument, saying that Goethe tarried a long time beside it and made many notes (Roethe 193).

The Igel monument is described in three places in the *Campagne*, and, as will be shown, it assumes a very significant symbolic role in the work as a whole. Goethe first described it on the trip out (7:21-8:29), then on the trip back (118:7-25), and lastly during his stay in Trier (119:27-121:24). Following Roethe's usage, these visits will be referred to as Igel I, II, and III, although the last two are only a page apart, and really make one lengthy entry. That the matter was important to Goethe can be seen from the fact that there is an extant note, corrected by Goethe, as follows:

> Nachzubringen als Noten
> Monument zu Ygel
> Flüchtige und unzulängliche Skizze in Pokows
>   Reise
> Englisches Kupfer
> Ausführliche Zeichnung in den Trierischen
>   Alterhümern (W. A. I, v. 33, 364).

On the basis of internal evidence, for instance the word "gegenwärtig" (8:3-4), as well as the time element in the journey out, both Roethe and Dove conclude, doubtless correctly, that the description was actually based on observations made on the trip back, about the twenty-second of October or later. The accounts given of the monument on this trip and in Trier must represent the results of his study in the 1820's. Here then Goethe has taken the contemporary account, pushed it forward two months in the chronological narrative, and filled its place with material written nearly thirty years later. The word "Nachzubringen" in the note quoted above would bear this out, indicating that it was written after reviewing a portion of the already completed manuscript. The note cannot be dated precisely, but it must come from a late part of the first period of work or from the second period. So the accounts of the Igel monument form an important instance of the re-casting for literary purposes to which Goethe subjected the raw material of his experiences. "Dichtung" must be separated from "Wahrheit." The passage as such, of course, demands a careful analysis.

It has been frequently pointed out that the strictly military parts of the *Campagne* are arranged in a dramatic rising and falling action, with the climax at the famous cannonade at Valmy. On the way to Valmy, places, persons, incidents and experiences are described with frequent undertones of apprehension for the success of the expedition. After the climax at Valmy, Goethe returns along almost the same route, recalling the incidents before mentioned, but in such a way as to underline by contrast how complete and devastating a fiasco the expedition had become. From the climax the "descending action" is progressively accelerated until the mournful references to previous experiences come like the hammer blows of complete disaster. Coupled with this acceleration is an abbreviation. Experiences related at length on the way out are recalled in a line or two on the way back. For instance, the famous mailbox at Grevenmachern is described in nearly two pages on the way out (9:13-11:2), in four lines on the way back (118:2-5).

The monument at Igel, however, is treated in a fashion just the reverse, for on the way out a page and a half were devoted to it, on the way back and at Trier, a total of three pages. So the very external form of its presentation calls attention to its special importance, the reason for which becomes clear when its content is examined. It forms not only a frame for the military parts of the work, it also serves as a symbol for the deeper meaning of the whole.

Stated briefly, the monument is a symbolic glorification of the family, in which Goethe saw the basic cell of human association, based on mutual love and confidence; its existence and development depend on peace, its ethos is diametrically opposed to that of war. It is the eternally solid and steady pole in the kaleidoscopic whirl of events. The monument, as described by Goethe, shows the family against a background of war.

> Hier stehen Eltern und Kinder gegeneinander, man schmaust im *Familienkreise*; aber damit der Beschauer auch wisse, woher die Wohlhäbigkeit komme, ziehen beladene Saumrosse einher, Gewerb und Handel wird auf mancherlei Weise vorgestellt. Denn eigentlich sind es Kriegskommissarien, die sich und den Ihrigen dies Monument errichteten, zum Zeugnis, dass damals wie jetzt an solcher Stelle genügsamer Wohlstand zu erringen sei (8:15-23; italics added).

The last lines concerning the monument pertain to its base, and the double meaning involved can hardly have been accidental:

> Die so manchem Jahrhunderte widerstehende Dauer dieses Monuments mag sich wohl aus einer so gründlichen Anlage herschreiben (8:27-29).

The family, then, as the "Urform" of human society, was used by Goethe to contrast with war and revolution, which are essentially crimes against the family. The Igel monument is ideally suited to become a symbol of this, for the ancient family it commemorated were "Kriegskommissarien," Goethe tells us, constantly near war and drawing their sustenance from it. The contrast seemed to be made for Goethe's purposes. His own fate in being torn from the bosom of his own family to go to war must have made it more poignant for him. But the family is more than a contrast to war; its deepest principles are at once a preventative and a cure for war. Furthermore, the family in its "Urform" and its "Metamorphosen" is the source from which the principles of proper social organization should flow naturally and organically. Thus what Goethe, sorely troubled at that time and later by the phenomenon of war and revolution, had to say about the family (both as "Urform" and as "Metamorphose") must be traced closely.

On the twenty-seventh of October, two months later, Goethe came again upon the Igel monument:

> Doch ein herrlicher Sonnenblick belebte soeben die Gegend, als

mir das Monument von Igel, wie der Leuchtturm einem nächtlich
Schiffenden, entgegenglänzte (118:7-9).

After the defeat at Valmy and the horrors of the retreat in the most miserable weather, the shaft of sunlight heightened the symbolic importance of the monument. First of all, Goethe saw here again the contrast between the family and war:

> ... ein Monument, zwar auch kriegerischer Zeiten, aber doch glücklicher, siegreicher Tage, und eines *dauernden Wohlbefindens rühriger Menschen* in dieser Gegend (118:11-14; italics added).

Secondly he emphasized again the importance of the activities on which family life must be based: " ... das Gefühl eines fröhlich-tätigen Daseins ... (118:19)." As has been seen in the examination of Igel I, the monument also had sharp meaning for Goethe in relation to his own family:

> ... da ich mich nur desto unbehaglicher in meinem erbärmlichen Zustande fühlte.
> Doch auch jetzt wechselte schnell wieder eine freudige Aussicht in der Seele, die bald darauf zu Wirklichkeit gelangte (118:21-25).

The account of the twenty-fourth of October, Igel III, which purports to be Goethe's reflections about it after he had reached the safety of Trier and gained time for reflection, is the most detailed of the three. It begins in the most general terms:

> Soll man den allgemeinsten Eindruck aussprechen, so ist hier Leben dem Tod, Gegenwart der Zukunft entgegengestellt und beide unter einander im ästhetischen Sinne aufgehoben (119:32-120:3).

This is the temporal view of the eternal role of the family in which the older, death-bound generation of the present nullifies the claims of death by calling into life the new generation of the future.

There follows then a description of the architectural construction of the monument, with Goethe's conclusion as to what era of antiquity it belonged (120:6-20). Goethe noted here " ... der antike Sinn, in dem das wirkliche Leben dargestellt wird (120:22)," in other words he emphasized the realism of the monument. Goethe did not draw attention to it specifically, but one is forced to recall the contrast between his own realistic views and the abstract, philosophic idealism of his friends in Mainz. The inability to come to an understanding with old friends, for philosophic reasons, is to become an ever more important element in the *Campagne* as we proceed, and so we see the Igel monument not only as a symbol of the family, but also, to a lesser extent, as a symbol of Goethe's side in this series of disagreements with old friends.

The description of the obelisk continues as follows:

> In dem Hauptfelde *Mann und Frau* von kolossaler Bildung, sich die Hände reichend, durch eine dritte, verloschene Figur, als *einer Segnenden*, verbunden. Sie stehen zwischen zwei sehr verzierten, mit über einander gestellten *tanzenden Kindern* geschmückten Pilastern (120:23-28; italics added).

This represents a marriage. The hand-clasp, the figure giving the blessing, as well as the dancing children, make that clear, as does the following paragraph:

> Alle Flächen sodann deuten auf die *glücklichsten Familienverhältnisse*, übereindenkende und -wirkende Verwandte, redliches, genussreiches Zusammenleben darstellend (120:29-31; italics added).

The description then proceeds with particular emphasis on the economic basis without which the family could not exist:

> Aber eigentlich waltet überall die Tätigkeit vor; ich getraue mir jedoch nicht alles zu erklären. In einem Felde scheinen sich Geschäft-überlegende Handelsleute versammelt zu haben; offenbar aber sind beladene Schiffe, Delphine als Verzierung, Transport auf Saumrossen, Ankunft von Waren und deren Beschauen, und was sonst noch Menschliches und Natürliches mehr vorkommen dürfte (120:32-121:5).

There will be repeated cause in the future to note the great importance that Goethe assigned to the economic factor in his view of family life, which this passage forecasts.

In concluding Goethe turned to the rich mythological decorations of the monument, mentioning, however, only four specifically (there are a number of others), Bacchus, fauns, Sol, and Luna. The first two are of course erotic symbols, while the last two symbolize husband and wife. Thus those mythological elements that are enumerated reinforce the family theme.

The passage ends as Goethe mentally celebrated Anna Amalia's birthday by wishing he could erect such an obelisk to her memory. A strong personal note here enters again, for Goethe's own family was only made possible by his position in Weimar, which, in the last analysis, he owed to the duchess, who had been chiefly responsible for bringing him to Weimar in the first place.

But the above analysis of the Igel monument is not yet complete. For one thing, the mention of Anna Amalia has only been partly accounted for, because she was far more to Goethe than an employer. In the second place, the description of the varied commercial activities on the monument include a large number of people, all of whom could not possibly have been members of the same blood-family, namely the merchants, the sailors required for the ships, the guides and grooms for the pack-horses, the clerks and customers involved in laying out, inspecting, and selling the wares.

To turn first to Anna Amalie. To Goethe she was first and foremost a patroness. From the point of view of the family, then, she was the center of a "family" of artists. She was also the center of her own blood-family, and, what is more important, she was long the actual political head of the state, thus head of the political family, the people of Sachsen-Weimar. Also, of course, she was the center of the court, that is to say of the cultured and educated people. In addition she was a member of many other such groups, metamorphoses of the family. Furthermore, the composition of these family groups in part overlapped, in part changed, for blood relationship is not the vital factor in the family as Goethe conceived it, nor is permanency. The latter becomes clear when we consider the commercial activities depicted in the monument. The participation of the customers, for instance, in the group would have been of quite short duration.

From the closing paragraphs on the monument it is apparent then that Goethe has enormously expanded the concept of the family. In fact it is now profitable to redefine it as *a group of two or more individuals working together under the leadership of a responsible head for the achievement of some mutually beneficial end.* Of course the head must be worthy and give conscious direction, and the collaboration of the various members must be organized to become effective.

Jockers has clearly recognized this multiplicity of family forms in the *Campagne*:

> Noch deutlicher wird das (der Eindruck eines gesetzlich bewegten Ganzen) bemerkbar in der 'Kampagne' in Frankreich, deren gesellschaftswissenschaftliche Bedeutung noch kaum erkannt worden ist. Nur wer das rechte Auge hat, wird da überall kleine Menschenkreise entdecken, aus denen wie die Gigantes in einer spa-

nischen Prozession Figuren herausragen, die den Charakter gewisser Stände und sogar Nationen klar ins Licht stellen.[20]

Looking ahead over the material to approximately the point of the *Zwischenrede*, it is at once apparent that Goethe has depicted a host of "families." It is valuable to review these in tabular form, grouping them under general headings wherever possible (the following list makes no pretension of completeness):

I. *Frankfurt.*
   1. Sommering group (vaterländische Luft) (4:19-5:4).
   2. Goethe's blood family (Letter from Frau Rath) (126-129).

II. *Weimarisches Regiment* (Karl August, head).
   1. von Fritsch (6:24-7:10) and (118:26-119:24).
   2. 11:17 ff.   9. 69:10 f.
   3. 13:19-15:31   10. 71:6-73:16.
   4. 37:27 f.   11. 74:1-34.
   5. 40:11 f.   12. 75:1-33.
   6. 49:1-5.   13. 77:7-20.
   7. 53:16-55:30   14. 79:9 ff.
   8. 63:27 f.   15. 94:3-20

III. *Grevenmachern Postkasten* 9:24-10:4. Almost all the letter fragments are parts of family life!

IV. *Kramladen in Longwy* 12:20-13:2. Mother and daughter save shop.

V. *Cities*
   1. Longwy 13:3-18. Divided "Volk."
   2. Verdun 30-33 and 99-103. Divided "Volk."
   3. Luxembourg and Trier. Architecture as evidence of past "families," particular emphasis on "Mönch- und Pfaffentum, Bürgerthum, Ritterthum." See especially 133:19-20.

VI. *Feld-und Zeltgespräche* (overlaps with "Weimarisches Regiment").
   1. 17:14-20.   6. 49:18 ff.
   2. 19:10-21:19.   7. 52:3-13.
   3. 30:14 ff.   8. 59:17-60:3.
   4. 34:26 ff.   9. 102:27 ff.
   5. 46:1-30.

VII. *Wissenschaft.*
   1. 25:10-27:7. Prinz Reuss.
   2. 40:20 ff.
   3. 57:27-59:16.
   4. 67:15 f.
   5. 122:11-32 Wyttenbach.

VIII. *Society of Flight* (overlaps with II and VI).
   1. 99:2-22.
   2. 101:16-102:8.
   3. 103:15-105:20.
   4. 112:22 f.

Roman Monument at Igel 49

IX. *Sivry Sketches* (89-93), including,
    1. first French family.
    2. second French family.
    3. Marketenderin, mother and child.
X. *Fragment of Goethe's own family*, himself and Götze (overlaps with II and VIII).
    1. 94:21-95:13.
    2. 98:14-19:02.
XI. *Fragment of Duke of Brunswick's family*, self and sick son.
    1. 95:13-96:11.
XII. *Fragment of King of Prussia's family*, self and Louis Ferdinand, *passim*.
XIII. *Étain family*.
    1. 105:26-107:34.
XIV. *Liseur families*.
    1. 111:17-113:10 (relatives at Arlon).
    2. 115:23-30 (parents at Luxembourg).
XV. *Rhenish principalities*.
    1. 125:20-26 (bad leadership by princes, "Volk" goes astray).
XVI. *Minor examples*.
    1. 80:21-81:19 (roast pig).
    2. 109:9-29 (four neat French soldiers at Spincourt).

In view of the many and exceedingly varied "families" enumerated above, it is at once obvious that the largest family is the Prussian army itself, which met its catastrophe due to faulty command, for it had two conflicting commanders. Goethe pointed out from the beginning the many and serious faults of the army and the whole military organization, and nearly all his criticisms were levelled either directly or indirectly at the leadership.

From this point of view, then, Goethe in the *Campagne* is always surrounded by and in contact with "families," whose existence and number changed as the need for them changed. The "families" then have shifting membership, old ones are constantly ending, new ones all being born. Thus the *Campagne* shows the individual as a member of a large number of "families" simultaneously, "families" that are varied infinitely according to the purpose at hand. The *Campagne* is then, among other things, also a sweeping social study of the forms of association ("families"), some temporary, some relatively permanent, some large and some small, in which man, the social creature, constantly has his being.

The Igel Monument still exists today, and it is profitable to turn to a short consideration of the work of art that Goethe chose as such an all-pervading symbol. Careful modern photographs of the monument allow one to recognize easily all the elements that Goethe described, as well as a number of others, but the main face of the monument (see plate I)[21] makes one thing immediately clear; namely that the three main figures are not as Goethe described them.

> In dem Hauptfelde *Mann und Frau* von kolossaler Bildung, sich die Hände reichend, durch eine dritte, erloschene Figur, als einer Segnenden, verbunden (120:23-26; italics added).

So Goethe saw the two outer figures as man and wife shaking hands across the third, central one. But reference to Plate I shows that the right and the left figures cannot possibly be shaking hands. Instead, the one on the right and the center figure are doing so.[22]

Below the main figures is an inscription, which is worth quoting verbatim. In it the capital letters in parentheses are Dragendorff's and Krüger's emendations, which represent the best informed opinion of modern archaeology on what the missing letters were. The lower case letters in parentheses represent those necessary to fill out standard Roman abbreviations.

> D P(UBLIO AELIO) SECU(NDINO PATRI SUO E)VOCAM
> T(O AUGUSTI ET SEC)URI(i)(S————ET————)
> NOD(F)ILIS SECUNDINI SECURI ET PUBLIAE PA
> CATAE CONIUGI SECUNDINI(i) AVENTINI ET L SAC
> CIO MODESTO ET MODESTIO MACEDONI FILIO EI
> US LUCI(i) SECUNDINIUS A VENTINUS ET SECUNDI
> NIUS SECURUS PARENTIBUS DEFUNCTIS ET
> SIBI VIVI UT (h)ABERENT FECERUNT

The italicized *D* and *M* at the beginning and the end of the first line are larger in size than the rest of the inscription, and stand for DIS MANIBUS, "to the gods of the shades," which was the standard Roman indication of a funeral monument. A translation, following approximately the Latin word order, is as follows:

> To Publius Aelius Secundinus, their father, army veteran, and to Securus————and————nodus, sons of Secundinius Securus, and to Publia Pacata, wife of Secundinius Aventinus and to Lucius Saccius Modestus and to Modestius Macedo, son of that Lucius. Secundinius Aventinus and Secundinius Securus have made (this monument) to their dead relatives that they (S. Aventinus and S. Securus) may have (it) in their own lifetimes.

From the inscription it is plain that the two main figures, as the only two colossal ones, are the brothers Secundinius Aventinus and Secundinius Securus. This can be seen from the fact that theirs are the only names in the nominative, therefore subject of both verbs. Also, the SIBI VIVI indicates that they were alive at the time the monument was erected. All this Goethe could read. Dragendorff and Krüger go on to explain that in Roman times, the living members of a family always had themselves represented on funeral monuments in life-size or larger, while the defunct family members were represented in smaller figures. The other individuals named in the inscription are then, including the one woman named, Publia Pacata, departed relatives. All the rest of the four sides of the monument were interpreted correctly, on the whole, by Goethe. Why should he have made this "error" in regard to the main face?

As Goethe returned from the military invasion, we know that he tarried long beside the monument, that he noted down many things, and, in Wagner's words: " . . . es ist ein Epitaphium eines römischen Commissairs . . . (Roethe 193, 196) . . . unter dem Kaiser Augusto im Jahr der Gebuhrt Christi erbauet (Bergemann 553)." In the *Campagne* Goethe used the word "Kriegskommissarien (8:20)." Where did he get the idea that the family were suppliers or officials for the army? Wagner's words indicate that Goethe got that impression at the monument. The local popular interpretations of the monument, according to Dragendorff-Krüger, were either that it commemorated the birthplace of the emperor Caligula (out of the "Volksetymologie" that Caligula came from Caius Igula), or that it was erected in honor of the marriage of Constantine and Helena. None of the various scenes with which the four faces of the monument are adorned specifically concern the army or military life. And yet Wagner's word "Commissairs" indicates that Goethe knew, as he examined the monument, that the people involved were some type of government officials, probably "Kriegskommissarien." The location in an area which in Roman times was the frontier might have given Goethe the idea of the military, but whence the "Commissairs," that is, the fact that they were some kind of government officials? This view of Goethe's must then have come from a correct understanding of the end of the first line and the beginning of the second line of the text, VOCAMT, as being all that is left of EVOCATO

AUGUSTI, army veteran. Wagner's reference to "dem Kaiser Augusto" makes it probable that some letters of the word "AUGUSTI," since obliterated, were still decipherable when Goethe passed the monument. Such an understanding on Goethe's part would betray a very respectable degree of knowledge of Roman antiquity. First he would have to realize what the *M* at the end of the first line meant, namely the MANIBUS of DIS MANIBUS, and thus exclude it from his reading of the text proper. Secondly he would have had to be familiar enough with Roman customs to realize that the extant letters VOCAT were to be emended into EVOCATO AUGUSTI, army veteran. He would have had to understand that these old soldiers in Roman times were commonly given the lucrative jobs of supplying the army.

That Goethe would have made a careful attempt to read the inscription we know from other sources. An outline of Goethe's account of the stay in Trier, a few days later, has survived. In relation to the various monuments that he described in that city, there is the cryptic note "Nicht zu dechiffriren."[23] In other words, in Trier Goethe made a careful attempt to read some inscription or other, and the very word "dechiffriren" shows that he realized the care, knowledge, and archaeological skill that must be brought to such a task. Goethe read the Igel inscription some one hundred sixty years ago, and it is quite possible that some additional important letters were still legible in his day which have since become effaced. This may well explain the reference to Augustus noted above. Whether or not this is so, his conclusion "Kriegskommissarien" represents a respectable amount of knowledge and amazingly accurate observation.

When Goethe passed the Igel monument he was no novice in understanding ancient art. Less than four years previously he had returned from Italy, where all manifestations of antiquity had claimed his absorbed and devoted study. Furthermore, he had been assisted in that study by excellent artists, Angelica Kauffmann and Tischbein; he had travelled with a copy of Winckelmann, and had excellent advice from Winckelmann's disciples, as for instance Reiffenstein in Rome. Then Goethe had pursued his studies of ancient art and life from one end of Italy to the other and back again with a single-mindedness that approached mania. The opinion of the modern archaeologists Dragendorff and Krüger on Goethe as an interpreter of ancient art is very high. In tracing the history of the interpretation of the monument, they have this to say of Goethe's *Campagne* description:

> Wenige Jahre später, 1792, kam Goethe auf seiner Kriegsfahrt nach Igel. Seine kurzen Bemerkungen in der *Campagne in Frankreich* zeigen, mit wie viel Verständnis und feinem Gefühl Goethe auch dieses Monument in seiner Eigenart erfasst hat, das sich ihm sofort in ein kulturgeschichtliches Bild einordnet. Wir fühlen, dass wir in einer neuen Zeit stehen. Goethes Worte sind, trotzdem sie alles andere als eine gelehrte Behandlung des Monuments sind, oder vielleicht gerade deshalb, das beste, was bis dahin über das Denkmal gesagt worden ist.[24]

Later, in 1829, Goethe wrote a short essay on the monument which will be considered below. In speaking of that essay Dragendorff and Krüger praise Goethe's method:

> Er knüpft daran die methodisch richtige Bemerkung, dass die Bilder, besonders die poetischen, nicht die Erfindung der ausführenden Künstler seien:

In other words, for his time Goethe must be considered an expert in matters of classical sculpture, and hence it is quite possible that he could correctly read the inscription, in fact, in view of Wagner's contemporary words "Commissairs," and "Augusto" we must conclude that he not only could, but did.

But let us turn from the inscription to the main figures of the monument. Another point is still to be considered. Goethe described one of the two outside figures as a woman. A careful look at Plate I shows that the left figure cannot be a woman; that figure wears a tunic, which was strictly masculine garb. The right figure, however, is apparently masculine also, for it is wearing a toga; and a careful examination of the breast shows no evidence of feminine characteristics. Furthermore, this figure exposes an ankle and several inches of leg, an attitude which, due to Roman notions of modesty, would have been improper for a woman, especially on a funeral monument.

In Italy Goethe sought out experts to assist him. In Trier in the evaluation of art monuments, he told about seeking out a young schoolmaster (122:11), without mentioning him by name. He was J. H. Wyttenbach, whom Goethe used as a guide to the artistic and architectural sights of Trier, as we know from another portion of the Trier outline:

> Mein Führer, indem er mich geschichtlich unterrichtete, machte
> mich auf Gebäude der verschiensten Zeitalter aufmerksam (Roethe
> 362).

Another disconnected notation on the same outline makes it certain that they must have discussed the Igel pillar: "Aber dem Geschmackgenusse nicht zusagend wie das Monument zu Igel." What Wyttenbach's interpretation of the monument was in 1792 is impossible to say, but in 1821 he wrote on it as follows:

> Commencing with the pier . . . we clearly see . . . three figures,
> and, as it seems to me, all of them men.[25]

Thus the matter of the clasping of the hands, the sex of one of the figures, the reading of the inscription and the expert advice that Goethe consulted would all seem to indicate that he interpreted the main face of the monument correctly in 1792. We know from Wagner that Goethe tarried long at the monument and took copious notes. Did these notes survive the bonfire that Goethe made of his written material on the *Campagne* at the Jacobis? It is doubtful, for there Goethe referred to burning "das ganze Heft (158:25)." Can a lapse of memory, not assisted by any notes, have caused the "error" in the present version of the *Campagne*? It is not likely. The visual memory of Goethe, the "Augenmensch," devotee of the plastic arts, and deep student of antiquity, was accurate and reliable. On this Dove says:

> Jedermann weiss, wie zuverlässig diese (die Erinnerrung) bei
> Goethe stets für alles war, was sich dem Auge im Raume darzu-
> stellen vermag (Dove xxxvii).

The explanation for this "error" in interpretation becomes apparent when we turn to the works that Goethe used in the 1820's in preparation for writing. In the paralipomenon quoted above, page 44, he mentioned "Ausführliche Zeichnung in den Trierischen Alterthümern," which referred to the work of Quednow.[26] Plate II is a reproduction of the Quednow illustration, which in fact shows a man on the left, a woman on the right shaking hands across a figure that is partly effaced. But a close examination of the figures will show that the left forearm of the left figure is disproportionately long, a point that cannot have escaped Goethe's attention, and which would have aroused his suspicion, if he had in fact forgotten the exact positions of the figures. In his explanation of the monument, Quednow says:

Über der Inschrift sieht man unstreitig das Hauptbild, aus drei Personen von 9 Fuss Höhe bestehend, von welcher die linker Hand eine männliche und die rechter Hand eine weibliche, die mittlere aber bis auf den unteren Teil des Gewandes ganz zerstört ist. Die männliche Figur reicht der weiblichen die linke, und diese der ersteren die rechte Hand; die hintere verstümmelte Figur hat wahrscheinlich auch eine ihrer Hände in die der beiden vorderen Figuren gelegt. Die Figuren sind vortrefflich gearbeitet, nur blos der Kopf der weiblichen Figur, unstreitig eine Ergänzung aus neuerer Zeit, ist schlecht und unverhältnismässig . . .[27]

To be noted here is the fact that the method of shaking hands is an unnatural one, a left hand and a right hand, instead of two right hands. Secondly, the head of the female figure, which Quednow assumes is a later substitution, is actually, according to Dragendorff and Krüger, a genuine part of the original. Furthermore, Quednow says on the following pages that he follows the explanation of a Professor Storck in seeing the outside figures as representing a marriage, the central one being a *deus fideus*. The suspicion is inescapable that the artist who did Quednow's engraving made it agree with the interpretation in the text. At any rate, the disproportionately long left forearm in the left-hand figure, as well as the fact that the two figures use the wrong hands in their clasp, would certainly have aroused the suspicions of such a careful observer as Goethe.

We return to the extant note on the Igel monument from Goethe's hand; in addition to the reference to Quednow, there is a note: "Englisches Kupfer," by which is meant the engraving of William Pars, which appears here as Plate III (taken from Dragendorff and Krüger's reproduction). Here the figures are depicted more accurately; they are all men; the right and the center figures are shaking hands. Why then did Goethe follow Quednow's inaccurate engraving and inaccurate interpretation, when Pars' accurate engraving must have reinforced his own memory of the monument?

The reason is obvious. In Quednow's inaccurate reproduction Goethe saw a welcome opportunity to strengthen the family symbolism of the Igel monument; thus, for artistic purposes, he consciously gave an inaccurate description. In this interpretation the main face describes a wedding, thus the founding of a family, while the other areas are devoted either to various economic activities, or to allegorical pictures which concern the family.

The appearance of the Igel monument in the *Campagne* did not by any means end Goethe's interest in the obelisk. When, in 1829, H. Zumpft made a small model of the monument, a casting of it was sent to Goethe, who was delighted to the point of writing an introduction for the accompanying pamphlet which described the model.

In this account, Goethe quoted from the description of the *Campagne*, material that is to be found 7:21-8:29 and 118:7-22, material which does *not* include the erroneous interpretation of the three figures. In 1829, Goethe interpreted the main scene quite correctly:

> D. *Familien- und häusliche Verhältnisse.*
>
> a) Grosses Bild der Vorderseite, eigentlich das Hauptbild des Ganzen; drei männliche Figuren: die eine rechts leicht bekleidet, scheint wegzugehen und von der in der Mitte stehenden kleinern, welche des obern Teils ermangelt, durch Händedruck Abschied zu nehmen; die grössere männliche links, hält in beiden Händen einen Mantel, als wollte sie solchen der scheidenden um die Schultern schlagen. Über diese Figuren sind drei Medaillons, aus Schildern oder Tellern hervorschauende Büsten angebracht, vielleicht die Hauptpersonen *der Familie* (J. A. v. 35, 268; italics added).

This description of 1829 is also interesting for the emphasis that it places on the family. Under the general heading *Mythologische Gegenstände*, he said:

> Sie sind gewiss sämtlich auf die Familie und ihre Zustände im allgemeinen zu deuten, wenn dieses auch im einzelnen durchzuführen nicht gelingen möchte (J.A. v. 35, 269).

Once again in this account he mentioned the importance of the family, for now that the main panel was correctly interpreted as three men, the family symbolism was no longer so obvious and had to be particularly emphasized.

The important point about this essay of 1829 is however, that it does not mention the inaccuracy of the *Campagne* interpretation. If the erroneous account of the *Campagne* had simply been an error caused by Quednow's engraving, Goethe surely would have taken the opportunity to correct himself, particularly if the *Campagne* were really merely a series of mildly interesting and rather inaccurate autobiographical sketches. The facts that he not only did not, but also that he failed even to mention the difference between the two descriptions, to say nothing of planning corrections to the *Campagne* in later editions, all this can mean only one thing: *the adoption of Quednow's erroneous version was a conscious, purposeful, step taken for artistic reasons to give heart and core to the Igel monument as a symbol of the family in the "Campagne," a literary work of art, in which capacity, then, the "erroneous" description of the Igel statuary could not have been corrected without damaging the "Campagne."*

Thus above and beyond the significance of the monument as a symbol of the family it is of key importance; it shows how Goethe transformed facts to fit his literary and social purpose in the *Campagne*. Goethe's freedom with the Igel monument is merely the most interesting and important of literally scores of such transformations of fact. Understood thus, Dove's full implications in the phrase referring to the *Campagne-Belagerung* as "Eine Poesie der Geschichte" become plain.

IV. INVASION

It is necessary to depart for a moment from the chronological account of events which Goethe used in part to disguise his critical comment, and to turn, instead, to a logical arrangement. His tendency in treating the facts and events will be seen more clearly. We must, furthermore, examine a fairly large volume of detail. A single discrepancy, or even a number of them, between the historical fact and Goethe's narrative could result from any one of several causes. Assurance that such discrepancies reflect a conscious artistic purpose can only be gained cumulatively, by noting a similar tendency in a large number of individual instances.

a) Inefficiency of Command

When he finally joined the army before Longwy on the twenty-seventh of August, Goethe described the situation of the army in dispassionate, matter-of-fact tones, but the total effect, as so often from now on, added up to a sharp criticism of the Prussian military leadership. He found no sentries or guards posted at the camp, no one to demand passes, not even anyone from whom to ask information or directions (11:10-13). Furthermore, to judge from the term that he used, "Zeltwüste," the camp was badly disorganized. The site of the camp was even worse. It was situated in a field that had been drained by a ditch, which through carelessness had become stopped up. As a result, the camp-site was flooded with the most revolting garbage and sewage. Rather than bed down on muddy, polluted ground, Goethe slept in a carriage and had others carry him on their backs when he had to move about (12:7-14).

At Massiges, on the nineteenth of September, is to be found the only reference in this part of the work to a camp-site that was properly laid out; " ... das Lager war abgesteckt, und wir bezogen den für uns bestimmten Raum (48:2)."

On the march of the twenty-ninth of August, Goethe managed to inject another doubtful note, this time in the unity of command. Who was really in charge, the Duke of Brunswick, or his social and political superior, the King of Prussia? The spectacle of the King of Prussia personally inspecting carriages along the line of march was hardly reassuring (16:14-19).

Then Goethe noted the king, surrounded by his own group, separated from the duke, with his own group.

> Wir nun, obgleich mehr zu Beobachten als zu Beurteilen geneigt, konnten doch der Betrachtung nicht ausweichen, welche von beiden Gewalten denn eigentlich die obere sei? welche wohl im zweifelhaften Falle zu entscheiden habe? Unbeantwortete Fragen, die uns nur Zweifel und Bedenklichkeiten zurückliessen (17:7-13).

This is strong language in reference to such exalted personages. Also interesting is the use of the "wir." Roethe has pointed out how frequently Goethe used this general, indefinite form to hide his personal opinions, as he doubtless is doing here.

Later, after the occupation of Verdun, camp was shifted a short distance (September sixth), and as a result, the King of Prussia, Goethe reported, occupied a chateau named *Glorieux*, the Duke of Brunswick one named *Regret*, which names caused all sorts of comment in the camp. It was a fitting play on words, for the king was well known for his youthful valor and, although, of course, Goethe did not say so, there was fear that it might really be irresponsible impetuousness. Brunswick on the other hand was inclined to be overcautious and hesitant to the point of missing opportunities. For the purposes of this investigation, this reported play on words becomes important only when it is ascertained that the headquarters of the respective noble gentlemen were in fact, just reversed! Massenbach, whose work we know Goethe consulted in writing of the *Campagne*, also gives the wrong names for the respective quarters,[28] and refers to the gossip in the camp about the symbolism of the names. In trying to find Carl August's new headquarters, Goethe gave a fairly detailed account of his confused journey, with all the various roads, directions, and turns. Roethe, with a detailed general staff map before him, retraced Goethe's steps from the description in the *Campagne* and proved that Goethe ended up near *Regret*, the headquarters of the king, and not near *Glorieux* (Roethe 165). Thus the suspicion arises, did the Goethe of the 1820's perpetuate a confusion of names that he knew existed? If he did not, but had only fallen into Massenbach's error, what is the point of his careful description of his route to find the new camp, unless it be a hint to those contemporaries who were there that he, Goethe, was consciously including an error? Roethe decided that Goethe included this error in order to make proper use of the characterizing names.

Goethe was also critical of the personal behavior of the leaders. On the twenty-ninth of August, he noticed the two leaders, both with isolated groups well in advance of the main body of the army, in an area where any bush might have concealed an enemy band. Wasn't this foolhardy? But then he took the sting from this reflection in a characteristic manner by musing that it is always the personal bravery of the commanders that assures victory (17:18-20). In a similar fashion he had toned down his criticism of the fact that the King of Prussia had wasted his time in such a subordinate job as inspecting carriages with the words: "Nicht leicht ist jemand von einem vornehmern Visitator angehalten worden (16:18)."

After the successful siege of Verdun, Goethe described two acts of pillaging, with the clear implication that high-ranking officers, and possibly the king and the duke themselves ("die hohen Militärpersonen" 33:18-19), participated in it. First, food stores were plundered, " . . . welches in unserer Lage bedenklich schien . . . (33:10)," then a weapon's storehouse was ravaged, in which latter act the "high military personages" were involved. It is typical that Goethe distracted attention from the gravity of this act in treating it in a humorous light ("Lustig dagegen war die Art . . ." 33:10). Acts of plundering, are of course, inescapable in any invading army. Nonetheless, all military theorists and all civilized armies unite in forbidding it on the purely military grounds (in addition to the obvious moral ones) that it diverts attention from the main military goals, that it incenses the civilian population, and that it actually impairs the combat-readiness of the troops. Goethe's report that the highest military personages initiated the plundering, which was then carried on by all the military ranks, puts the entire allied army, but most especially the leaders, in a very bad light. And the sentry, for a tip, permitted others to enter and leave with their plunder!

Goethe then concluded with a paragraph on hypocrisy that is remarkably frank and which, although it ascribes the main fault to war as such, has the effect of excusing the Prussian leadership and the army:

> So zwischen Ordnung and Unordnung, zwischen Erhalten und Verderben, zwischen Rauben und Bezahlen, lebte man immer hin, und dies mag es wohl sein, was den Krieg für das Gemüt eigentlich verderblich macht. Man spielt den Kühnen, Zerstörenden, dann

wieder den Sanften, Belebenden; man gewöhnt sich an Phrasen, mitten in dem verzweifeltsten Zustand Hoffnungen zu erregen und beleben: hierduch entsteht nun eine Art von Heuchelei, die einen besonderen Charakter hat und sich von der pfäffischen, oder wie sie sonst heissen mögen, ganz eigen unterscheidet (34:4-14).

Finally, the personal behavior of the Duke of Brunswick did not escape Goethe's critical eye. The gloomy note struck by the description of the valley of the Tourbe, the night of September 19th, as the army was approaching action, was reinforced by the peculiar behavior of the duke. When halt was called at Somme Tourbe, the duke personally reproved some units several times for building fires that were too large. This is amazing: fires of any size would betray an army's position. Instead of permitting fires or prohibiting them, the duke objected to big ones, and personally reproved some, not all, of the men. The waste of a general's time in such perfectly futile half-measures was used by Goethe to characterize Brunswick's character and methods. And, as Goethe's comrades at once pointed out, the position of the army was doubtless well-known to the French anyway (50:12-13).

Even Prince Louis Ferdinand, though he was not in the top echelon of command, and even though he later became a friend of Goethe's, was subject to veiled criticism on the basis of his personal behavior. During the advance to Valmy, the prince had ridden beyond the Prussian vanguard, though expressly warned that that was specifically prohibited. Goethe's personal intervention had been necessary to persuade the prince to return, on which Goethe commented: " . . . man ersicht hieraus, dass ein Vermittler überall willkommen ist (43:13)." But the very fact that Goethe, a civilian observer, was needed to recall a prince, and hence a high-ranking officer, to disciplined behavior constituted an unfavorable comment not only on the personal behavior of the prince, but also on the discipline of the army. Furthermore there is doubt that Goethe actually did take the part that he claims for himself. The memoirs of the Prince Royal mention the incident, but make no mention of Goethe by name, instead they state that it was another Weimar officer that did the warning.[29] There will be cause later to doubt some of Goethe's other accounts of his own personal participation.

On the score of financial dealings also Goethe was very

critical of the army command. On the twenty-eighth of August, at the camp near Pillon, occurred the incident of the seizure of the flocks of the French shepherds (18:10-19:4). Not only was the destruction of the livelihood of the French shepherds painted in heart-rending colors (and, of course, families depended on that livelihood!), but the Prussian army was placed on the same moral level as the émigrés as far as financial ethics are concerned: to pay for the flocks, they used worthless printed slips (issued in the name of Louis XVI) on which only the amounts needed to be filled in. Such financial dealings were just as questionable as the use of the false "assignats" by the émigrés, for the French king did not know of this use of his name, could not have consented to it if he had, and was unable, at the time they were issued or later, to redeem them with cash. How seriously Goethe viewed the human tragedy of this confiscation can be seen from his final remarks on it: "Die griechischen Tragödien allein haben so einfach tief Ergeifendes (19:3-4)."

Later, on the seventeenth of September, when riding near the advance units of both the king and the duke, Goethe commented on the fact that the army was burning villages that showed any sign of resistance, but that the troops were following strict orders to spare the vineyards (45:15)! Goethe expressed his doubt of the efficacy of this order, and it is also worthy of comment that he weakened the condemnation in advance by noting how theatrical the landscape seemed with columns of smoke here and there, and by wishing for a van den Meulen to be able to paint it properly.

Furthermore, the command, in the person of the Duke of Brunswick, had perpetrated a colossal stupidity in the form and tone of a manifesto that he had published on the twenty-seventh of July of that year. It was addressed to the French people, and threatened all sorts of dire consequences if they failed to cooperate with their invaders, return to the allegiance of their proper king, protect that king, and overthrow the revolutionary government. Naturally, the revolutionary government then dealt even more harshly with the French king. This Goethe managed both to convey and conceal in the words on the fourth of September, on receiving news from Paris,

... wo, dem braunschweigischen Manifest zum Trutz, der König gefangen genommen, abgesetzt und als Missetäter behandelt wurde (35:13-15).

There were examples of poor discipline in the Prussian camp. On the thirtieth of August, Goethe reported two incidents which become more interesting when viewed together. To be considered first is the second of the two, the case of the pretty girl of Samogneux, who, in attempting to flee the invaders, ran directly into them (20:21-21:19). The gallant Prussians had her escorted home, and then follows a remarkable paragraph:

> Es gibt dergleichen Pausen mitten in den Kriegszügen, wo man durch augenblickliche Mannszucht sich Kredit zu verschaffen sucht und eine Art von gesetzlichem Frieden mitten in der Verwirrung beordert. Diese Momente sind köstlich für Bürger und Bauern und für jeden, dem das dauernde Kriegsunheil noch nicht allen Glauben an Menschlichkeit geraubt hat (21:20-26).

This self-congratulatory comment to be sure fits well with the incident preceding, but when considered in conjunction with the one previous to that, the contrast becomes painful.

This first anecdote had concerned the capture of an armed French peasant who had discharged his gun, so he claimed, to scare the birds out of his vineyard, and who was turned loose by the Prussian patrol with a couple of lashes with a whip. This leniency of the officer in command was in violation of a universally recognized principle of war, namely that ununiformed irregulars who take up arms are to be punished with death on the spot. In this connection, the reference to "Mannszucht" in the third following paragraph is uncomfortable. Here, then, Goethe can be seen using the association of incidents and events to indicate and yet to disguise his critical attitude.

The vineyard sharp-shooter is of further interest in that the account in the *Campagne* differs in important details from a dinner-table account of the same event that Goethe gave in 1794. To Böttiger on June sixth of that year he said that the Frenchman had fired directly at the Prussians, but was permitted to escape hanging only because there was no convenient tree near-by (Roethe 202). No doubt the milder final version reflects Goethe's desire to avoid too direct a condemnation of the Prussian military.

A few pages farther on is to be found the same sort of judgment by association, or expression of opinion by arrangement of material, used this time in a different and even more effective manner. Just before and just after the fall of Verdun, Goethe described four incidents, two of which occurred in the Prussian camp, two in the French; the contrast speaks for itself. In the Prussian camp, an officer, trying to water his horse, fell into the river and drowned, due to his ignorance of local conditions (29:11-16). Thus it is evident that the Prussians had not taken the trouble to choose and designate proper watering places for their animals, or, if they had, that the officer had disregarded these. In the second place, there was an explosion in the Austrian camp, due to carelessness with gunpowder while filling bombs (probably shells—29:17-27). Carelessness with ammunition is a prime symptom of poor discipline.

On the French side, the first anecdote concerned the commandant of the city of Verdun, Beaurepaire, who, while the city council met to consider surrender, warned against it, then, when it had been decided against his will, pulled out a pistol and shot himself (29:27-30:4). Goethe characterized this as ". . . ein republikanischer Charakterzug," and " . . . ein Beispiel höchster patriotischer Aufopferung (30:3)."

Then, after inserting an account of the ride into Verdun and a few other matters, Goethe related the story of the French grenadier, which will be treated below, only to connect it, at the end, with Beaurepaire's suicide. Thus, even a straight arrangement of the incidents in 1, 2, 3, 4 order would have conveyed an implication that would have been, apparently, too direct for Goethe, so he adopted the order 1, 2, 3, then changed the subject, then related incident 4, and linked it with 3.

The patriotic French grenadier, according to Goethe's report, fired a shot that injured no one, as the Prussians entered the city. Too proud to deny his guilt, he was arrested, and, while sitting on a bridge railing under guard, he committed suicide by throwing himself over backwards into the river. Goethe claimed to have seen the man, and gave a very sympathetic description of him, characterizing his deed as " . . . diese zweite heroische, ahnungsvolle, Tat" (32:15), thus connecting it with Beaurepaire's suicide. He ended the account with the highly significant remark: " . . . und noch sah man nicht die geringste Bewegung unter den fränkischen Truppen, zu uns überzugehen (32:21)."

Even more important than the choice of anecdotes and their arrangement is the fact that Goethe's account in each one of the four differed in important points from the actual events, as far as they can be ascertained. To summarize the differences, there was no Austrian camp before Verdun. It was many miles away, so there is something wrong about Goethe's report of an explosion there. It was not a Prussian officer who drowned while watering his horse, but an enlisted man. In Verdun the patriotic French grenadier had actually shot and killed a Prussian officer, not discharged his piece harmlessly, as Goethe wrote. Finally, the commandant of Verdun, Beaurepaire, had not shot himself in the council-session, as Goethe has it, but some time later in the privacy of his own quarters, apparently out of fear of a later court-martial for having surrendered the city, not from patriotic motives. It is to be noted, however, that all these changes point in the same direction, namely to make the Prussians appear in a poorer light than the French. Goethe was here proceeding as he had with the Igel monument—twisting facts to fit his purpose. The above account of the facts must be pieced together from Roethe, Chuquet, Wagner's diary, and from the *Briefe eines Preussischen Augenzeugen über den Feldzug des Herzogs von Braunschweig gegen die Neufranken im Jahre 1792,* Hamburg, Germania, 1793. Though published anonymously, this latter work was actually written by C. F. Lauckhard, from whom another account of these events is to be found in his autobiography, *Magister C. F. Lauckhards Leben und Schicksale, von ihm selbst beschrieben,* in Petersen's *Memoirenbibliothek,* Series II, vol. 15, Stuttgart, n.d.

Lauckhard's praise of the patriotic attitude of the French seems to have strengthened Goethe in his pro-French and anti-Prussian bias, but it would be a mistake to see this as a lack of patriotic feeling on Goethe's part or even as sympathy for the cause of the French Revolution. Goethe was never impelled by reasons or motives that were primarily political. When his attitude seems to be political, it is only because, as has been shown, to him politics were only a surface manifestation of deeper sociological factors which are determined by and subject to the laws of nature, just as science and art are so determined. The natural form of society is the family, or, collectively speaking, the "Volksfamilie," an organic entity held together from within by natural and eternal laws, not, like transitory political forms, held together externally by man-made laws.

In contrast to the allies, the French appeared to Goethe to be a "Volk," a homogeneous, organic unit, "eine gesteigerte Familie," justified in their existence and in their defense of that existence. The allies, on the other hand, represented the outmoded, dynastic, and cynically Macchiavellian political units, in that the rulers were out of touch with their people; thus were not leaders of a "Volk." Hence the allied undertaking was unjustifiable, because it was directed against an organic unity, the French "Volk" or "Volkheit," which was a manifestation of nature; and the allies were, therefore, acting contrary to nature itself. At Verdun, the grenadier and the commandant, in patriotically sacrificing themselves for their people, acted in accordance with the deeper laws of nature, as Goethe understood them, and thus were representatives of nature, while the allied nations were acting contrary to nature's deepest laws in that they were following an arbitrary "Staatsraison," which was motivated by selfishly dynastic and political considerations. This is the underlying meaning of Goethe's apparent bias toward the French, of his apparent prejudice against the allies. From the same source sprang his exceedingly critical attitude toward the French émigrés, who had excluded themselves from their own "Volksfamilie" out of the selfish desire to preserve their own individual privileges at the expense of their "Volk" as a whole.

b) Émigrés

The unfavorable impression that Goethe obtained from the émigré ladies at Mainz and on the road to Grevenmachern has already been discussed. Later Goethe met émigrés at Grevenmachern, where, while waiting for post horses, he noted a number of high-ranking French nobles who, due to their lack of servants, were watering and tending their own horses. This approving note, however, is followed by one that is definitely disapproving:

> Was aber den sonderbarsten Kontrast mit diesem demütigen Beginnen hervorrief, war ein grosser, mit Kutschen und Reisewagen aller Art überladener Wiesenraum. Sie (the émigrés) waren mit Frau und Liebchen, Kindern und Verwandten zu gleicher Zeit eingerückt, als wenn sie den inneren Widerspruch ihres gegenwärtigen Zustandes recht wollten zur Schau tragen (9:5-12).

The "inner contradiction of their present position" was a double one. First, they were embarking on a warlike expedition with all their possessions, including their entire families and excessive baggage. Second, after having been thrown out by their own people, they were advancing again into their native land, due only to the aid of foreign armies. Not to be overlooked is the reference here to the fact that many were accompanied by their "Liebchen." Goethe's disapproval of such liaisons has already been noted in the discussion of his experiences in Mainz.

Under the date of the eleventh of September is to be found an incident which, of all those centering about the émigrés, placed them in the sorriest light. Goethe met an émigré marquis who was very deeply disturbed because the Prussian king, by departing from his headquarters *Glorieux* (actually *Regret*) in a cold downpour without any protective clothing, had forced the French royal princes in his retinue to do likewise. Of this "inhuman" treatment of the noble and royal blood the marquis complained bitterly. He apparently did not realize, nor did Goethe explain, that Prussian military custom dictated that all officers, from the king down, undergo the same hardship in regard to clothing as the common soldier (Roethe 210). The contrast between the Prussian king, hardened to military life from youth by many expeditions and maneuvers, and the sheltered, pampered French princes, was glaring. That this softness was merely symptomatic of a weakness that was far more serious is shown by Goethe's comment:

> ... (dem Marquis) konnte die Betrachtung nicht tröstlich werden, dass der Krieg, als ein Vortod, alle Menschen gleich mache, allen Besitz aufhebe und selbst die höchste Persönlichkeit mit Pein und Gefahr bedrohe (39:26-29).

But the marquis refused to be consoled by this reasonable and obvious comment. In other words, translated from Goethe's veiled language into plain English, it means that the émigrés were unable or unwilling to give up their privileges and share the hardships to which war exposes everyone; they refused to face facts.

Not all of Goethe's comments on the émigrés, however, were negative. In an inn at Longwy the name of the French marquis de Bouillé had been mentioned. The officers had praised him, " ... als einen bedeutenden und in die Operationen kräftig eingreifenden Fremden ... (13:28-29).'' Hearing the name de Bouillé, the inn-keeper, who had been hovering about, broke into the conversation to show great respect for the marquis and express hope in the effectiveness of that worthy and active man's efforts. The reason for Goethe's favorable mention is clear— de Bouillé had been an able and patriotic Frenchman, and so a true member of his "Volk."

During the sleepless night before the action at Valmy, on the nineteenth of September, Goethe had met by chance the Marquis de Bombelles, whom he had known in Venice when there with Anna Amalie two years previously. They fell to discussing the pleasure they had had in Venice, where the marquis was French ambassador, when the latter interrupted. Goethe records the marquis' words in direct discourse, a rare thing in the *Campagne*, and, as Roethe showed (Roethe 22 ff.), always a sign that Goethe attached great importance to the material:

> "Schweigen wir von diesen Dingen! jene Zeit liegt nur gar zu weit hinter mir, und schon damals, als ich meine edlen Gäste mit scheinbarer Heiterkeit unterhielt, nagte mir der Wurm am Herzen: ich sah die Folgen voraus dessen, was in meinem Vaterlande vorging. Ich bewunderte Ihre Sorglosigkeit, in der Sie *die auch Ihnen bevorstehende Gefahr* nicht ahneten; ich bereitete mich im Stillen zu Veränderung meines Zustandes (53:5-13; italics added)."

This important pronouncement was given by Goethe in direct discourse for several reasons. First of all, the marquis was an old friend; secondly, pleasant days in Venice were recalled; but most important was the fact that these words reflected Goethe's own fears at the time and later as to the course of the revolution. Vitally important are the words " . . . die auch Ihnen bevorstehende Gefahr . . . ", for the "Ihnen," of course, refers not just to Goethe as an individual, but to the Germans, and the possible spread of the revolutionary ideas to German soil was a worry that obsessed Goethe from the time of the "affair of the necklace" on.

Whether or not this conversation actually took place is not too important, for as Roethe says:

> Die historische Verlässlichkeit dieser Nachtszenen braucht man nicht hoch einzuschätzen: ihr künstlerischer Wert wiegt umso schwerer (Roethe 216).

The reason that Goethe treated these two émigrés in such a

friendly and even highly respectful fashion lies in the fact that, in contrast to all the others, they had shown themselves to be responsible men of foresight, who had served their country effectively, because they felt themselves to be members of the French "Volk."

c) French "Volk"

The first member of the French "Volk" as such whom Goethe met was the postmaster at Grevenmachern (10:5-29). As Goethe was awaiting a change of horses, he fell into conversation with the French official who, on finding Goethe not so rabidly anti-revolutionary as others, gradually gained confidence and began to speak openly. The man was not a fanatical revolutionary, nevertheless he was no friend of the invaders. "Er sagte manches Bedenkliche; ihm schien der Zustand der Dinge wenigstens sehr zweifelhaft (10:13-15)." All in all, Goethe gave the impression that the man was a reasonable, well-informed public servant who, though not an extremist, was nevertheless a patriotic Frenchman. That Goethe was no extremist is seen from the fact that the postmaster took him for a "republican," which means in essence that here two moderates from opposing camps were able to discuss the situation rationally and sensibly.

In the captured Longwy the French "Volk" appeared to Goethe first in the family of the shop-keeper from whom he bought woolen blankets. This family, consisting only of mother, daughter and baby, was pleasant and told of their successful efforts to save the baby's life during the bombardment of the city. Also, though a shell had hit their property, they were able to escape without serious damage. Later the party was warned about the terrible Jacobins, meaning the same family from whom Goethe had just bought the blankets! Wild stories about poisoning were told of certain inns (13:3-18). Goethe saw clearly that the citizenry of the town were divided, though the royalists appeared in the worse light because of their fantastic fears and their exaggerated charges against their opponents.

After the capture of Verdun the Weimar headquarters had been set up (September sixth) in a house run by a "good natured" host who was also a real member of the French "Volk," for he had given Goethe's servant Götze, as the latter was leaving, a letter to his sister in Paris, but with the remark: "Du wirst wohl nicht hinkommen (38:10)." And on the eleventh of September the author's party took refuge in a French peasant house, the arrangement of which pleased Goethe, for

> ... sie (die Wohnung) zeugte von einem stillen, häuslichen Behagen; alles war einfach naturgemäss, dem unmittelbarsten Bedürfnis genügend. Dies hatten wir gestört, dies zerstörten wir (38:20-23).

This is the first of several instances in which Goethe expressed admiration for the houses of the French peasantry and for the peasants themselves. There are only a few such instances before Valmy, but after that they become more frequent and significant. That it was particularly painful for Goethe to be one of a group that disturbed or destroyed a family unit is obvious. But even this impression of the matter is not allowed to stand without modification, for fear that it would be too plain. In the next few lines Goethe weakened it by referring to the plight of the invaders, namely plunder or starve.

Later at Valmy Goethe was able to obtain some French bread captured by raiding hussars. Naturally it was white, for: "... der Franzos erschrickt vor jeder schwarzen Krume (56:32)." Here then white and black bread are used to symbolize the French and the German peoples respectively, and consequently the contrast between them. This is the sense of the remark that Goethe made later in describing the "desertion" of the two French boys who had gone along with the allied armies to be able to care for their requisitioned horses:

> ... ich glaube aber, dass eigentlich das dargebotene Kommissbrot sie zu dem letzten entscheidenden Schritt bewogen habe. Weiss und schwarz Brot ist eigentlich das Schibboleth, das Feldgeschrei, zwischen Deutschen und Franzosen (66:16-19).

The same symbolic use of the two kinds of bread appears again in the second half of the *Campagne,* when an inn-keeper gave an émigré a meal at reduced prices, because, as he told Goethe, he was the first Frenchman he had ever seen eat black bread (164:13-15).

The French "Volk" then had won Goethe's approval as a reasonable people who placed great importance on the family and family life, who were ready to make sacrifices for their "Volk," and who possessed a sense of unity with each other.

That they were at the moment engaged in a revolution of which Goethe sharply disapproved did not alter that fact.

In the "rising action" of the *Campagne* then a number of incidents have been noted which seem, in their deviation from reality or in the manner of their presentation, to reveal a consistent artistic purpose. It will be necessary to watch closely from now on to see whether enough additional incidents can be found to confirm the present possibility and transform it into an assurance.

V. VALMY

That the unhappy cannonade at Valmy should have ended in disaster is not surprising in view of the fact that disunity of command had prepared the way. Scouts had reported a new movement of the French, and the king, against the will of the Duke of Brunswick, had ordered a pursuit. Almost immediately, however, it appeared that the original information had been in error. Karl August, among others, checked personally and found this to have been the case, a fact which Goethe recorded (48:13-28. See also Dove 276-277). Nonetheless, the order stood and the march continued through the evening and all night. Strategically, this order was the fatal flaw in the Prussian campaign, for it brought the Prussians and allies into contact with the French at the wrong place and in the wrong direction; the Allies were facing back the way they came, the French stood between them and their bases, facing Paris. The decision that had such an unhappy result had been given in unseemly haste by the Prussian king, over Brunswick's objections, and, when the facts on which the decision were based were proved to be erroneous, the orders were not rescinded (Roethe 215). Goethe's account in the *Campagne* does not make the situation clear, doubtless out of respect for the personages involved, though he could count on the fact that contemporaries or students of military affairs would have known the actual situation.

In effect the inconclusive nature of the action at Valmy, a mere cannonade, is a fitting climax to the ill-starred and ill-led campaign. Goethe's account of this important turning point not only contains numerous inaccuracies, but also gives a distorted overall picture of the action. The reason for this is not far to seek; Karl August had led a cavalry attack that had been sharply repulsed (Dove 277-278), after which his units had been withdrawn from the immediate battle-line as can be seen from the fact that later Goethe had to go forward to subject himself to the "Kanonenfieber" experiment. Out of regard for his patron, of course, he carefully omitted the inglorious role of the duke. As a climax to this list of incompetencies, during the battle, if it can be so termed, the Weimar regiment came under allied artillery fire, which Goethe reported, although in such a fashion as to extract the sting from the account.

In the universal discouragement and dejection at having

achieved no decisive results that followed the end of this cannonade, when his friends turned to him for comment, " ... denn ich hatte die Schar gewöhnlich mit kurzen Sprüchen erheitert und erquickt ... (60:1-2)," Goethe made the famous remark of Valmy: "Von hier und heute geht eine neue Epoche der Weltgeschichte aus, und ihr könnt sagen, ihr seid dabei gewesen (60:2-4)."

This "Valmyspruch" is of importance for our investigation, for it must be determined whether or not Goethe actually made the remark at the time, and more significant, exactly what he meant by it. Mommsen noted that the date of the cannonade is wrong, for Goethe gave it as the nineteenth, while it actually took place on the twentieth. That is a minor point, however, in view of Mommsen's later objection that Goethe could not have known *then* that the cannonade represented a turning point. The real reason for the Prussians' failure to press the affair was their decision to give up the west in order to be able to concentrate on Poland.[30] In searching Goethe's correspondence of the time, Roethe cited a letter to Knebel to show that it did not repeat the remark:

> In diesen vier Wochen habe ich manches erfahren und dieses Musterstück von Feldzug giebt mir auf viele Zeit zu dencken. Es ist mir sehr lieb, dass ich das alles mit Augen gesehen habe und dass ich, wenn von dieser wichtigen Epoche die Rede ist sagen kann: *et quorum pars minima fui* (W.A. IV, v. 10, 25).

Mommsen concluded that if Goethe actually had made such a remark, it represented a momentary flash of intuition and did not indicate that Goethe realized the deeper implication of political events. But Mommsen failed to take into account the pervasive sense of history that this letter expresses; Goethe was well aware he had witnessed an historical event, and the solemnity of the realization was heightened by his use of Latin.

However, there is another reason to doubt whether Goethe actually made the remark. Massenbach, in his account of the affair, said: "Der 20. September 1782 hat der Welt eine andere Gestalt gegeben; es ist der wichtigste Tag des Jahrhunderts."[31] Goethe had read Massenbach's work not only when it first appeared in 1809, but he had also referred to it while writing the *Campagne*. In view of the strikingly similar wording, did Goethe simply adopt Massenbach's conclusion or was his final formulation of an actual remark at Valmy merely influenced by Massenbach's wording?

Another factor must be considered before a satisfactory answer can be arrived at. On the twentieth of September the French Assembly reached the end of its term of office and among its last acts decreed universal suffrage with abolition of the property qualifications on the right to vote, and appointed a Convention to succeed it. More important, it abolished the monarchy as of the twenty-first of September, and, on the twenty-second, voted that henceforth the date should no longer be written Year IV of Liberty, but Year I of the Republic. And this without making any provision for a republican form of government! The news of these actions had reached the Prussian and allied armies at Valmy by the twenty-seventh. In the second entry under that date Goethe described how the news had filtered through, and the consternation that it had aroused (70:8-30).

With his proven intuitive foresight, Goethe understood that the events in Paris meant an acceleration and accentuation of revolutionary violence, in which course of events he naturally clearly saw the stimulating effect that the allied threat had produced. Coupled with the fact that he must have seen, after Valmy, that there could be no more advancing for the allies, it is evident that Goethe was in a state of mind that would make such a pronouncement a probability. The report that a year later at Mainz his fellow officers recalled his remark at Valmy in connection with the inauguration of the famous revolutionary calendar, which was decreed to begin retroactively as of 22 September, 1792, could not have been a fabrication as the officers were of the Weimar regiment and many were doubtless still alive in 1822. It must then be assumed that Goethe actually did say something about the historical significance of the event at Valmy. He could not have made the remark on the nineteenth, as he states; it must have been made on the twentieth at the earliest, probably several days later, when the news from Paris on the disenthronement of the king and the commencement of the republic had had a chance to reach the allied camp. One must agree with Chuquet's judgment of the "Valmyspruch:" ". . . il (fait) honneur à la pénétration et l'étendre de son esprit."[32]

For the purposes of this examination, the Valmy remark is

illuminating because it shows that the Goethe of 1792 was aware of the historical significance of the moment. But it is more than an historical insight. Roethe summed up the military aspects of the affair by saying that Valmy represented the end of the great army of Frederick the Great (Roethe 218-219). Later on, in the humorous incident with the "Marketenderin," the contrast between the "good old days" of the great Frederick and the Prussian army of 1792 was underlined. But Goethe, typically, extracted the sting from the contrast by placing the pronouncements in the mouth of a ridiculous old woman (75:31-76:12). Years later, in 1797, Goethe made remarks showing that he understood the significance of the "Volksheer," to be sure. But at this time he did not refer to the French armies. This cannot be the deeper sense of the remark, then, as Roethe was inclined to believe. Still Roethe was close to the truth.

Gothe's realization that the French represented a more or less united "Volk" has been indicated above several times, particularly in reference to the suppressed introduction. Viewed in this light, then, the famous words of Valmy mean that Goethe understood that this cannonade represented a turning-point in the European political order. The old order of the dynastic, monarchical political system, divorced from and yet imposed on the "Volk," was on the downgrade, while the new nationalistic state, represented by France, founded on a united "Volk," was on the rise. At this point in history, the old order was not yet weak enough to fall, nor the new strong enough to be completely victorious. The result was a draw, a stalemate, which Goethe, in his concern with "die Sitten der Völker," "die menschliche Gesellschaft," thoroughly understood in all its portents for the future.

VI. RETREAT

The fact that the advance to Valmy and the retreat from that place follow the same pattern in Goethe's description has been noted by most of the critics and commentators on the *Campagne*. So here, as in Chapter IV, we shall depart from the chronological order and arrange the material under the same headings used there, a procedure that will reveal a definite "Steigerung" in the way in which Goethe presented the events.

a) Inefficiency of Command

In the uneasy days of truce following the battle, Goethe turned to science, this time mineralogy. He discovered natural crystalline balls that were first mistaken for cannonballs (67:15-68:14). This discovery, in turn, led him to tell of the order issued by the higher command to the effect that, in view of the fact that the finest chalk was to be found everywhere just below the surface of the soil, the soldiery should use it to clean their uniforms. And this at a time when the army was starving and soaked in the most miserable cold, rainy weather, and without tents!

Furthermore, the transport had broken down. It had been interrupted by French raids, due to Prussian failure to secure the supply lines by eliminating French strong-points on the march out. As a result, there was no bread for several days. To allay hunger, the command had given "eine etwas wunderliche Vorsichtsmassregel . . . (69:1)," namely that the men should thresh barley and cook the grains until they burst, whereupon they could be eaten.

During the remaining days of inactivity and throughout the following retreat, food became an increasingly vital subject. At the end, it became an acute problem of life or death. At this point, however, it still had its humorous aspects, although the incidents show the military organization in a very poor light. First, a transport destined for the Austrians was commandeered by the Weimar unit; and later, when the bread finally did arrive, it was so mouldy as to be inedible (73:17-74:02). Here, too, Goethe hinted for the first time at the dread disease that had already incapacitated many and was to kill thousands before the end—dysentery.

The stupidity of the manifesto of the Duke of Brunswick has

been referred to. Its disastrous effect was recalled as Goethe noted that the French had issued a similar manifesto, offering, by contrast, good will and hospitality to any who wanted to join them, which had the result of weakening the opposition rather than helping the French cause (65:20-28). It will be remembered that the duke's propagandistic effort helped the opposition without doing his side any good!

During this period of truce, the Duke of Brunswick showed an astounding lack of understanding by repeating (as Goethe said: actually it was a new manifesto) his first notice to the French. Not only did this new pronouncement fail in its intended effect of freeing the French king, it gave confidence to and solidified the revolutionary forces. It was recognized as an empty threat. The following passage was said to have been greeted with roars of laughter in the French Convention:

> Le soussigné déclare que Leurs Majestés l'Empereur et le Roi de Prusse, invariablement attachés au principe de ne point s'immiscer dans le gouvernement intérieur de la France, persistent également à exiger que Sa Majesté très Chrétienne ainsi que toute la famille royale, soient immediatement remises en liberté . . . que la dignité royale soit rétablie sans délai dans la personne de Louis XVI et de ses successeurs.[33]

The second manifesto had an even more serious result in that it caused Dumouriez, the French general, to break off the armistice and resume hostilities (74:3-18). Here again Goethe diverted attention from the full meaning of the incident with humor by joking about the duke's unfortunate pride in authorship!

The actual retreat began on the twenty-ninth of September, fittingly enough in disorganization and bad weather. Now the bill of indictment against the allied leadership lengthened incredibly. On the first day sick and wounded were abandoned to the mercies of the weather and the enemy (76:20), although there was no pursuit, nor even contact with the enemy! Again on the retreat there was evidence that no organized camp was used by the allies. On that same night "kein Lager ward bezogen (77:7)," which roused Goethe's lively fears of surprise attack (78:7-19). On the next night the same thing happened (79:1); and on the first of October "einige Zelte wurden aufgeschlagen (79:29)." The disintegration of the army had begun.

At the two bridges over the Aisne on the second of October

Goethe pictured the army as a whole for the last time. Disorganized, grim, filthy, and sick, it filed past in silence as the king with his staff paused beside the bridge. Later Brunswick paused beside another bridge to watch the retreat of the weary troops (82:8-83:10). On the third of October more sick were abandoned (83:15-20), and on the next day Goethe tried to escape into his scientific studies with Fischer's *Physikalisches Lexikon*. On the same day Goethe's comrades reproached him for failing for the first time to have ready a cheerful word of encouragement (85:1-2). As if to climax this tragic mismanagement, the horse of a cavalryman, requisitioned in the area weeks before, escaped, for which the man was threatened with dire disciplinary measures (85:22-27).

In the *Campagne* Goethe and the Duke of Brunswick came face to face only once: on the seventh of October. The account, as Goethe has written it, sounds innocent and harmless enough. When Goethe's party heard that the duke was behind them, they stood aside to let him pass. Stopping before the group, the duke addressed these words to Goethe:

> "Es tut mir zwar leid, dass ich Sie in dieser unangenehmen Lage sehe, jedoch darf es mir in *dem* Sinne erwünscht sein, dass ich einen einsichtigen glaubwürdigen Mann mehr weiss, der bezeugen kann, dass wir nicht vom Feinde, sondern von den Elementen überwunden worden. (95:20-24)."

Goethe then made a fitting reply, the duke bid them farewell, and Goethe closed with these words:

> Er hatte mich eigentlich niemals geliebt, das musste ich mir gefallen lassen; er gab es zu erkennen, das konnt' ich ihm verzeihen; nun aber war das Unglück eine milde Vermittlerin geworden, die uns auf eine teilnehmende Weise zusammenbrachte (96:7-11).

The fact that Goethe used direct quotation in giving the duke's speech shows the reader that he attached special importance to it. Actually, this seemingly unimportant and even cordial meeting expresses Goethe's sharp condemnation of the duke. For one thing, if the meeting had actually been as pleasant as it seems, why did Goethe dwell on the fact that the duke had never liked him, and had taken no pains to conceal it? That he should have referred to an old antipathy is unusual. Roethe speculated that the ill-feeling must have arisen during a state visit in 1784, judging from one of Goethe's French letters to Frau von Stein:

> Du reste, la conduite du duc envers tout le monde . . . est incomparable . . .
> Je te parlerai au long de sa conduite envers moi . . . (W. A. IV, 6, 350).

The noble duke was, of course, the brother of Anna Amalie, to whom, the duke realized, Goethe would soon be recounting the events of the ill-starred expedition. Furthermore, the duke was well aware of Goethe's literary reputation; he would be quite likely to write about the expedition. The duke's words are thus a clear hint as to what point of view Goethe should adopt in telling of the affair. But, of course, a hint from a man who was not only a duke, but also a general amounted, in those days, to an order, a fact of which the courtier Goethe was well aware. In addition, the duke was speaking before witnesses, and as a courtier and diplomat he was naturally well versed in the art of speaking directly to another without letting bystanders realize what was going on. Thus both he and Goethe understood perfectly that his words were an order to Goethe how to explain the failure of the expedition, not only to Anna Amalie, but in any eventual literary accounts as well. It has been shown throughout that Goethe clearly placed a large part of the blame for the failure of the expedition on the incompetence of the leaders. Goethe's report of the meeting, therefore, showed one of those principally responsible for that failure trying to save his reputation behind the screen of the admittedly bad weather. And how characteristic is the last sentence ("das Unglück eine milde Vermittlerin") in distracting the attention of the casual reader from the real point. And yet Goethe has told all the facts!

There are two later indications that Goethe was worried about possible censorship in the account that he planned to write. In Trier, on the twenty-eighth of October, he met an old officer who told others that Goethe would not write of the expedition (again direct discourse),

> "Glaubt es nicht, er ist viel zu klug! Was er schreiben dürfte, mag er nicht schreiben, und was er schreiben möchte, wird er nicht schreiben (124:22-24)."

Still later in Coblenz Goethe met a general at table to whom he talked of the expedition rather unguardedly, at which the latter, "mit einer bestimmten Gewissheit," invited Goethe to his quarters for a detailed discussion of the matter;

> Ich schien es anzunehmen, blieb aber aus und gelobte mir innerlich, das gewohnte Stillschweigen so bald nicht wieder zu brechen (141:17-20).

In the invasion, Goethe had criticized the command for various sins of omission and commission, thus pointing to potential dangers. In the retreat, the command was criticized as thousands of men paid with their lives for the same and other faults of the leaders. And as a final touch, one of the leaders tried to influence Goethe's report of the causes. In a letter to Herder from Luxembourg, written on the sixteenth of October, Goethe summed up his opinion of the leadership:

> Wenn Ew. Liebden Gott für allerlei unerkannte Wohltaten im Stillen danken, so vergessen Sie nicht, Ihn zu preisen, dass er Sie und Ihre besten Freunde ausser Stand gesetzt hat, *Torheiten ins Grosse zu begehen* (W.A. IV, 10, 36; italics added).

b) Émigrés

In the retreat also the self-exiled French nobility were, with a few exceptions, treated very harshly. During the short stay in Verdun, Goethe learned that the Baron de Breteuil was staying in a neighboring house, which fact recalled to him the part which that nobleman had played in the catastrophic affair of the necklace. Goethe had always attributed an exaggerated importance to that affair, and the terms in which he recalled it in Verdun show clearly that, to him, it represented the beginning of the revolution. Goethe here was mentally reviewing the course of the whole revolution to date. The time was apt, since now, with the retreat of the allies final and complete, the revolutionary government was confirmed in power, at least for a time. The reference is important for the purposes of our investigation because of the opportunity it gave Goethe to speak of the moral degeneration of the French nobility of the pre-revolutionary era:

> ... denn leider alles, was zur Sprache kam (in der Halsbandgeschichte), machte nur das greuliche Verderben deutlich, worin der Hof und die Vornehmeren befangen lagen (102:24-27).

During the invasion we noted the derogatory manner in which Goethe referred to the excess of émigré baggage. On the retreat Goethe saw this baggage, including whole carriages, now abandoned alongside the road. Naturally the abandoned goods were ransacked, and Goethe reported one instance (110:19-30) in which whole cases were found to contain nothing but playing cards! In regard to dead bodies along the road, stripped by ghouls, Goethe made:

> ... traurige Betrachtungen über den Zustand des wohlhabenden, gutmütigen Bürgers in schrecklichem, diesmal ganz unerwartetem Kriegsunheil (111:14-16).

The bearing of these observations on the family and family life is, of course, clear.

At Arlon Goethe visited the respectable middle-class family of his guide Liseur, who was apparently the black sheep of the family. Goethe enhanced the solid, honest, and hard-working character of the family, however, by putting into their mouths the strongest condemnation of the use of the false "assignats" of the émigrés. In the street of the town Goethe had noticed two carriages, larger than most, which, on inquiry, were found to contain the facilities for printing the false money. The use of this unsecured paper currency, really counterfeit, formed the basis of one of Goethe's strongest accusations against the émigrés, as has been shown. The following passage outlines fully for the first time the evil that resulted from their use, as told by the family mentioned above:

> Denn da man sich seit einiger Zeit der *echten* Assignate kaum erwehren könne, so habe man nun auch, seit dem Einmarsch der Alliierten, diese *falschen* in Umlauf gezwungen. Aufmerksame Handelsleute hätten dagegen sogleich, ihrer Sicherheit willen, diese verdächtige Papierware nach Paris zu senden und sich von dorther offizielle Erklärung ihrer Falschheit zu verschaffen gewusst; dies verwirre aber Handel und Wandel ins Unendliche; denn da man bei den *echten* Assignaten sich nur zum Teil gefährdet finde, bei den falschen aber gewiss gleich um das Ganze betrogen sei, auch *beim ersten Anblick niemand* sie zu unterscheiden vermöge, so wisse kein Mensch mehr, was er geben und was er empfangen solle; dies verbreite schon bis Luxemburg und Trier solche Ungewissheit, Misstrauen und Bangigkeit, dass nunmehr von allen Seiten das Elend nicht grösser werden könne (112:19-34; italics added).

Later on Goethe repeated the indictment in detail (123:1-19) from Trier, with the new note that the false "assignats" undermined the value of the genuine ones, so that the disaster was comparable to the burning of a city. Thus, though the "assignats" of the Parisian government were bad enough, the false, counterfeited ones of the émigrés were inexcusable. It is to be noted also that Goethe presented the indictment from the point of view of the solid middle class, namely as a threat to the economic basis of family life.

Later, in Trier, Goethe was shown about an abbey by the abbott, who complained bitterly about the émigré French princes who had been quartered there. The words "Übermut und Verschwendung (134:21)" were used by the church dignitary in describing them. On his boat trip down the Mosel, Goethe had stopped in an inn where he had found the innkeeper's wife outraged at the behavior of some émigrés, who had wastefully wadded bread into balls to throw at each other. In tears she had swept up the bits of bread (137:6-14). Later still, in Coblenz, Goethe complimented the local citizenry for their willingness to supply the Prussian forces with much good wine. The local people replied that they were glad to give to the Prussians, but hated to give to the émigrés, as they resented their insolent behavior toward their own prince and their attempt to usurp his prerogatives in his absence (142:23-30).

The most revealing occurrence concerning the émigrés, however, is one of the first mentioned in this chronicle of retreat. At Sivry the news of a peasant uprising against the émigrés was received. On the previous night a brother of the host had appeared in a house that Goethe was occupying, then had disappeared again mysteriously. Goethe had connected the incidents (88:4-16 and 94:2). According to Goethe's account (90:30-33), no great harm was done in the uprising though actually an officer was killed and, in retaliation, four villages were burned by the émigrés. This, in turn, caused a series of vengeful acts by the populace against the émigrés (Dove 283). The salient point here is the fact that the French peasantry allowed the allied units to retreat in peace, but singled out the émigré units for attack, as if to emphasize the fact that the émigrés were excluded from the French "Volk." They had never been members of the "Volk" and now, as allies of the enemies of France, were traitors, facts which members of the French "Volk" themselves, the final judges, recognized and expressed through their actions.

There is only one favorable reference to the émigrés in this section, the story of Goethe's unnamed émigré host in Verdun.

Reflecting on the affair of the necklace in connection with the presence of the Baron de Breteuil, Goethe reported that he had found in the host's house a series of note-books kept by the latter when he had been a member of the assembly of the notables in Paris in 1787 (103:3-14). Actually his host was Baron de Manonelle, who had not been a member of that assemblage of 1787 (Roethe 235). But Goethe invented the notebooks to contrast the émigré of the type of the Baron de Breteuil with the good émigrés, those who had borne a sense of responsibility for the people and for France. The latter, then, were really members of the French "Volk," while members of the *ancien régime* like Breteuil, showed that they were not. At the same time the situation allowed Goethe to review mentally the course of revolution:

> Die Mässigkeit der damaligen Forderungen (1787), die Bescheidenheit, womit sie abgefasst, kontrastierten völlig mit den gegenwärtigen Zuständen von Gewaltsamkeit, Übermut und Verzweiflung (103:9-12).

The next morning the exodus from Verdun began; and Goethe with sympathetic respect, described the departure of his émigré host on foot, followed by his servant, carrying a bundle on a stick (103:25-30).

c) *French "Volk"*

In this section Goethe showed again a highly respectful attitude toward the French common people. During the truce after Valmy, the French soldiery treated the Prussian soldiers with great friendliness and consideration (65:11-29). On the people and the landscape Goethe commented as follows:

> ... (das Land) ... das aber denn doch seine wenigen, arbeitsamen, ordnungsliebenden genügsamen Einwohner allenfalls ernährt ... ich aber habe keineswegs Ungeziefer und Bettelherberge dort getroffen. Von Mauerwerk gebaut, mit Ziegeln gedeckt sind die Häuser, und überall hinreichende Tätigkeit (66:22-29).

Children from every village spoke with satisfaction of their diet, and Goethe concluded:

> ... so schien es doch, als ob in Friedenszeiten hier nicht gerade Hunger und Ungeziefer zu Hause sein müsse (67:4-5).

On the fourth of October Goethe arrived at the little town of Sivry, where he interrupted his account of the flight with a series of sketches of the life of the peasants (85:29-87:21). The life of these simple "Landvolk" is described in the most sympathetic tones, "idyllisch-homerisch (85:32)." First the construction of the house, then the internal arrangements of the fireplace, the seating accommodations, etc., received Goethe's admiring examination. Finally he fitted the family into the one large room, and then described the family life and praised the institution of the "pot au feu." Goethe's pleasure in what he saw is clear throughout: "Nett und der Ordnung gemäss (86:33)." Finally the customs and manners of the family are described in detail. The children, for instance, kissed their parents' hands and wished them good night on retiring (87:29-31).

In this highly important passage, several points are worthy of special mention. The description of the family life at Sivry, like all of Goethe's family pictures, reminds one of the two causes for metamorphosis which Goethe laid down in his botanical writings. First there are the external causes which in the plant world are environment, heat, light, altitude, degrees of moisture or lack of it, etc. Transferred to the social sphere, we note Goethe here, as elsewhere, detailing the external environment of the family or "Volk," namely the land, the house, the trade or occupation. The second causes of metamorphosis, in the botanical world, were internal, the juices of the plant which, in Goethe's explanations, lead to the "fortschreitende Metamorphose" from leaf to calyx, to sepal, to petal, etc. This internal metamorphosis, in the lives of the people, is represented here at Sivry, as elsewhere, by the customs of the people, their manners and morals.

The family is, of course, the center of the picture, not the individual members as such. No individual is named or described in detail. Furthermore it is not the relationships between members of the family so much as family life viewed as a whole that Goethe presents here. The economic life, as seen from the tools, instruments and arrangements; the customs of the family, as seen from the chair of honor by the fire for the guest and from the well-mannered children; this is family life seen organically, with due attention devoted to realistic matters such as the economic foundation on which it rests and to the role of material things. Finally, and most important, this picture of the family is clearly meant to be symbolic of the life of the whole "Volk," which Goethe made clear at the beginning when he used the terms "Häuslichkeit" and "den französich-ländlichen, idyllisch-homerischen Zustand (85:31 and 86:01)." This family at Sivry, then, represents the family, both as "Urform" and in its rural French "Metamorphose."

The stay at Sivry had other important elements. While bargaining for a pig in a neighboring house, Goethe saw an old "Marketenderin" break in with a young mother and her newly-born child. With a definiteness that brooked no opposition, she had the mother and child fed, gotten into dry clothes, and put to bed.

> Wir betrachteten sie mit Verwunderung: sie verstand sich aufs Requirieren (90:19).

In other words, the useful but morally questionable abilities of the "scrounger," the "organizer" or "promoter," as such figures have been termed more recently, are here shown in a favorable light because they are here devoted to the protection of the family, or at least the indispensable elements of a family, namely mother and child.

The pig was finally purchased by Goethe's own "promoter," Liseur, and butchered against a picturesque background of family life (90:27-92:4). The thread of the family runs through the entire stay at Sivry, even to the end, when, upon leaving, Goethe's party gave their hosts useful advice on how to avoid being looted by the irregular elements that were sure to follow (93:11-25).

The first stop after Verdun was the town of Étain, where Goethe described another family. A tragedy was acted out as Goethe watched: "eine wahrhaft ergreifende Familienszene (107:4)." A son, originally seduced by the ideals of the revolution, had gone to Paris. Recalled, at the insistence of his family but against his own will, to take part in the "restoration" in the wake of the invading allied armies, he arrived just in time to have to join the general flight. As a deserter from the new government, he could not, of course, stay, but had to flee with the émigrés whom he despised. His parents, overjoyed to see him again, had to hasten his departure (107:6-34). This exemplifies Goethe's indictment of the revolution; *that it breaks up families.*

Later that night at Spincourt, in a lodging found for them

by the clever but unscrupulous Liseur, Goethe noted a group of French royalist soldiers, in whom he recognized a party that he had noted during the retreat from Verdun because of their neat and clean appearance in the general mud and bad weather (105:1-3). Here he found them cleaning and drying their footgear before the fire (109:12-29) and admired them for their cleanliness in spite of adversity, contrasting it with the German attitude:

> Ein musterhaftes Betragen, an das man sich in manchen Fällen des Lebens wohl wieder zu errinnern hat! Auch dacht' ich dabei meiner lieben Kriegskameraden, die den Befehl zur Reinlichkeit murrend aufgenommen hatten (109:25-29).

That Goethe should praise émigrés is unusual; but the reason is plain. These men were simple soldiers, not members of the corrupt upper classes, but instead members of the French "Volk," and as such admired by Goethe.

On the next day, at the request of their guide Liseur, the group made a detour via the latter's home in Arlon. Liseur wished to show off his important friends to family and neighbors. To the family Goethe vouched for Liseur's services,

> ... und ob wir gleich an die Bekehrung dieses verlorenen Sohnes nicht sonderlich glauben konnten ... (111:30-31).

The Arlon scenes also are important for our purposes. The life in a small French town is outlined in the most complimentary terms:

> ... diese Personen (zeigten sich) in bürgerlicher Würde, Freundlichkeit und gutem Benehmen zu unserer Verwunderung, wovon in den französischen ernsten Dramen alter und neuer Zeit ein Abglanz herübergekommen ist (113:2-6).

Here again Goethe draws attention to a French family unit as an organic entity and at the same time as a symbol of the "Volk." In this case however, the picture is intensified by the contrasting human type, the prodigal son Liseur. In him, as in the "Marketenderin," Goethe saw that peculiar human type, half rootless ne'er-do-well and half rascal whose particular talents fitted him to profit from the dislocations of war, but who is of little use in the stable middle-class conditions of peacetime.

Thus in the retreat are to be found in accentuated form (Steigerung) the same elements that were developed in the invasion. The incredible incompetence of the allied command finally resulted in catastrophe which was climaxed by the shameful attempt of the Duke of Brunswick to hide the effects of his own failings by means of censorship. On the subject of the émigrés Goethe is clearer than before—they merit condemnation for being traitors to the French "Volk." This is sharply emphasized first by the fact that the rebellious peasants attacked only émigré units during the retreat, letting the allies pass unmolested, and secondly by Goethe's sympathetic portrayal of those few émigrés who had been responsible and patriotic Frenchmen, hence real members of their "Volk." And finally resulted in catastrophe which was climaxed by the dwelt upon with loving care. The perceptive reader is led to the inescapable conclusion that the people and institutions condemned by Goethe were those which violated the principles or ethos of the family as Goethe understood them, namely the allied armies and the bulk of the émigrés; while those which Goethe treated sympathetically embodied those same principles, namely the French "Volk" and particularly the family at Sivry.

VII. INTERLUDES AT LUXEMBOURG — TRIER — COBLENZ

a) Goethe's Personal Role

Before leaving Trier, Goethe at the request of the Duke Karl August paid a call on the Marquis Luccesini, an official high in the Prussian councils, only to have his unspecified request (apparently for information) refused. As Luccesini had had a hand in the second of the Duke of Brunswick's fateful manifestos, Goethe's questions were doubtless about the manifesto or the following diplomatic negotiations, or both (135:15-25).

For the purposes of this examination, the most important example of Goethe's personal role is connected with a letter that he received at this time from his mother (126:5-129:14). The amount of space he devoted to it is an indication of its significance for Goethe. The letter inquired whether or not he would accept a post as councilman of the city of Frankfurt. Whether this was a *bona fide* offer or only a respectful gesture really makes no difference here since Goethe treated it as if it were genuine. This offer confronted Goethe with a personal choice between the republican type of government and the monarchical. He had just participated in a military campaign which showed him that the monarchical, at least insofar as it was represented by Prussia and her allies, was inefficient, outmoded, and suffered from poor leadership, while the same campaign showed him that the democratic or republican form of government, at least in France, was full of a frightening "Dämonie." But what a difference between the "republic" of Frankfurt and that of France!

The post was offered to Goethe at this time because of the recent death of his uncle. This fact and the role his grandfather had played in the city council indicate that by custom only one member of an outstanding family was chosen to the "Rat" at one time. In other words, the city government, insofar as the council was concerned, was founded on family principles, a situation that led Goethe into family reminiscences about his grandfather, who had been "Schultheiss." That Goethe referred consciously to this role of the family in Frankfurt affairs becomes clear when he related that, on his last visit to the city, he had found his now deceased uncle

> ... der als wackerer Sohn, dem Vater gleich, die höheren Stufen freistädtischer Verfassung erstieg ... im traulichen Familienkreis (127:11-13).

In this connection also Goethe recalled his youthful feeling of republican pride and hope that some day he would participate in the affairs of his native city.

Goethe then considered his life in recent years and was inclined to refuse the offer from a sense of loyalty to Karl August and the ducal family, to the country which he had served for so long, to his circle of friends in Weimar, and, most important of all, to his own family in memory of " ... so manches andern häuslich Lieben und Guten (128:20)."

Here again he noted, as he had previously at the Igel monument and in the St. Louis anecdote, the inspiring effects of thoughts about home and family. Thus Goethe saw himself torn between family and family; that of his parents, aunts, cousins, etc., of Frankfurt, which tried to draw him there, while the blood family of his own founding, namely Christiane and their child, tended to keep him in Weimar. Furthermore the most important, his own family, was not the only one in Weimar to claim his loyalty; there were the manifold "families" involved in his official and unofficial activities there, which latter also, of course, formed his profession, the economic foundation for his own blood family. It is clear where his deepest roots lay.

So Goethe reported that he declined the offer, citing diplomatically his recent lack of touch with events in Frankfurt, saying that his experience would not be useful in that city, and hinting at the fact that he had recently been raised to the nobility which would have disqualified him as "Bürger" and hence also as member of the council. In the last line of his report on the matter he noted that his mother had to wait a long time for his reply. He did not answer her letter until the twenty-fourth of December after having been prodded by a second note from her on the subject. The choice was a hard one for Goethe to make; and it is certainly no accident that he delayed the final refusal until after he had been reunited with his own family (the tenth of December); until the eve of the great family festival of Christmas.

Thus this letter, and the recollections that it aroused in Goethe, showed neatly the number and variety of families in which an individual, in this case Goethe himself, may be a member at any given time. The following families can be distinguished here:

I. *Frankfurt*
   1. Goethe's blood family — mother, uncle Textor, grandfather.
   2. "Stadtrat" — influential, respected leaders of the city.
   3. "Die Frankfurter Graduierten" — the intelligent, energetic younger generation of which Goethe had been a member before leaving for Weimar.
   4. Boyhood companions who were filled with patriotic republican sentiments.
   5. "Frankfurter Bürger" — that is the family of the citizens of the free city as a whole.

II. *Weimar*
   1. Loyalty to his patrons Karl August and Anna Amalie; two important subdivisions, first: the family of those interested in art and culture, second: of those charged with political leadership.
   2. Family of his own founding — Christiane and child.
   3. "Das Land" — the "Volk" he had served in official capacity.
   4. "Family" of his own circle of friends, Meyer, Herder, etc. (overlaps II, 1).
   5. Nobility (129:7-11) — family of political and social leaders, transcending political boundaries (overlaps II, 1 and 4).

We noted above in the discussion of the Igel monument that one family or form of the family may overlap another. The individual is presented as the *nexus* of a large and varying number of separate families, some of which exist separately side-by-side, others interlock, still others exist for relatively very short periods of time, while some, of course, are as nearly permanent as the life of the individual. This letter, then, was used by Goethe to show himself in the center of such a complex of families, to show clearly how he was, as all men are, forced to choose between conflicting "family" loyalties.

b) Families in Trier and Coblenz

Under the date of the twenty-ninth of October Goethe surveyed the advances that the revolutionary arms and ideas had made on the German side of the border. His disgust with the inaction of the princes and rulers up to that time is as evident as his fears for the future:

> Vom unseligen Neutralitätssystem die nächsten Fürsten paralysiert, desto lebendig-tätiger die von revolutionären Gesinnungen ergriffene Masse. Sollte man (die Franzosen), wie Mainz bear-

beitet worden, nicht auch die Gegend und die nächst anstossenden Provinzen zu Gesinnungen vorbereiten und die schon entwickelten schleunig benutzen (125:20-26)?

Here again Goethe's criticism was levelled at the rulers, for only where they, the proper leaders of the "Volk," failed in their duty of leadership did the "Volk" (Masse) fall victim to the seductive foreign ideas.

In Coblenz Goethe witnessed an incident which he retold to contrast the Austrians with the Prussians. A Prussian sergeant had tried unsuccessfully to insert his wagon into an Austrian column crossing a bridge. An Austrian sergeant had prevented the attempt. Goethe called the incident:

... ein Streit ... welcher den Charakter beider Nationen klar ins Licht setzte (143:16-17).

His contrast of the two individuals was quite sharp:

... der Gelassene (Österreicher) war stämmig und stark, der Wütende (Preusse) — denn zuletzt erwies er sich so — hager, lang, schmächtig und rührig (144:5-7).

There is more here than a contrast between a Prussian and an Austrian. The key here lies in two factors. First the Austrian: "... rührte sich nicht und hielt auf Ordnung nach wie vor (144:1-2)," in other words, as Goethe himself had so often done, upheld order, and secondly the Austrian sergeant was functioning as the effective leader of his "family," in this case the detachment of troops under his control.

In this section also Karl August is presented as an effective "father" of his particular "family," namely the Weimar regiment. He arranged for the transportation of the sick from Trier to Coblenz by water, a manner of transportation far more suitable than a jolting journey overland. Later in Coblenz Goethe had high praise for the foresight of his duke for choosing the water route (139:27-140:2). Also in Coblenz the duke exhibited intelligent care for the members of his "family" in helping them acquire new footgear after the ravages of the campaign. He bought leather and had the shoemakers among the troops convert it into shoes. Goethe was most specific in his family reference: "... die väterlichste Sorgfalt für seine Untergebenen (142:1)."

Goethe's own boat trip down the Mosel from Trier to Coblenz exhibited several "families." The first was the family of those in the boat, under the leadership of the pilot, or "Schiffer."

This family was soon in trouble because the leader failed in his responsibilities; he lost his way (137:29-30).

The party finally landed at Trarbach, where a most hospitable family took them in, dried their clothes, kept them for the night, and provided them with mattresses to make their trip pleasanter the next day (138:9-139:14). The generosity of the host in offering them mattresses for their journey and the hesitancy of the wife to give up such valued household possessions gives a heart-warming glimpse of family life.

It is rather astonishing that Goethe then (140:7-141:3) quoted an entire page from the memoirs of General Dumouriez.[34] Several questions are raised by this circumstance and the fact that later (201:23-204:24) Goethe copied verbatim three pages of a description of some antique cut gems published by Meyer. Why, on two occasions, should Goethe have copied lengthy passages from the works of others? He cannot be accused of dishonesty or laziness, and he certainly could write German better than Dumouriez could French, or Meyer, German. Dove (296) correctly draws attention to the differences between Meyer's pedestrian language of the catalogue and an instance in which Goethe vividly described a few of the gems earlier (186:29-34). And why, if Goethe did choose to copy from the works of contemporaries, did he fail to give credit?

In the introduction, we mentioned the fact that in the *Campagne-Belagerung* Goethe used the works of others to an extraordinary extent. Roethe devoted no less than five chapters to Goethe's sources (Roethe 158). Nevertheless, he did not exhaust the matter despite his thorough and conscientious work. For instance, he did not show the full extent of the influence of the two works of Lauckhard. This is not the place for a detailed account of the influences evident in the *Campagne*. But a review of the main instances of indebtedness is instructive: *Wagner*. That this man's journal was one of Goethe's prime sources of material has been referred to repeatedly. Unfortunately, the original has not been published and is not available; but it is evident from Roethe's account that Goethe used Wagner in dozens and scores of instances, in the *Campagne* as far as Coblenz, and in almost all of the *Belagerung*. It is certainly not an accident that of all the source works used Goethe gave credit to Wagner alone, and that, significantly, this acknowledgment follows the direct translation from Dumouriez by less than a page:

> Auch kam mir des treuen Kämmerier Wagner Tagebuch zu Ergänzung des meinigen gar wohl zu statten, das ich in den letzten Tagen ganz und gar vernachlässigt hatte (141:29-32).

Dumouriez. In addition to the direct translation noted above, Chuquet[35] lists eleven instances in which Goethe's wording is suspiciously close to that of the memoirs of the French general.
Massenbach. The striking similarity between Massenbach's words on the meaning of the Valmy cannonade and Goethe's phrases has been noted. Fifteen further instances of great similarity between Massenbach and Goethe have been counted in this study. Of these the most important are doubtless the frequent and merciless criticisms of the Duke of Brunswick. Massenbach characterized him finally by quoting the remark of a General Gaudi in 1787: "Grosse Talente, tiefe Einsichten, aber in entscheidenden Momenten Charakterlosigkeit!"[36]
St. Louis Anecdote had been told by Goethe after Valmy (71: 15-72:16) and was taken from the memoirs of a Sire de Joinville. We know that he took it from a republication of 1785[37] because Goethe mistakenly "corrected" a misprint.
Attila Anecdote (72:23-73:3) was doubtless suggested to Goethe by Massenbach.[38] But we also know that Goethe used another work on the subject when he came to write the *Campagne*.[39]
Journal officiel ou Moniteur universelle—official journal of the French government: Goethe read it regularly, and quoted it once inaccurately in the *Campagne* (44:16-17). The news from Paris to which Goethe referred constantly came in large part from the "Moniteur."
Lauckhard, Briefe eines Augenzeugen, etc. Fifteen similarities have been counted. For instance, Lauckhard, like Goethe, was enraged at the sight of émigrés throwing bread at each other[40] and dwelt at length on the terrible effects of the second manifesto of the Duke of Brunswick.
Lauckhard, Leben und Schicksale, etc. Some twenty instances of influence on the *Campagne* were counted in this study. Lauckhard is intemperate in reviling the French émigrés[41] and complains about the Rhenish princes who permitted the spread of revolutionary ideas among their peoples.[42]

There are, of course, other sources, such as Laue and Goethe's servant Götze. Roethe gives a complete account. The foregoing shows, however, that the military portions of the *Campagne-Belagerung* represent the work of a group of writers. Almost all of them also participated in the events, and all the accounts, except that of Joinville, were written at the time of the events. Although they never met as a group, all the writers contributed some elements to the finished literary account of the eventful time, namely Goethe's *Campagne-Belagerung*. We see here a metamorphosis of the family, presented under the responsible "leadership" of Goethe, producing a literary account of the times and of the experiences of contemporaries. Thus Goethe made a virtue out of the necessity, for lack of his own notes, of using the works of others!

In this interlude of recuperation after the military campaign Goethe then wove into the narrative an examination of additional family forms which at the same time expand the concepts and define them more closely. The letter of his mother, the Frau Rat, gave him an opportunity to show an individual, himself, as a member of a number of different families who is torn by conflicting loyalties. That he also saw the military organizations as metamorphoses of the family is proved by his account of how well Karl August had discharged his fatherly responsibilities to the Weimar regiment. Goethe, furthermore, looked on the peoples of political units as metamorphoses of the family as is shown by his description of how poorly the princes of the Rhenish principalities responded to the challenge posed by the advancing ideas of the French Revolution.

VIII. ZWISCHENREDE

This insertion of five pages addressed directly to the reader forms an important transition in the *Campagne*. It will be recalled that, in the *Verfolg* to *Geschichte meines botanischen Studiums*, Goethe told that, after his return from Italy, he felt a deep sense of loss. The things lost were of three main categories; art, science, and the forms of association of human society, the "family" or "Volk." This study is particularly concerned with the last of these three, to a lesser extent with the second, and only slightly with the first. In the *Campagne* up to this point we have observed Goethe examining all the forms of human association encountered from the point of view of the "family" as "Urform" and "Metamorphose" of human society. He expressed judgments on many of the examples though often in such veiled form that the "gulping" reader would miss them.

On his return from Italy, Goethe had found no "Volk" in Germany, corresponding to the Roman "Volk" as described in *Das Römische Karneval*. The preceding pages of this examination have demonstrated that he sensed such a "Volk" among the French as well. Why was there no German "Volk" comparable to those found in Italy and France? In the remaining pages of the *Campagne-Belagerung* Goethe explores this question indirectly by examining in detail the attitudes of various individuals and circles of individuals among the Germans. Naturally these circles, or "families," were all his friends, and since he had come to insights that they did not possess, the account becomes a recital of the reasons, varying with each group, which prevented Goethe from seeing eye to eye with his old friends. But, what is far more important, the total of all these disagreements with old friends shows clearly in what respects the Germans were not yet a "Volk;" what still needed to be done to weld them into such a "Volk."

The frictions and deep uneasiness aroused in contacts with the Sömmering circle were detailed above. It will be recalled that the misunderstandings were fundamental and far-reaching, and that they were on three levels, the political, the psychological, and the philosophic. It will be recalled also that Goethe's personal disappointment was so keenly subjective that he, in the paralipomenon, characterized his reaction to the mental, spiritual, and philosophical horizons of his old friends by saying: "Mir ward unwohl in der Gesellschaft."

It is worth noting, however, that this subjective criticism does not begin after the *Zwischenrede*. It was made also on several previous occasions. We must consider those previous instances here before proceeding to a discussion of the *Zwischenrede* proper.

First, on the thirtieth of August, while observing color effects in a pond (23:3 ff), Goethe fell into conversation with Prince Reuss who, like his Mainz friends, was surprised to find Goethe, the poet, involved in scientific matters, and asked for the reasons.

The conversation between the two, during the shelling of the city, continued throughout the night and concluded after dawn with a significant Goethean comment to the effect that it was much easier to discuss such matters with "Geschäfts- und Weltleute,"

> ... weil sie den Geist frei halten und dem Referenten aufpassen, ohne weiteres Interesse als eigne Aufklärungen; da Gelehrte hingegen gewöhnlich nichts hören, als was sie gelernt und gelehrt haben und worüber sie mit ihresgleichen übereingekommen sind. An die Stelle des *Gegenstands* setzt sich ein *Wort-Credo*, bei welchem denn so gut zu verharren ist als bei irgend einem anderen (27:1-7; italics added).

It was typical of Goethe to contrast the man of the world favorably with the scholar or abstract idealist. His criticism seems to be directed primarily against the scholars who belittled his optical ideas; but, at the same time, it expresses clearly the grounds for the misunderstandings between Goethe and the groups of his old friends, first in Mainz, and later in Pempelfort and Münster. His opposition to their way of thinking is expressed in the word "Gegenstand," by which Goethe was clearly referring to his own position, and the term "Wort-Credo," which refers to that of his opponents. The use of this general and unfamiliar term also has the effect of veiling and lessening the contrast, a stylistic device common in this work. For what does "Wort-Credo" mean? Either the belief in the mere words of others, *i.e.* authority, or in abstract ideas. Goethe had serious reservations about both.

The fact that Goethe had consulted with Johann Hugo Wyttenbach in Trier has been mentioned above. Wyttenbach, like the others, expressed amazement at finding Goethe immersed in science, rather than poetry. To make his position understandable to the young man, a devotee of philosophy, Goethe cited Kant's *Kritik der Urteilskraft*. He must have felt the wry irony here, that he, with his realistic distrust of abstract philosophy, should have taken recourse to that philosophy to justify his preoccupation with what was to him the most obvious thing in the world, nature. In this connection Brion's words deserve attention:

> On pourrait résumer toute la pensée de Goethe, savant naturaliste dont la philosophie, si tant est qu'on puisse employer ce mot en parlant d'un homme qui a refusé tout dogmatisme, dans un simple phrase: tout ce qui est biologique, qui est organique, est bien. Le mal, c'est l'arbitraire, c'est l'intelligence sortie de ses gonds, c'est l'absence de raison ou la raison ratiocinante en dehors de la vie.[43]

Later on we shall find that the question of the value of abstract philosophy was one of the important causes for his disagreements with his old friends, the Jacobis, Princess Gallitzin, and Plessing, as it had been with the Sömmering circle.

Goethe closed the first account of his contact with young Wyttenbach with the highly significant words:

> Es ist wundersam, wie eine jede Zeit Wahrheit und Irrtum aus dem Kurzvergangenen, ja dem Längstvergangenen trägt und mit sich schleppt, muntere Geister jedoch sich auf neuer Bahn bewegen wo sie sich's denn freilich gefallen lassen, meist allein zu gehen oder einen Gesellen auf eine kurze Strecke mit sich fortzuziehen (122:26-32).

This is another of the passages in which Goethe expressed general ideas whose real inner meaning becomes clear only on careful analysis. An interpretation or deciphering of these words, on the basis of what has gone before, would yield this: truth and error refer to abstract philosophy, that of the recent past probably refers to rationalism, that of the distant past possibly to the Greeks. Goethe himself is "der muntere Geselle" who must travel alone on a new path (science), unless he can find a comrade (Wyttenbach) to accompany him for a short distance.

Later Goethe spoke highly of Wyttenbach's assistance in exploring the antiquities of Trier (129:15-20). According to Roethe, the man did indeed become an expert in archaeology. Furthermore, the description of the monuments of Trier that follows in the *Campagne* is, as Roethe has demonstrated, largely taken from the Zeiller-Merian[44] and from Quednow. Why, then, did Goethe attribute this to Wyttenbach? The latter, beginning about 1808, published a series of articles in learned journals. Goethe must have been familiar with at least some of them. Thus Goethe, in 1822, memorialized a cordial acquaintanceship of previous years.

We return to the chronological thread. After he learned that the military operations would continue on the right bank of the Rhine for some months, Goethe's desire to flee became overwhelming. Since the direct route homeward was blocked by the French occupation of Frankfurt, he obtained leave and planned to proceed down the river to Pempelfort to his friends the Fritz Jacobis. Two motives accounted for this flight of Goethe's, for a flight it was: "... das Fluchtgefühl ergriff mich abermals (144:22)." First it was a flight from war: "Mir bangte vor jeder Fortsetzung des kriegerischen Zustandes (144: 21)," and secondly the flight was motivated by an intense desire to reestablish contact with friends. Of the Rhine, he said:

> ... er floss zu Freunden, mit denen ich, trotz manchem Wechseln und Wenden, immer treu verbunden geblieben. Mich verlangte aus der fremden, gewaltsamen Welt an Freundesbrust ... (144:27-30).

The reasons for Goethe's keen desire for "Freundesbrust" are plain. He had just completed a disastrous military adventure that had proved to him, beyond all doubt, that the political states then dominant in Germany were completely unfit to become the nuclei of the desperately needed "Volkheit." With a sense of urgent anxiety about the future, then, he sought sympathetic hearts and minds to whom he could unburden himself, with whom he could share his apprehensions. He was to be bitterly disappointed.

At this point Goethe inserted the *Zwischenrede*, which seems to divide the work in two. Up to now the material has been presented in the form of diary entries, mostly short, with day and month given. There has been a wealth of external objects and incidents to be described and commented upon. The author was almost submerged in a vast "family" (to be sure a "rückschreitende Metamorphose" thereof), namely the army, with little or no control over his own daily comings and goings. In the following portions the diary form is modified sharply. With but a few exceptions, the work up to this point had been objective, dealing with actions and conditions. But beyond this point it becomes much more subjective, expressing feelings, thoughts, reactions, and reflections. The author steps much more into the foreground. The member of a group under military discipline now becomes an independent individual, still moving in groups to be sure, but with perfect freedom to break or join associations as he desires.

Of course the *Zwischenrede*, as a five-page "bridge," could not possibly unite two parts of a work as dissimilar as these. Of the two parts, Roethe said: " . . . dass nur eine äussere Einheit besteht." The *Zwischenrede*, he continued, is " . . . eine solche Einlage, die den Zusammenhang mehr schädigt als fördert (Roethe 246)." Such a misunderstanding was due to Roethe's theory that the main theme of the second part of the work was that of the productive individual *versus* society. Although this is partly accurate, it is insufficient. Dove was much closer to the truth in his belief that the "Leitmotiv" of the whole work is the French Revolution. On the *Zwischenrede* particularly his sensitive remarks are excellent:

> Der sehnsüchtig idealistischen Jugendzeit . . . steht hier (in der Zwichenrede) der männliche Realismus späterer Tage gegenüber (Dove xxiv).

Actually, the *Zwischenrede* welds the work into one organic whole by making use of the family as the "Urform" of human association.

In the *Zwischenrede* Goethe next explained how he had gotten into the extroverted habit of living from day to day, saying:

> Der Vorteil, der daraus entsteht, ist gross; man braucht von einer vorgefassten Idee nicht wieder zurückzukommen, nicht ein selbstbeliebig gezeichnetes Bild wieder auszulöschen und mit Unbehagen die Wirklichkeit an dessen Stelle aufzunehmen; . . . (147:12-16).

Goethe thus avoided a frame of mind that is typical of the individual whose deepest reality is within rather than in the external world; in modern terms, the frame of mind of the introvert.

However, Goethe also saw clearly the disadvantages of living thus from day to day:

> . . . dass wir mit *Unbewusstsein* in wichtigen Augenblicken nur *herumtasten* und uns nicht gerade in jeden ganz unvorhergesehenen

> Zustand aus dem Stegreife zu finden wissen (147:17-20; italics added),

by which, of course, he was preparing the reader for the unexpected shock that the attitude of his Jacobi friends gave him.

The remainder of the *Zwischenrede* is to be understood as an explanation in outline, from a vantage point removed from the time of the events by twenty-eight years, of the differences that existed between himself and the various circles of his own friends, particularly the Jacobis. And, as has been shown, these circles represented the best in German society. But in view of Goethe's characteristic reticence in regard to the faults of others, it will be necessary to read between the lines with great care in these pages. Of the Jacobis Goethe said only: ". . . sie hatten sich getreu an ihrem Lebensgange gehalten (147:32-33)." Just what Goethe meant by this can be seen only from the contrasting course of his own development, which he then proceeded to outline in some detail. Here again, we must look for what he does not say; for what he implies.

He referred to his many stages of testing, testing through action and testing through maintaining steadfastness in the face of challenge (147:34-148:2); vicissitudes which had changed him into a different person, vicissitudes, which " . . . doch alle *dem gottgeführten Menschen* zu Nutz und Frommen gereichen müssen (148:7-8; italics added)." "Der gottgeführte Mensch" is of course Goethe. The implication here is that his friends were not led by God through various tests.

After a frank admission that these conclusions are the result of mature consideration of later years (148:5-10), Goethe noted the effect of "das Sehnsüchtige" in making youth attractive, but said of himself at this juncture:

> (das Sehnsüchtige) . . . wollte dem Manne nicht mehr ziemen, nicht mehr genügen, und er suchte deshalb die volle, endliche Befriedigung (148:20-22).

That he had outgrown this youthful attribute carried the implication that his friends had not.

The full and final satisfaction had been Italy, for which, as a younger man, he had longed for years: " . . . bis ich endlich durch kühnen Entschluss die wirkliche Gegenwart zu fassen mich erdreistete (148:25-27)." In reporting his bold choice to act, Goethe implies that his friends had not done so.

In Italy he felt that he had been relieved gradually of "kleinlichen Vorstellungen" and "falschen Wünschen" (148:34), to which his friends, presumably, were still prey. In Italy the study of art had filled him with great objects and attitudes, and, significantly, " . . . das Bedürfnis der Mitteilung ward immer geringer (149:10-11)." To this psychological turning outward, out of himself, which indicated a more mature independence, his scientific interests [" . . . die entschiedenste Wendung gegen die Natur (149:16)"] had made an important contribution. This turn to science had also the effect of taking him away from all companions, of a lonesomeness that was relieved (and, at the same time, a "Sehnsucht" that was satisfied) by his relations to Christiane, of which he said simply:

> . . . wär' ich ganz einzeln geblieben, hätte mich nicht ein *glückliches häusliches Verhältnis* in dieser wunderlichen Epoche lieblich zu erquicken gewusst. Die *Römischen Elegien,* die *Venezianischen Epigramme* fallen in diese Zeit (149:21-25; italics added).

The outlook of his friends had not been broadened like his own by his Italian experiences, his scientific background, and his military and diplomatic experiences in the earlier abortive Silesian campaign, which had: " . . . mich in einem bedeutenden Lande durch manche Erfahrung aufgeklärt und erhoben . . . (149:29-31)." Finally, in reference to the effect of the military expedition just concluded, he said of himself: " . . . so hätte alles, was noch Zartes und Herzliches sich ins Innerste zurückgezogen hatte, auslöschen und verschwinden mögen (150:9)."

We spoke of the need of henceforth reading with even greater care. Goethe's closing words of the *Zwischenrede* tell us so directly:

> Fasse man dies alles zusammen, so wird der Zustand, wie er nachstehend skizzenhaft verzeichnet ist, nicht ganz rätselhaft erscheinen (150:10-12).

Later, just before the Plessing episode, he becomes even more specific in his admonition to the "assimilating" reader:

> Wer Vorgesagtes in Gedanken festhält und *sich davon durchdringt,* wird nachstehendes Abenteuer . . . weder unwahrscheinlich noch ungereimt finden (167:20-24; italics added).

Roethe saw the *Zwischenrede* as striking the keynotes for the rest of the work: "innere Einsamkeit," "Alleinstehen" and "Entfremdung." This critic held that Goethe stood "trotz missbilligender Selbstkritik auf der Seite des fruchtbaren Individuums gegen die Ansprüche der Gesellschaft (Roethe 248)." However, Goethe here was not primarily the individual opposed to society, but rather the social being, willing and able to devote his talents to a "family" and to a "Volk," seeking such groups into which he could fit. Thus, when Goethe later fled from Pempelfort, it was not as an individual fleeing society but rather as a socially inclined man who, while searching for the elements of a German "Volk," had found instead an isolated, peculiar group which had no roots in its people and had no understanding for his wider concepts of family and "Volk."

In the final lines of the *Zwischenrede* Goethe says that the sketches to follow represent his urge: ". . . diese vor vielen Jahren flüchtig verfassten Blätter nach gegenwärtiger Einsicht und Überzeugung umzuschreiben (150:13-15)." He thus here repeats that the picture he is about to give represents his convictions of 1822, not those of 1792. This represents also an admonition to the reader to examine the actual Pempelfort experiences with care and see, by comparing the facts with the *Campagne* version, what Goethe's "present insights and convictions" were.

IX. PEMPELFORT

At the very beginning of the Pempelfort sketches, Goethe noted the lack of complete harmony between himself and his hosts, the Jacobi family and their friends. The first subject for comment was, naturally, the military experience that Goethe had just come through, "wobei mein Realismus, zum Vorschein kommend, die Freunde nicht sonderlich erbaute (151:6-8)."

The group then turned to Goethe's literary work, from which he chose to read *Die Reise der Söhne Megaprazons*, which had been inspired by his reaction to the French Revolution. Only fragments remain. The work is a description of the voyages of political discovery taken by six brothers (family), which led them to lands with differing political institutions. The work, apparently influenced by Rabelais, was to have been allegorical. The reaction of the Jacobi circle was not favorable. Because of this, Goethe said, he left his "Familie" in some port or other and dropped the subject. To be noted here is the fact that the choice of reading matter was left to Goethe who then read material of social and political application. Goethe's statement that it was the lack of understanding which caused him to drop the work permanently must be challenged, for the subject of the work, namely the examination of various political forms, was of superficial importance, as Goethe came to realize either then or later, in comparison with his developing concept of the "family," in "Urform" and "Metamorphose," as the core to problems of social organization.

Next Goethe's friends suggested he read aloud to the circle, first his own *Iphigenie*, and then Sophocles' *Oedipus Coloneus*. The sensitive and introspective nature of both of these works Goethe found intolerable. After the *Iphigenie* he referred to the Sophocles work as " . . . einen höheren Grad von Folter (151:31)."

Literary memories of former years formed a much safer topic of conversation, as the group soon found; but even this aroused Goethe to an analysis of the conditions of twenty years previously. It was inevitable that he would state why he could no longer fit into them. In those former days, he reported, important and dissimilar individuals had gathered into groups, each showing his compatible and congenial side and covering up his incompatible ones. In such a society of "Weltkinder" there was naturally "eine gewisse Kunst (152:25)." In this fashion mutual misunderstandings remained hidden for a long time. Goethe's own position in this society, which of course the Jacobi circle of 1792 still represented, was assured by his talent. Nonetheless, Goethe recalled that he frequently, even in those days in the 1770's, would turn with " . . . gehässiger Ungezogenheit gegen irgend ein scheinbar falsches Bestreben (152:33-34)" and would persist "im Dünkel des Rechthabens" with "der Ingenuität des Voltaire'schen Huronen (153:2-4)." We must keep two things in mind: first, the society here characterized by Goethe was not only that of his friends in the 1770's, but also that of the Jacobis in 1792, and, secondly, his derogatory reference to his own behavior must be discounted as an evidence of his efforts, by now familiar, to distract from adverse comment, in this case by blaming himself. This self-blame will be noted frequently in his account of the Pempelfort visit.

The psychological reason for his behavior Goethe outlined later anent his optical studies, saying that he could proceed "nur didaktisch und dogmatisch," and confessed "eine eigentliche dialektische und konversierende Gabe war mir nie verliehen (156:24-26)."

But there is more involved here than the fact that Goethe's forthright and undiplomatic behavior did not fit well into the polished social circle around the Jacobis. Goethe had just returned from a military campaign against the forces of the French Revolution, and while he by no means could be called a soldier of the sword in the fight to prevent the ideas of that revolution from spreading into Germany, he was certainly a soldier of the pen, as witnessed by his "Revolutionsdichtung" as a whole. So Goethe would have had to feel the intensification of the extremes at the expense of the middle way which accompanies any such struggle. He would have been in a mood to demand that people show themselves for or against, that they stand up to be counted. Consequently he could only have felt sharp impatience with a circle that consciously included everyone, even himself, as he said later, "(Kreis) . . . welcher nichts ausschloss, also auch mich nicht (154:10-11.)." Thus the artificiality ("eine gewisse Kunst)" of the social tone of the group would have been apt to incite him to harshness against what he considered false goals ("ein scheinbar falsches Bestreben)." One must not be misled by the qualifying modifiers here, "gewisse" and "scheinbar." How intense his convictions were, and consequently how intense his reactions would have been when challenged, can be seen from the reference to himself as "der gottgeführte Mensch (148:8)."

The stylistic devices which Goethe used on occasion to soften and disguise criticism are by now familiar. It is no surprise, then, to find at this point a short seeming change of subject, a reference to French literature, to find, further, high praise of Jacobi's personality, appearance, and manners. Goethe then proceeds with the characterization of that former period in their friendship, namely the 1770's. Each element is connected with the Jacobi circle. Goethe was actually enumerating the number and extent of French influences on the Jacobis.

He began with Voltaire, "... der eigentlich die alten Bande der Menschheit aufgelöst ... (153:19-20)" (from Goethe a damning comment!), and proceeded to link Voltaire with the Jacobis through the former's disciple, de Pauw. Hemsterhuis, a neighbor and frequently a guest, was inclined toward: "... zartere Beruhigung ... ideelle Befriedigung ... platonische Gesinnungen ... Religion (154:1-3)," with all of which, except the last, the realistic Goethe of 1792 would have been out of sympathy. Diderot had been a frequent guest at the Jacobis, and he, as a "Dialektiker," would not have been compatible with Goethe. Lastly, he noted the circle's devotion to Rousseau's superficial and sentimental views on nature, which again were anything but harmonious with his own at that time.

The comment on Goethe's personal disappointments in this circle is now continued. First, as though to soften the impact of what followed, Goethe noted the impossibility for friends to follow the internal development in an author as it occurs, which would explain their surprise when a new work does not resemble the previous ones (154:18-24). For this reason *Megaprazon* was disliked for its complete lack of resemblance to *Iphigenie. Der Gross-Kophta,* already published, was not even mentioned. Referring to this, Goethe said that he felt like a composer who was prevented from repeating his most recent melodies (154:33).

It was in the field of science, however, that his personal disappointments in this circle of old friends were deepest. For Goethe, nature was a vital matter, a manifestation of God—*deus sive natura.* Thus science, the study of nature, was not only necessary for a poet, but in addition had, for Goethe, deeply-felt religious overtones. His friends, on the other hand, felt that science was a waste of time for a poet, and they were tactless enough to say so. Their "Denkweise" not only did not connect with his, but revealed ". . . Vielmehr in den meisten Punkten gerade das Gegenteil (155:10)." His friends accepted the deistic concept of the universe as a machine that God had set going, then left. Thus the physical world, to them, was dead matter. Goethe, as a pantheist, couldn't tolerate ("unleidsam" 155:15) this view of a mechanical universe of dead, lifeless matter. In support of his own views Goethe cited "die Urpolarität aller Wesen (155:23-24)." Thus the disagreements with his old friends appear on the deepest levels. And, a fact which Goethe did not bring out, he was nonetheless well aware that the deistic view was largely a French development of the eighteenth century.

On these scientific subjects, Goethe found, his Pempelfort friends shut themselves up consciously and willfully within the circle of their own beliefs and ideas, " . . . und das taten sie redlich (155:30-31)." Goethe was irritated to the point of playing "das böse Prinzip (157:2)," when his *Metamorphose der Pflanzen*, which had been printed some time before, turned out to be unknown to the group, and when his optical ideas were countered with Newton's "dead" hypothesis. Once again his use of words in reporting the disagreements betrays his intense feelings: " . . . höchst langweilig . . . nichts als beschränkte . . . Vorstellungsarten . . . bornierter Streit (156:29-32)." But, of course, the Goethe of the *Campagne* did not speak in such strong terms without using stylistic devices to weaken the indictment, in this case by embedding the foregoing expressions in phrases which reduce their force. But in spite of all these personal disappointments, Goethe experienced one unqualified success in his report on Italy. On that subject complete harmony existed (157:11-23).

At this point Goethe inserted a paragraph on the Jacobis as a family (157:24-158:13), starting with the countryside, the location of the house, the house itself, the rooms inside, then finally the members of the family seen at a typical family occasion, the dinner table. This is the same organic method of presentation that was noted above in describing the Sivry family, a method by which careful attention is paid to the environment as one of the vital factors in causing metamorphosis. And although the Jacobis seemed to be a family in the best sense of the word, with fine children and valued friends, Goethe's point of departure, the external environment, leads the reader to the realization that the internal environment, so to speak, the mental, spiritual and cultural horizons of the group, are not favorable. He has been criticizing those aspects of the internal environment, noting their mistaken literary values, the excessive French influence, and the unfortunate deistic philosophy.

After reporting the destruction of his *Campagne* sketches and satiric "ordres du jour (158:16-28)," an action which he took out of excessive severity with himself as he came to understand many of his own errors in those pieces, he returned to a characterization of the family group in its internal environment. The result of this analysis was that the Jacobis were unsuited to become members of the future German "Volk."

The first of these comments is contained in the incident in the gallery of paintings that the circle visited (158:29-159:14). After viewing works by the most outstanding painters, including such Flemish immortals as Rubens (who, though accounted a member of the Flemish school, was German born), the group turned to go. But one unidentified member, catching sight of an Italian masterpiece, exclaimed: "Ist einem nicht zu Mute, als wenn man aus einer Schenke in gute Gesellschaft käme (159:7-8)!" Attention is called again to the stylistic importance of the direct quotation. Goethe had already mentioned the injustice of the group toward the northern, the Dutch school of painting, and, although he too admired the Italian, he said that he profited for life from the Dutch masters. The contrast of "Schenke" and "gute Gesellschaft" shows a liking for what is foreign and distant in art and scorn for what is local and native. In other words, this circle was spiritually estranged from its own "Volk" in regard to art.

In the succeeding paragraph Goethe reported the democratic tendencies of the group, by which he clearly meant tendencies friendly to the French Revolution (busts of Mirabeau, Lafayette, etc., were on display 159:15-29). And this in spite of the impending danger to the left bank of the Rhine through the advancing armies of that revolution. This circle, then, was also politically estranged from its own people. It is quite clear from the phrases that the patriotic note is here intentional: " . . . schwankte schon die Gesinnung der Deutschen . . . leider nach deutscher Art und Weise zur Nachahmung aufgeregt . . . (159:24-27)."

But these words refer not only to the Jacobis but also to the better German society of the time as a whole, of which they were typical representatives. This is evident from Goethe's words "der Deutschen," "nach deutscher Art und Weise." Goethe repeated what he had done in the Sivry sketches; while characterizing an individual family, to be sure, he also raised it to the status and force of a type.

After showing the Jacobi group to be spiritually and politically estranged from the "Volk," Goethe turned to a description of the émigrés, again, of course, in an uncomplimentary light. The first mentioned are the French princes whose ridiculous ride in the rain beside the King of Prussia Goethe remembered. The incident was mentioned above. It will be recalled that it was cited as evidence of the fact that they couldn't or wouldn't face facts. Then Goethe described the absurd picture of Mme. de Bueil making her morning toilet in an apothecary shop. Although he failed to say so, the lady was the longtime mistress of Herr von Grimm (mentioned on the next page of the text). Goethe, then, in speaking to his contemporaries, recalled those loose, amoral liaisons which he noted in Mainz at the beginning. Thus, when these émigrés were freely taken up into the Jacobis' circle, Goethe obviously meant to imply that, as the émigrés were divorced from their "Volk," so were the Jacobis from theirs. This international society around the Jacobis represented, then, a rootless, "Volk"-less society, not supra-national, but rather a-national.

There is no lack of other derogatory statements anent the émigrés. Frau von Coudenhoven is mentioned (160:9). It will be recalled with what overtones her name was associated previously in Mainz. The group's parties are referred to as "Halbsaturnalien (161:15)." In this way Goethe indicated that he was by no means to be considered a member of the group. At table the conversation turned to the patriotic behavior of the Frankfurt "Bürger," and Frau von Coudenhoven exclaimed that she would give anything to be a citizen of that city. Goethe replied that he knew a method by which she could, namely by marrying him! Thus Goethe subtly emphasized his own membership in a "Volk," that of the city of Frankfurt. But the individual and the group must agree who is and who is not a member. Goethe had just excluded himself from the Jacobi group, when Herr von Grimm excluded Goethe, to all intents and purposes, by telling an incident which had occurred at the table of the king after Goethe's "Kanonenfieber" experiment. The officers and diplomats around the king also belonged to the "international" set. The repetition of the story, which placed Goethe outside of the set around the king, underlined Goethe's distance from the Jacobi group. Some of the officers had reported meeting Goethe on his ride into fire, which action had puzzled the company at the king's table, until they had concluded:

> ... dass man sich nicht darüber wundern müsse, weil gar nicht zu berechnen sei, was man von einem seltsamen Menschen zu erwarten habe (161:12-13).

In characterizing him as a "seltsamer Mensch," they are definitely excluding him from their own group. And no one could have been more typical of both the king's circle and the Jacobi set than their spokesman, Herr von Grimm, a German with a French mistress.

Towards the conclusion of the Pempelfort visit, "ein gewaltiges rheumatisches Übel (161:18)" put Goethe to bed for a few days. He reported that he contracted the illness "durch Verkältung." We analyzed, above, the reasons why Goethe's Jacobi visit was a series of bitter disappointments to him. The last disappointment, and surely one of the keenest for Goethe, was to see his friends associating freely and on a cordial and equal footing with the émigrés, to Goethe the living symbols of "Volk"-lessness. It was noted that Goethe's reaction to the loose political thinking of the Sömmering circle at Mainz was one of revulsion so keen that it may have been physical as well: "Mir ward unwohl in der Gesellschaft." In view of this strong reaction it is well to examine with some care what Goethe has to say about his illness at Pempelfort. First of all, it was preceded by wild parties ("Halbsaturnalien)." Secondly, Goethe's account of the treatment administered by the physician contains veiled irony, as it would if Goethe felt that the doctor was using physical means to combat an affliction that had partly psychological origins. He was treated with camphor:

> ... welcher fast als Universalmedizin galt. Löschpapier, Kreide
> darauf gerieben, sodann mit Kampfer bestreut, ward äusserlich,
> Kampfer gleichfalls, in kleinen Dosen, innerlich angewandt. *Dem
> sei nun, wie ihm wolle,* ich war in einigen Tagen hergestellt
> (161:23-28; italics added).

This is the same man who, less than two months previously, had withstood all sorts of privation, sleeping on cold, muddy ground, without ill effects. As recently as his trip down the Rhine, he had refused to enter an inn for the night, but had slept in the boat. After six weeks of sleeping in the open, he said, "(mir graute) vor Dach und Zimmer (145:32-34)."

Another circumstance concerning this illness must be mentioned. The illness and the convalescence: "... liess mich meine Lage bedenklich finden (161:30-31)," and through his worry about his chaise, "... vermehrte sich die Ungeduld, die mich in den letzten Tagen ergriffen hatte (162:7-8)." The conclusion does not seem far-fetched that (as was often the case with Goethe), psychic and spiritual factors played a definite role in this illness if one considers that Goethe's health, before reaching Pempelfort, had been robust; that he had been fairly skeptical of the treatment the physician administered; that the Jacobi visit, instead of giving him the hoped-for relaxation among sympathetic and like-thinking people, had turned out to be a series of deep and bitter disappointments; that he had seen these friends place themselves on a level with the émigrés; and finally that the departure from Pempelfort was actually a flight.

We remember that Goethe used the words "unconscious" or "unconsciousness" twice in the *Zwischenrede*:

> Wie ich überhaupt ziemlich unbewusst lebte ... (147:6) ... dass
> wir mit Unbewusstsein in wichtigen Augenblicken nur herum-
> tasten ... (146:17-18).

It was the illness that brought Goethe to the full realization and consciousness of his situation which, in turn, caused his impatience and decision to depart without awaiting his chaise. One is reminded of Thomas Mann, who repeatedly shows how illness is one of nature's devices to raise material that has been dormant in the subconscious mind into the bright daylight of consciousness. In his cautious way Goethe expresses this thought thus:

> Die Langeweile jedoch des Leidens liess mich manche Betrachtung
> anstellen, die Schwäche, die aus einem bettlägerigen Zustand gar
> leicht erfolgt, liess mich meine Lage bedenklich finden (161:28-30).

His departure from Pempelfort constituted a flight, as he himself admitted: "... von dem Strome mit fortgezogen der unaufhaltsam eilenden Flüchtlinge, *selbst mit Flüchtlingsgefühl* (162:20-21; italics added)." From what was he fleeing? Not from a natural, but from a distorted famliy, a family strangely misshapen in its internal environment, devoted to the wrong ideas and goals, divorced from the only soil proper for healthy growth, its own "Volk."

This is the picture of the stay in Pempelfort presented by the final version of the *Campagne*. Actually the break with Jacobi did not come until years later. The contemporary letters show that, instead of a break, the visit of 1792 led to a cementing of old ties. He wrote to Christiane from Düsseldorf on the fourteenth of November that he was staying with his old friend Jacobi, "... in dessen Umgange ich mich so wohl befinde als ich mich vor einem Monat übel befand (W. A. IV, 10, 39)." To Körner, on the same day, he wrote that he felt, "... wie neu geboren und fange erst wieder an gewahr zu werden, dass ich ein Mensch bin (W. A. IV, 10, 40)." From Münster, on the tenth of December, he wrote Jacobi a letter of thanks in the warmest terms:

> Das Bild was ich von dir und den deinigen mitnehme ist unauslöschlich und die Reife unserer Freundschaft hat für mich die höchste Süssigkeit (W.A. IV, 10, 41).

Furthermore, Helene Jacobi wrote later to the countess Sophie Stolberg:

> Er (Goethe) ist und bleibt der wahre Zauberer, und auch Sie werden ihn lieben und bewundern, sobald Sie ihn kennen ... Ihm war unendilch wohl unter uns, und der Abschied kostete ihm viel. Fritz und er haben sich tiefer durchdrungen und inniger erkannt wie je.[45]

The final break between the old friends did not come until 1805, a fact which caused Dove to speculate that Goethe was here anticipating that disagreement (Dove, xxv). Actually, of course, the break, as pictured in the *Campagne*, was imaginary, so presented for literary purposes. A perusal of the correspondence for the ensuing year shows that Goethe wrote Jacobi no less than seventeen times, the largest number of missives to any one correspondent, more even than to Christiane, who received ten. And those seventeen include comments on and ask for reactions to subjects very close to Goethe's heart, including the "Revolutionsdichtung."

In the account of the visit to the Jacobis Goethe is thus to be seen developing more clearly the elements of disagreement with his contemporaries which had been only sketchily indicated in his accounts of the meetings with the Sömmerings and Hubers in Mainz, with Prince Reuss, and with Wyttenbach. And, as in the case of the Igel monument, Goethe has added considerable portions of "Dichtung" to the "Wahrheit." And here as there the reasons for the changes are clear. They explain why Goethe, a socially-inclined individual, was bitterly disappointed when he sought in the Jacobis, who exemplified the better German society of the time, elements and seeds of a sorely-needed future German "Volkheit." Consequently he excluded himself from the group as they, in turn, excluded him. He continued his journey, or flight.

Furthermore, it can now be said with assurance that discrepancies between the actual visit to the Jacobis and Goethe's account of it in the *Campagne* were conscious and purposeful. It is now evident that only a conscious artistic purpose—namely to develop and expound his family concepts—can explain the discrepancies. It is conceivable that faulty memory or inaccurate sources could have explained many or possibly all of the discrepancies in the military portions of the *Campagne*. But it seems inconceivable that Goethe's faulty memory should be sufficient explanation for such a complete distortion of an account of a visit to such old and good friends as the Jacobis.

X. DUISBURG

"Schreckbild Plessing"

On the trip to Duisburg, Goethe again met émigrés. He was forcefully reminded of his own continuing flight. At an inn where he stopped for a meal, two incidents were described. The first, that of a senile old man pampered and sheltered from reality by his attendants, was a symbol of the condition of these people, at once pitiable and senseless (163:9-21). This incident contrasts with the story of the young and realistic French émigré, who had been travelling on foot and eating German black bread (163:27-164:15). The young man could face facts, while the old man could not and the marquis near Verdun had been unwilling to do. The innkeeper under-charged the young man, saying (as quoted directly by Goethe) that he was the first émigré he had seen who would eat black bread (164:13-15).

In Duisburg Goethe then looked up his old acquaintance Plessing with whom he exchanged reminiscences. The Plessing episode, including the introductory sketches, must have been extremely important to Goethe to judge from the amount of space, fifteen pages, devoted to it.

Before going into the story proper, Goethe sketched briefly the atmosphere of the time against which it occurred. He began by telling of the "Werther" sickness that had overwhelmed Europe twenty years before (164:23-165:11) and characterized it as "Sentimentalität . . . zärtlich-leidenschaftlicher Ascetik . . . leidige Selbstquälerei . . . (164:31-165:4)." He noted that this sickness was due in a large part to English influence, but that it lacked the saving grace of the British irony. Thus it represents an important contrast to the "sickness" of the Jacobi circle which was in part due, as has been shown, to excessive and poorly assimilated French influences. It is to be emphasized that Goethe did not criticize the French or the British as such, but rather those of his countrymen who imitated them too slavishly.

In his picture of the spiritual environment of the 1770's Goethe sketched next the activities and theories of Lavater, both as a symptom of the ills of the time and as a factor contributing to them. The essence of Lavater's activities was the glorification of the individual, " . . . so hielt er sich am einzelnen Falle, am Individuum (165:23)." Consequently many a person who had not become prominent until that time "im bürgerlichen

Lebens- und Staatsgange (166:6)" was praised as possessing extraordinary individual value. The irony in this remark is of course clear, and it is continued as Goethe noted that even an individual's foolish errors were included in the complex "seines *werten* Daseins (166:14; italics added)." These analyses were made, ". . . ohne Rücksicht auf die allgemeine Vernunft, die doch alle Natur beherrschen soll (166:17)," and they proceeded with time through " . . . eine sich immer mehr entscheidende Selbstgefälligkeit . . . (166:21)," to the point of " . . . geistlicher Stolz, der es dem natürlichen an Erhebung auch wohl zuvortat (166:23-24)."

For Goethe however, these interests of Lavater had special value because they were made on the assumption of that organic unity of mind and body which was always Goethe's fundamental creed. The collection of portraits of important people that they inspired, and the good that was accomplished through Lavater's stimulus in the Weimar group (167:4-19) turned out to be of considerable importance, resulting namely, among other things, in stimulating Goethe's interests in science, as he hinted in the words "Saat . . . Kotyledonen . . . Ernte (167:15-16)."

At this point there is inserted the clear admonition to the reader, mentioned before, to "assimilate," not to "gulp," what has been said:

> Wer Vorgesagtes *in Gedanken festhält* und *sich davon durchdringt*, wird nachstehendes Abenteuer, welches beide Theilnehmende . . . vergnüglich in der Erinnerung belebten, *weder unwahrscheinlich noch ungereimt finden* (167:20-24; italics added).

In regard to his early contact with Plessing, Goethe spoke of the letters from a complete stranger, in which he believed he saw:

> . . . statt des Duldens Eigensinn, statt des Ertragens Hartnäckigkeit, und statt eines sehnsüchtigen Verlangens abstossendes Wegweisen (168:6-9).

Under the excuse of a detour to check the mines at Ilmenau, Goethe had journeyed into the Harz in the winter of 1777 to find this strange correspondent. The journey, incidentally, formed the basis of his poem *Harzeise im Winter*. In 1820 Goethe had written an explanation of the poem at the request of a "Gymnasialrektor," which he closed with the note: "In meinen biographischen Versuchen würde jene Epoche eine bedeutende Stelle einnehmen (Dove xxvi)." Consequently Dove saw this section merely as a welcome opportunity for Goethe to develop in detail the conditions of the 1770's. This is hardly a satisfactory explanation, for, as we have seen, practically every element in the *Campagne* so far considered has some specific function in this cryptic work. We shall demonstrate that Goethe is here delineating, in his presentation of the man Plessing, the completely asocial man and the conditions that helped make him so. So far Goethe has been examining families of all types, good and bad. But now he portrays an individual who was unsuited and disinclined to enter into any close social relationship.

Goethe's first stop on the trip into the Harz was at the inn at Nordhausen where he witnessed the banquet of an unnamed group celebrating the successful conclusion of a difficult and lengthy business transaction. The contrast to the individual that we are about to meet shows itself on several levels. The group was concerned with practical business; wit and happy banter circulated freely, despite the varying rank of the individuals involved. This was a "family," then, composed apparently of representatives of two different governments, assembled to accomplish a specific task which they have concluded successfully.

On the next morning Goethe journeyed on to the "Baumannshöhle" to which he had been attracted by his scientific interests in mineralogy. Significantly, we see him correcting his preconceived ideas by comparing them with reality.

It is at this point that Goethe quoted stanzas five, six, and seven of his ten-stanza poem *Harzreise im Winter*. In the second half of the sixth stanza Goethe showed Plessing as consuming his own worth in "ungnügender Selbstsucht," and in the last half of the seventh stanza, the reference is to external nature and science:

> Öffne den umwölkten Blick
> Über die tausend Quellen
> Neben dem Durstenden
> In der Wüste!

In this fashion Goethe characterized Plessing at two separate places before the reader meets him. In connection with Lavater's ideas Goethe was curious as to whether or not the actual meeting would confirm his impressions from the two long letters. The attention of the reader is also drawn in advance to Plessing's peculiar shortcomings, thus strengthening the intended impression when the man is finally introduced in person.

A waiter in Wernigerode, Plessing's town of residence, informed Goethe that local people found fault with Plessing's "finstere Laune," and said furthermore, " . . . dass er mit unfreundlichem Betragen sich aus der Gesellschaft ausschliesse; gegen Fremde sei er zuvorkommend . . . (173:4-6)." The reason for such behavior on Plessing's part was of course, clear; local society would involve him in obligations, which would be unwelcome to his selfish nature, whereas association with strangers would not.

Goethe then described the meeting, with evident relish in his incognito. As Plessing prepared to read his letter to Goethe, the latter reflected that he knew it by heart, thus showing his unusual interest in the case. During the reading Goethe found his impressions and the Lavater theories confirmed, namely that:

> . . . ein lebendiges Wesen [sei] in allem seinen Handeln und Betragen vollkommen übereinstimmend mit sich selbst und jede in die Wirklichkeit hervorgetretene Monas erzeige sich in vollkommener Einheit ihrer Eigentümlichkeiten (175:21-25).

Goethe analyzed Plessing's actions and behavior, noting that the latter had never devoted himself to "die Aussenwelt," and attributing his lack of attractive qualities to "eine ganz eigens beschränkte Selbstgefälligkeit . . . (173:35)." Instead, Plessing had turned with all his force into himself " . . . und sich auf diese Weise, da er in der Tiefe seines Wesens kein produktives Talent fand, so gut als zu Grunde gerichtet (176:9-11)." He had even missed the comfort and advantage of the ancient languages. Goethe realized that in such a case "eine rasche, gläubige Wendung gegen die Natur und ihre grenzenlose Mannigfaltigkeit das beste Heilmittel sei . . . (176:16-17)," and attempted to induce it in Plessing by praise of "his own" profession of landscape painting. Plessing interrupted irritably, revealing his lack of interest and understanding (177:5-8).

When Goethe went on to describe specific beauties of the "Baumannshöhle," Plessing stated that he had started once to view them, but since they were so far from what he had imagined, he turned back rather than destroy his beautiful imaginings (177:33). In other words, he preferred his own imagination to reality, which Goethe rightly termed "krankhafte Symptome

(177:35)," a preference that Goethe, to be sure, had seen and regretted more than once in others as well. When Goethe asked him what his imaginary picture of the "Baumannshöhle" was like, Plessing's flights of wild imagination described the very fore-courts of hell.

At this point Goethe excused himself deftly and continued the next day on his inspection of the Harz mines. Then he spoke of their next meeting without incognito and their continuing correspondence. In the intervening years Plessing had become devoted to ancient mystic philosophy, from which he tried to derive the origins of man, a pursuit, of course, that has almost no contact with the facts of life. How that impressed Goethe, deeply suspicious as he was of abstract thought, is clear. In the letter to Jacobi of the tenth of December, 1792, already noted, Goethe referred to Plessing as involved in "antediluvianischen Untersuchungen (W. A. IV, v. 10, 40)."

Plessing had changed little in the intervening years. Goethe's account in the *Campagne* contains some inaccuracies, mostly of a nature to make Plessing appear in a better light; but none of them are of importance to this investigation. Dove has summarized the inaccuracies (Dove 292). At the time of Goethe's visit in 1792 Plessing was ill-kempt, in ill health, due to immoderate study, and in straitened financial circumstances (180:21-30); in short, he was still asocial. He had never married although Goethe failed to mention the fact. "Noch immer schien er einem Unerreichbaren nachzustreben (180:30)."

After reminiscing over former days, there was nothing left to talk about and Goethe departed. The Plessing episode contrasts significantly with another during Goethe's sojourn at Duisburg. He also called on Professor Merrem, from whose knowledge of natural history he profited greatly (181:4-12). From the Plessing call, Goethe carried away little of positive value; but he gained a great deal, according to his report, from the one on Merrem, who was a practical, active, and productive man.

It is interesting to compare Plessing and Jacobi. Both were suffering from poorly assimilated foreign ideas. While the Jacobis represented, to a certain extent, outgrown stages in Goethe's own development, Plessing represented a tendency towards self-isolation which was no less dangerous in Goethe's view. Plessing, the egocentric individual, was unable or unwilling to enter into relationships of any kind, while Jacobi's family was founded on the wrong basis and directed towards the wrong goals, creating an intellectual island, which was only another form of irresponsible, intellectual snobbery.

We note striking similarities in the elements of disagreement with the Sömmering-Hubers in Mainz, in the Huber letter quoted above, in the scorn for science and the immoderate devotion to abstract, speculative thought. We have heard Goethe voice similar complaints in the Prince Reuss conversation, in the talks with Wyttenbach and the Jacobis. Goethe was describing in extreme terms tendencies in contemporary German life that deeply disturbed him because, from a national standpoint (taken in its widest meaning), they were little short of suicidal. In other words, Goethe intended Plessing as a "Schreckbild" for his fellow Germans, a warning to them to overcome their Werther-like egocentricity, to face reality and heed the "Forderung des Tages," to associate with their fellow citizens in the defense and preservation of the common good as he had forcefully depicted it in *Hermann und Dorothea*:

> Denn es werden noch stets die entschlossenen Völker gepriesen,
> Die für Gott und Gesetz, für Eltern, Weiber und Kinder
> Stritten und gegen den Feind zusammenstehend erlagen.
> (Urania, 308-310).

XI. MÜNSTER

Princess Gallitzin

On his way to visit the circle of the Princess Gallitzin in Münster, Goethe again ran into the eternal flood of émigrés and exiles that had accompanied him almost everywhere in the Campagne. This time some of them were Germans. Again they reminded him that his own journey was a flight and, at the same time, recalled the unpleasant associations he had had with the French émigrés: he was forced to spend the night sitting up in a chair in an inn as all the accommodations had already been taken (181:17-27).

On the next morning, the eighth of December, Goethe presented himself to the princess, the "schöne Seele" of the *Campagne,* as he himself later described her in a letter to Jacobi (W.A. IV, v. 10, 46). "Das Verhältnis meinerseits war ganz rein, . . . (181:31)" he said, as he entered the group around the princess, meaning that he was quite aware of the present otherworldly, religious atmosphere of that circle. As a result, bitter disappointments like those at Pempelfort were spared him.

In his characterization of the princess, Goethe was highly complimentary, ending with the comment that one could not judge her personality properly, " . . . wenn man eben diese Individualität nicht in Verbindung wie im Konflikt mit ihrer Zeitumgebung betrachtet (182:13-14)." In identifying this "Zeitumgebung" he cited three names, Hamann, Hemsterhuis, and Fürstenberg, by whom, of course, the mystically religious tone was set. The Princess had been one who had felt since early in life, "dass die Welt uns nichts gebe (183:2)," and consequently had withdrawn into a small circle, where one " . . . um Zeit und Ewigkeit besorgt sein müsse (183:4-5)."

Goethe then proceeded to describe this small circle, speaking first of the children, as the main concern of any family. He approved of her way of raising her family with the naturalness preached by Rousseau. The daughter, especially, attracted his attention, and it is instructive to contrast his description of her with what he had said about the daughter of the Jacobi family. The delicate contrast delineates the differences between the two groups. The Jacobi girl was "wohlgebildet (158:7-10)," while the young lady at Münster, to judge from Goethe's surprise at the fact that she had become "stämmiger," must have been inclined to corpulence. The latter was "verständig," the former "tüchtig, treuherzig." The Jacobi girl was "liebenswürdig," the other "liebenswert." The Jacobi girl had reminded Goethe of her mother, Betty von Clermont, an attractive and intelligent woman whom Goethe had known and admired in her younger days, and who had found her life in a large and happy family. The Gallitzin daughter, however, he found "haushälterisch, dem halbklösterlichen Leben sich fügend und widmend (183:15)." In the Jacobi girl then, Goethe saw the happy willingness and desire, as well as the capacity, for motherhood, for the founding of a family, while the Münster girl, fine as she was, seemed already on the road to the nunnery.

The religion of this circle was Catholicism, in which they had found "das ewig Künftige" (183:16)," a phrase in which the ironic overtones must not be ignored. Goethe praised the charities of the group, as the "Vermittelung" between the world of this side of the grave and that beyond, and their moderate ascetisism, which was evident from the house and the modest furnishings lacking signs of pretense or show. Here again, Goethe examines with care the external environment of the family as he had done at Sivry and Pempelfort. Of the general impression, he said: " . . . es sah eben aus, als wenn man anständig zur Miete wohne (183:28-29)," a phrase that not only shows the moderation of the family, but also throws light on the fact that their real existence was not of this world, which they only inhabited temporarily, as tenants, as it were.

Since the external environment was of little importance to the Gallitzin family, Goethe soon turned to a consideration of the internal environment of the group. Of the various factors to be enumerated there, the first is the appreciation of art, on which Goethe dwells, an area in which he and his hosts could largely agree.

The artistic interests and discussions in the house centered around the collection of carved gems that Hemsterhuis, recently deceased, had willed to the Princess. Although Goethe and his hosts were both deeply interested in art, their views on the subject differed greatly. He describes their differing definitions of what is beautiful. In the terms of Hemsterhuis, whose influence was still paramount in the house, the beautiful was achieved " . . . wenn wir die grösste Menge von Vorstellungen in *einem*

Moment bequem erblicken und fassen (185:8-10)," while for Goethe it could be obtained only

> ... wenn wir das gesetzmässig Lebendige in seiner grössten Tätigkeit und Vollkommenheit schauen, wodurch wir, zur Reproduktion gereizt, uns gleichfalls lebendig und in höchste Tätigkeit versetzt fühlen (185:10-14).

Although we should not lose sight of the similarities, the differences here are essential. It is to be noted that the Hemsterhuis definition is couched in abstract terms: the contemplated object and the observer are in a completely passive state. Goethe's definition, on the other hand, is alive and dynamic. It is given in concrete, even organic language ("Lebendige ... Reproduktion"); the objects viewed are at the peak of natural development, and the beholder is to be stimulated to activity. The processes that Hemsterhuis described end in the subject, while Goethe's lead to external action. For Hemsterhuis beauty ended in the passive enjoyment on the part of the beholder, while for Goethe it aroused a more intense interest in nature and life, that is to say, in society also since the latter is the human side of nature. The attitude of art for art's sake, if Goethe had ever adhered to it, had definitely no place in the philosophy of the older Goethe for whom life in its collective manifestations was of primary concern. The older he became, the more art, like any other occupation of the human mind, assumed a pragmatic obligation.

From Goethe's point of view, then, Hemsterhuis was saved from falling into the Plessing error of immoderate introversion by the saving grace of art. To be sure, he was devoted to "das Geistig-Sittliche," as Plessing was devoted to abstract philosophy; but the former was saved from extremes by his equal devotion to beauty, to "das Sinnlich-Ästhetische (184:13)." Furthermore, as Goethe went on to relate, Hemsterhuis had avoided the implied Jacobi error in his dealing with "Sehnsucht." It will be recalled that Goethe characterized longing as attractive in youth, but something that did not suit the adult man, thus implying that the Jacobis were still enmeshed in that youthful emotion. Hemsterhuis had satisfied his aesthetic "Sehnsucht" by purchasing gem stones. This satisfaction was only temporary, but as soon as longing again arose, he satisfied it with the purchase of another stone. Thus longing and satisfaction alternated in Hemsterhuis like polar opposites in a natural and organic fashion.

Although this "Sozietät" was very sensitive to art and to ideas and discussions about art, Goethe could not help but remark on the fact that these stones, a treasure of and monument to heathen antiquity, should hold a place of such esteem in a house so deeply Christian. He was naturally quite aware of the contrast:

> Doch konnte man sich nicht verbergen, dass die reinste christliche Religion mit der wahren bildenden Kunst immer sich zwiespältig befinde, weil jene sich von der Sinnlichkeit zu entfernen strebt, diese nun aber das sinnliche Element als ihren eigentlichsten Wirkungskreis anerkennt und darin beharren muss (187:7-13).

Goethe was describing material on which he and his hosts could agree, to be sure. But, at the same time, he delineated the bases for the differences between them, a procedure he had followed in his discussion of the Jacobis. Nevertheless, Goethe enjoyed such conversations, " . . . die ungeachtet ihrer Höhe und Tiefe nicht Gefahr liefen, sich ins Abstruse zu verlieren . . . (187:3-5)." His aversion to abstract thinking, far removed from real life, is noted again.

On the spur of the moment Goethe dashed off some verses to celebrate the union of the sensual, erotic elements in art on the one hand, and the moral elements, on the other (187:15-24). He pictured Amor mating with Venus Urania and the offspring, a new Amor whose arrows inflamed the stricken with the love of art. Although the company accepted in the main the idea of these verses, the pagan gods and the sensual images were a bit too strong for them, and so:

> . . . beide Teile machten sich's zur Pflicht, von ihren Gefühlen und Überzeugungen nur dasjenige hervorzukehren, was gemeinsam wäre und zu wechselseitiger Belehrung und Ergötzung, ohne Widerstreit, gereichen könnte (187:27-31).

In Pempelfort the "Weltkinder" had used "eine gewisse Kunst" in avoiding unpleasant subjects. Here at Münster Goethe observed the Gallitzin circle doing the same.

Goethe even differed from his hosts in the manner in which he appreciated the gem stones. They formed, he noted, an excellent bit of common ground between them; but still:

> Ich von meiner Seite konnte freilich nur das Poetische schätzen, das Motiv selbst, Komposition, Darstellung überhaupt beurteilen

und rühmen, dagegen die Freunde dabei noch ganz andere Betrachtungen anzustellen gewohnt waren (188:1-6).

The other considerations that his friends were accustomed to observe dealt, all of them, with the technical side of the art of cut gems. In other words, Goethe, without technical knowledge, appreciated the most important, the vital thing, namely the artistic value. The friends in their relatively less important technical appreciation remained on the surface. We shall see later, when we come to Goethe's departure, that they did not really appreciate art profoundly, that it was not of real importance to them.

The difference between the value Goethe assigned to the carved gem collection and that given it by the Gallitzins is evident even from such an external factor as the stowage of the gems. The princess had not bothered to take any special pains in storing them, and as a result, some had disappeared, doubtless stolen (189:10-20). One of Goethe's first acts, after the princess had loaned them to him, however, on arriving in Weimar, had been to have them carefully housed in specially made boxes (200:8-20). Baumgartner and Stockmann sum it up by saying that for the princess the stones were merely an interesting hobby, while for Goethe they were "ein Stück Religion."[46]

While at Münster, Goethe tried to avoid scientific subjects. But Fürstenberg brought up the matter, expressing the same amazed and disapproving disbelief that his Mainz friends, Prince Reuss, Wyttenbach and the Jacobis had expressed, at finding Goethe, the poet, involved with as "unprofitable" and "unsuitable" a subject as science. Goethe in reply tried to explain that his anatomical and osteological studies had been stimulated by Lavater's theories on physiognomy (189:29-190:22). Von Fürstenberg, because of his typically Christian dualism of good and evil, of this life and the next, of mind and body, of spirit and matter, could not see the organic unity of mind and body, the core of Lavater's theories and the starting point of Goethe's investigations. The Jacobis misunderstood Goethe's scientific preoccupations on philosophic grounds, on the grounds of their deism. The Gallitzin circle's misunderstanding, also on philosophic grounds, was based, however, on the religious conviction that the things of this world are of no real importance.

Goethe was more successful at Münster with his reports on

Italy. He emphasized the festivals of the church with such good effect that some of those present were moved to inquire secretly whether he was really a Catholic (190:29-191:32). These Roman stories are interesting because they show that Goethe could be diplomatic. To both the Jacobi and the Gallitzin groups he had related bits of his Roman experiences. But they were tailored to fit the attitudes of the groups. As we know from *Das römische Karneval,* the most important thing for Goethe's Roman experiences is the Roman "Volk." At Pempelfort and Münster we see him giving sketches in the resigned and ironical certainty that neither group can or will see what he considered important. We also notice a tragic note here: in his search for understanding Goethe has reached the point of despairing resignation.

Literature was another basis for misunderstandings as it had been with the Jacobis. At Münster, too, he was invited to read aloud. A copy of Voss' *Luise* was placed ready for him whenever the mood should strike him. Despite the fact that the situation was more tactfully handled in Münster, Goethe was just as unable to read *Luise* as he had been to read *Iphigenie.* This time the material was of the unrealistically sentimental and pastoral sort Goethe had outgrown long ago. His self-recriminations, "... ich wundere mich noch über diese unerklärliche Verstocktheit (192:24)," serve merely to distract the reader's attention from the real reason.

It is to be noted that there is no reference of any kind in the Münster sketches to the Gallitzin family's membership or lack of it in the German "Volk." Yet such considerations formed a large part of the Pempelfort sketches. The reason, of course, is plain: this circle was living in this world only temporarily, and therefore the things of this world, even revolution and the threats of war, were not really important to it. The question of political and social organization did not exist for them.

As Goethe was preparing to depart, the Princess pressed the gem collection on him a second time. At his renewed refusal, she explained her insistence by saying that she had been warned not to offer it to him because she did not know him well enough to entrust him with such valuable things. She wanted to make him this gift so as to prove to herself that she trusted him (192:26-193:6). Goethe was, of course, unable to withstand this remarkable motivation, remarkable in its complete subjectivity. The Princess did not consider the value of the stones.

Her own impression of Goethe was the most important thing to her. She preferred subjective impressions to objective facts even as Plessing did at the "Baumannshöhle." Baumgartner and Stockmann correctly explained her attitude toward the collection as nothing more than "eine vornehme Kunstliebhaberei."[46]

The good Princess accompanied Goethe a bit along his way, and then took leave of him with the pious formula that she hoped to see him again, if not this side of the grave, then on the other. The manner of leave-taking was familiar to Goethe, and he remarked significantly: " . . . ich sehe nicht ein, warum ich irgend jemand verargen sollte, der wünscht, mich in seinen Kreis zu ziehen . . . (193:28-29)." At Pempelfort Goethe had not fitted into the group, a fact that was recognized by both sides in the cryptic exchange of anecdotes (160, 161). The princess wished to make him a member of the Münster group. But this, too, was impossible for Goethe although he naturally concealed the fact. His departure symbolized his self-exclusion from the pious circle of the "schöne Seele." So the wanderer Goethe, fugitive from war, again disappointed in his search, continued his flight. Apparently it was more difficult for him to find the "Urfamilie" than it had been to discover the intermaxillary bone or the "Urpflanze."

XII. THE WINTER IN WEIMAR

On the eleventh of December Goethe continued his journey to Weimar, a journey full of difficulties, dangers, troubles, and apprehensions. Once more in the midst of a crowd of émigrés (194:7), he was again made to feel like a refugee. Furthermore, there were no roads part of the way, there were breakdowns and heated arguments with the postillions. The report had been spread that his carriage (a very heavy one borrowed from the Jacobis) was loaded with gold, silver, and valuables (195:10), which caused the company to be apprehensive of highwaymen or of foul play at some questionable inn. To add to the discomfort, the weather was bad and the postillions had hurried his trip to the point of making him travel at night (195:18). Finally the dreaded thing happened. The party was forced to stay the night at a disreputable inn (195:19). It is to be noted that the postillion was to blame for this unscheduled and worrisome stop. He had failed to provide proper leadership for the "family" of travelers under his care by losing his way in the night. The party had been forced to put up at the first opportunity in a potentially dangerous house.

It is possible that in his report Goethe exaggerated the difficulties and apprehensions of this journey in order to contrast them more strongly with the order and peaceful security of family life, for in his worry and fear he turned to the memories of such a life for comfort and consolation (195:24). And when he arrived in Cassel after dark the next evening, he saw most effectively

> ... alle Vorteile eines bürgerlich-städtischen Zusammenseins, die Wohlhäbigkeit eines jeden einzelnen *in seiner von innen erleuchteten Wohnung* (195:35-196:2; italics added).

Here, too, the émigré problem faced him again forcefully and unpleasantly. He was at first refused a room in the inn. When it turned out that he was a German, not an émigré, the apologetic landlord expressed his dislike of the émigrés:

> ... denn mitten in ihrem Elend, da sie nicht wüssten, wo sie sich hinwenden sollten, betrügen sie sich noch immer, als hätten sie von einem eroberten Lande Besitz genommen (196:20-23).

The innkeeper was enraged about the émigrés because they declined to face facts, just as the French marquis near Verdun had done.

Finally the goal of the journey was reached; Goethe was reunited with his own family in Weimar. In the remaining pages of the *Campagne* we note a number of families. But his own family is in the foreground, of course. Modesty prevents Goethe from going into great or intimate detail concerning his own homecoming. He merely said that his arrival: ". . . gab Anlass zu einer Familienszene, welche wohl in irgendeinem Roman die tiefste Finsternis erhellen und erheitern würde (196:28-31)." There are a few more lines about his house. The remodeling was almost finished. We learn about the happy exchange of news and impressions, and about his friend and collaborator Heinrich Meyer. In all, Goethe devoted only twenty lines to his family reunion. Here, as elsewhere, Goethe started the description of the family with the external environment. At this point, however, there is no space devoted to "internal environment." In a sense, the entire remainder of the work is a description of it.

Concerning the account of the winter in Weimar that follows Dove said: "Die Unvollkommenheiten des angehängten Kapitels über den Winteraufenthalt in Weimar (überrascht uns) (Dove xxvii)." As was noted above, Roethe also failed to understand Goethe's plans here inasmuch as he referred to this portion of the work as "angeflickt (Roethe 249)." Actually the story of these winter months forms the climax, the heart and core of the whole work in accordance with Goethe's intention.

From the description of the Igel monument onward, we have noted the great stress that Goethe laid on the practical and economic bases of family life. Now he turned to a description of his "professional" activities, the duties of court and government on which his livelihood and that of his family depended. His duties were manifold: he was "resident artist," manager of the court theater, advisor to the government, and also stimulating member of the society of the court. But his Weimar duties were far more than a means of making a living. In the first place, Goethe showed himself working for specific goals in several varying "families," and, in the second place, these activities at the same time formed the real "inner environment" of his own family. So we see him as intellectual, spiritual, and artistic leader discharging his duties as head of several "families," first, of his own family, secondly, of the "family" of the theater personnel, thirdly, of the "family" of the "Weimarische

Kunstfreunde," with its three subdivisions, and, lastly, of the most important one, the "family" of all Germans.

Several matters should be mentioned concerning this important section of Goethe's literary work, the winter in Weimar. There was no mention of it during the first period of preparation. Not until the third of February, 1822, did Goethe discuss the outline in detail with Meyer (Dove xxvii). This apparently led Dove to the impression that Meyer bore much of the responsibility for this section which is, in Dove's view, unfortunate in concept and execution. Goethe carefully outlined the material to be included (W.A. I, 33, p. 367 ff). The outline differs in one material detail from the order actually used in the finished work. According to the original plan, Goethe intended to discuss his own family, then the theater, then the "Revolutionsdichtung," and finally the gem-stones and the optical matters. In the final version, the "Revolutionsdichtung" is treated last for reasons that become obvious once the central function of the family is understood. This shift in arrangement permitted Goethe to describe his activities in ever larger, concentric circles. The facts that the outline was carefully used (each item was checked off after completion) and that Goethe discussed it with Meyer can only mean that the matter was of unusual importance to him.

We turn to *Family II*, the personnel involved in the Weimar theater. Goethe spoke of the origin of the group; it consisted partly of the remains of the Bellomo troop of travelling actors, including North Germans and South Germans, and in part of a group around the actor Fischer from Prague. He was successful having these people work together productively, Goethe said, because there still existed at that time a "Schauspielerhandwerk (197:23)." The goal of achieving a diversified and successful theater united this "family" under Goethe's leadership.

Then Goethe discussed the techniques of acting, saying that a "grammar" was necessary before one could reach the "poetry" or rhetoric. But he interrupted himself:

> ... so sage ich nur so viel; dass ich eben jene Technik, welche sich alles aus Überlieferung aneignet, zu studieren und auf ihre Elemente zurückzuführen suchte und das, was mir klar geworden, in einzelnen Fällen, ohne auf ein Allgemeines hinzuweisen, beobachten liess (198:4-8).

This is obviously a generalized description of the first stages of

Goethe's scientific methods, which were examined above. Notable here also for present purposes are the facts that Goethe used of tradition only whatever withstood careful examination, and that generalities were avoided.

Goethe sought to control, he said, the natural or conversational tone then in vogue among actors, and gradually "einer höheren Bildung entgegenführen zu lassen (198:19-20)." Again he interrupted himself:

> Doch darf ich hievon nicht weiter sprechen, weil, was getan und geleistet worden, sich erst nach und nach aus sich selbst entwickelte und also historisch dargestellt werden müsste (198:22-24).

The paramount importance of the organic method is also evident here.

Twice on one page Goethe interrupted himself to make a summarizing statement. The material concerns the theater, which, as is well known from *Wilhelm Meisters Lehrjahre* and from the preliminary study to it, the *Theatralische Sendung,* he was accustomed to look on as a parallel to, and symbol of, human society. It is also apparent that both summaries have political implications. In this light the picture becomes interesting. First of all, the theatrical troop is a "family," under Goethe's leadership, banded together for a specific purpose. In addition it is symbolic of the potential, not the actual, German "Volk." Thus the theatrical group symbolizes the social ideal so dear to Goethe's heart, the potential German "Volk" of the future. This troupe was composed of Germans from different areas. They were North Germans, South Germans, and Germans from Prague. The Italianate names "Bellomo" and "Malkomi" should not mislead anyone, for all the personnel involved were Germans, harmoniously united by devotion to a common task.

The discussion of the theater led Goethe to the consideration of *Family III,* "die Weimarischen Kunstfreunde," as he himself termed them later. The theater was only one of three spheres in which this group was active. In this family Goethe, as the leader of the "audience family," was also consciously at work in the selection and production of dramatic works of all sorts. The works of Iffland were valued because they pilloried the "Philister;" those of Kotzebue because of their condemnation of loose morals. Schröder, Babo, and others provided the necessary amusement; Hagemann and Hagemeister, the novelty, while

Shakespeare, Gozzi, and Schiller were used to elevate the intellectual tone (198:24-199:19).

In the field of opera, Goethe followed a similar procedure. Of the German composers the easy and light Dittersdorf was adopted, also a number of the lighter Italian operas. As a culmination of the "Steigerung" in the operatic offerings, the works of Mozart were played (199:20-200:7). Here, of course, Goethe was consciously leading the audience, "die Weimarischen Kunstfreunde," to a higher state of "Bildung."

The second field in which Goethe functioned as leader of the same family was that of art, specifically in the appreciation of the carved gems that he had received from the Princess Gallitzin. Actually, the members of the audience family of the theater and of the family of those interested in the carved gems were not necessarily the same people; but, as has been shown before, families change, in Goethe's understanding, with the changing purposes. Goethe's first concern in regard to gems was proper storage. He reports how he collected the group of art lovers and led them in their efforts to understand and appreciate the stones. Then he appended a catalogue of some of the more interesting of them. The descriptions evoke the sunny, uncomplicated and extroverted life of antiquity which contrasts with the more complicated, introverted, speculative, and mystical northern atmosphere. It has been shown that antiquity, for Goethe, was an invaluable subject of study. For him it was the only time in recorded human history when man had lived in complete, voluntary harmony with nature (see above, p. 18). As might be expected, all of the descriptions are "apollinisch" in nature, rather than "dionysisch."

This section has been subjected to severe criticism by some commentators. Dove says:

> Mit Betrübnis sehen wir ein Goethesches Meisterwerk, das sich an ein grosses historisches Interesse der Mit- und Nachwelt wendet, hier plötzlich entstellt durch den greisenhaften Zug verfallender künstlerischer Selbstbeherrschung (Dove xxviii).

Dove did not see that this section serves a specific and valuable purpose in the construction of the work as a whole. It revolves, as will be demonstrated, around the axis of the whole work—the family.

The gem catalogue consists of twenty items selected from

sixty-odd described by Meyer under the title *Nachrichten von einer Sammlung meistens antiker geschnittener Steine*, published in the *Jenaische Allgemeine Literatur-Zeitung* in 1807. Goethe copied verbatim from Meyer as he had used direct translations from the memoirs of Dumouriez earlier. In constructing the *Campagne*, Goethe used the works and reports of other contemporaries. A "family" was collaborating under Goethe's leadership in order to portray their common social environment. Viewed in this light, there can be no criticism of the gem catalogue in the *Campagne* on the grounds of either plagiarism or poor taste.

Goethe continued to report on the third activity of "Weimarische Kunstfreunde," their studies of Goethe's theories of color. The original purpose of the studies had been to assist painters and lovers of painting by placing the matter of color on a scientific basis. The same procedure was followed by the Weimar group also. There is no hint in the *Campagne* account of the full scope of the theories, or of the polemics against Newton. Goethe did report that he had Meyer make model sketches which served as instructional aids (205:16-18). It is apparent that Goethe here also was consciously working as the leader of the family to increase and guide their "Bildung."

Goethe then commented on his own "Revolutionsdichtung," which involves *Family IV*. In reference to the "Revolutionsdichtungen" as a whole he made an interesting comment:

> . . . allein ich vergriff mich im Stoff, oder vielmehr ein Stoff überwältigte meine innere, sittliche Natur, der allerwiderspenstigste, um dramatisch behandelt zu werden (206:17-20).

It is true, as all commentators have observed, that the "Revolutionsdichtung" does not succeed in giving a great and complete panorama of the French Revolution. But that was not Goethe's primary purpose, not even in *Die natürliche Tochter*. Goethe's primary purpose was "tendenziös." He attempted to unify his own people into a real "Volksfamilie" to enable them to defend themselves against the ideas of the revolution which he considered so harmful. The picture of the revolution presented by the various works of the "Revolutionsdichtung" is neither objective nor complete.

Goethe began the section with a review of his earlier dramas, noting that the first ones had been too inclusive and panoramic

(*Götz*) to do well on the stage while his later ones had been too sensitive and intensely individualized to appeal to a very large audience (*Iphigenie*). So he resolved to try "eine mittlere Technik" (206:20). Then follows a discussion of his *Gross-Kophta* with a revealing paragraph on the affair of the necklace. The exaggerated importance that Goethe attached to this incident as a forerunner of the French Revolution has been amply discussed elsewhere.[47] He was obsessed by the material before, during, and after the Italian journey, of which last period he said: ". . . alsdann nahm die weltgeschichtliche Gegenwart meinen Geist völlig ein (206:29-30)."

After sketching the original conception of *Gross-Kophta* as a comic opera and the final re-working into a dramatic comedy, Goethe described the reception the Weimar audience had given it. The fact that it was very carefully produced and most excellently played only increased the revulsion of the spectators: "Ein furchtbarer und zugleich abgeschmackter Stoff, kühn und schonungslos behandelt, schreckte jedermann . . . (207:30-32)." The characterization of the subject matter as terrible and tasteless is interesting. The theater audiences of the time endured far more terrible material in many of the French plays, and much worse taste in many a contemporary German comedy. But the audience was shocked by the play because it preferred not to face reality. That is what Goethe meant as may be seen from his emphatic reference to the excellent staging, expert acting, and bold treatment of the material: "Aber eben deswegen, weil das Stück ganz trefflich gespielt wurde, machte es einen um desto widerwärtigern Effekt (207:28-30)." "Kein Herz klang an," he said, and the contemporaneity of the subject matter "liess den Eindruck noch greller empfinden (207:34)." This complete failure on the stage was due to the all too common human failing of ignoring a really vital unpleasant challenge rather than accepting it. The play opened up vistas into the sad conditions of the upper classes of the time, boldly and effectively presented; but the reaction was sharply negative. Acceptance of the challenge of the play meant tackling a difficult matter, social reform. Like the French marquis and Plessing the Weimar audience could not face reality. The displeasure of the masons, feeling that their order was being criticised, and the shock of the ladies at a bold love-affair were far-fetched. Both groups were seeking excuses to condemn a play which directed their attention to things they didn't want to face or admit to themselves. Any excuse for condemnation was welcome.

In the *Gross-Kophta*, then, Goethe had tried to speak to his fellow countrymen, and had not only been misunderstood, but also sharply condemned for his efforts. His reaction to this rebuff was relatively objective and undisturbed (208:6-8).

He now turned to the revolution itself in *Der Bürgergeneral* with a comment that must be quoted. It outlines precisely the situation that Goethe was trying to combat with the "Revolutionsdichtungen." "Vaterland" is here used in its broadest connotation, including all Germany, whereas Goethe had earlier used it for his native city:

> ... (ich hatte) leider zu bemerken, dass man im Vaterlande sich spielend mit Gesinnungen unterhielt, welche eben auch uns ähnliche Schicksale vorbereiteten. Ich kannte genug edle Gemüter, die sich gewissen Aussichten und Hoffnungen, ohne weder sich noch die Sache zu begreifen, phantastisch hingaben; indessen ganz schlechte Subjekte bittern Unmut zu erregen, zu mehren und zu benutzen strebten (208:22-29).

From his account of the origin of *Der Bürgergeneral* it is quite clear that Goethe had not meant it to be anything more than a dramatic bagatelle. There is ample proof: the derivation from Florian, through Anton Wall's *Stammbaum*; the fact that the play was to be a vehicle for Beck as Schnaps, the beloved comic character of the original play.

Staging and acting were excellent, "Aber vergebens! das Stück brachte die widerwärtigste Wirkung hervor... (209:18)." His friends, even, thinking they were doing him a favor, denied his authorship. It is strange, indeed, that the popular reaction to such a harmless and relatively amusing bit of farce should have been violently negative. Here also Goethe, in reporting the incident in the *Campagne*, went to some pains to emphasize the excellence of the production:

> Dies (Austattung und Vorstellung) geschah auch mit Neigung und Ausführlichkeit; wie denn das gehaltreiche Mantelsäckchen ein wirklich französisches war, das Paul auf jener Flucht eilig aufgerafft hatte. In der Hauptszene erwies sich Malkolmi als alter, wohlhabender, wohlwollender Bauersmann, der sich eine gesteigerte Unverschämtheit als Spass auch einmal gefallen lässt, unübertrefflich und wetteiferte mit Beck in wahrer, natürlicher Zweckmässigkeit (209:9-17).

This completely unfavorable reception and the complete failure of the *Gross-Kophta* outlined above were due to the same causes; the public was determined to ignore the challenge. Actually, the play enjoyed a moderate success, though Goethe was correct in that its real meaning was not understood.

Goethe then went on to tell of the other works of the "Revolutionsdichtungen,"—"Bekenntnisse dessen, was damals in meinem Busen vorging (209:29-30)," and he again laid emphasis on his deep personal concern in the course of events: ". . . es war nicht leicht jemand . . . gedrückter als ich . . . (210:3-5)." Of course, all of the works in this category were misunderstood by his contemporaries. So Goethe turned to *Reinecke Fuchs* because it afforded him a welcome opportunity to portray mankind "in seiner ungeheuchelten Tierheit (210:21)."

We review and summarize briefly Goethe's reaction to the failure of his efforts to communicate with and influence his fellow countrymen. At the sight of his friends in Mainz in the pursuit of false goals, he became "unwohl." When face to face with a similar situation in Pempelfort, he came down with an illness that may have been psychological as well as physical. When his "Revolutionsdichtungen" failed, Goethe, in the bitterness of his disappointment, pilloried the human race with pleasure in *Reineke Fuchs*. These reactions of Goethe's to progressively more serious misunderstandings by friends and by the public show, as little else could, the intensity of his convictions and the purity of his own patriotic emotions.

Following the discussion of *Der Gross-Kophta* and *Der Bürgergeneral*, Goethe mentioned three other "Revolutionsdichtungen" without going into details: *Die Unterhaltungen deutscher Ausgewanderten, Die Aufgeregten,* and *Hermann und Dorothea*. In them also Goethe was trying to speak directly to the family of his countrymen, to lead them toward his ideal for "Volkheit." We consider them briefly.

The locale of the *Unterhaltungen*, which was begun in 1794 and printed in 1795, Goethe laid in the close vicinity of the besieged Mainz in the summer of 1793, that is, under the shadow of the French Revolution. The German family involved had been forced to flee from their possessions on French soil. They symbolized the better German society of the time inasmuch as they were sadly split among themselves over the ideas of the Revolution. Karl and the tutor were heatedly in favor of them, while Friedrich, Luise, and the Abbé were opposed to them.

A discussion of the "Klubisten" of Mainz (pro-revolutionary Germans who were functioning as part of the French-supported revolutionary government of Mainz), between Karl and a visiting "Geheimrat" developed into a blistering argument that ended in insults. The latter terminated his visit in anger, a social crisis that presented the theme of the work: how to live in family harmony despite the divisive ideas of the French Revolution. Thus at the beginning the revolution is shown as disrupting families, a note that is intensified when the reader learns that Luise has been separated from her fiancé by the same force.

The baroness blamed lack of self-control, a vital family virtue, as the cause of the outbreaks, and decreed that the whole family should exercise mutual forbearance and tolerance on the subject (J. A. v. 16, 180:5-24), recommending science as a suitable subject for conversation (J. A. v. 16, 182, 183). But the abbé went beyond this merely palliative measure by proposing to tell stories to the assembled group. Though the abbé did not say so, these stories have inner meanings which, if properly understood, could cause a permanent cure for the disagreements rampant within the family.

The abbé is the central figure of the work, one of those figures, like the abbé of the *Lehrjahre* or the "Pfarrer" of *Hermann und Dorothea,* through whom Goethe was apt to speak apodictically. The abbé was a member of the family, and how thoroughly the family idea permeates the work as a whole can be seen even from such a minor matter as Luise's snippy attitude toward the abbé. As a future wife and mother, she tended to respect men who were constructively active and thus economically capable of founding a family. In the harshness of her youthful inexperience, she was led to scorn the celibate, "idle," clergyman.

To distract from the topic of the revolution, the abbé proposed to tell stories which dealt with love, that is, the natural human emotion from which true families must organically spring (J. A. v. 16, 187:21-24). As if to emphasize the universality of the tales, he stressed their timeless quality. Consequently special consideration must be given to the four that he tells although all eight deal with the theme he has proposed, love.

Of the tales told by the others, Fritz and Karl each tell two. Fritz' first, like that of the abbé about the soprano Antonelli, concerned a girl who did not want to enter into a family relationship. An orphan raised in the large family of friends of her dead parents, she seems, shortly after suitors for her hand have put in an appearance, to be pursued everywhere by strange tapping noises, everywhere, that is, except in the room of her adored foster mother. The tapping ceased only after the foster father threatened her with a whip if it should continue. Thus the girl, whether consciously or unconsciously, in some manner unexplained by Goethe who delighted in such mystifications in this work, caused the tappings herself in order to avoid having to accept a fiancé. Fritz' heroine, then, declined to take even the first step toward founding a family.

Karl tells the two Bassompierre stories (J. A. v. 16, 209:6-212:30 and 213:7-30), both about men unable to enter into permanent unions with their lady loves because they were already married. These stories of Karl's deal with adultery and conflict with the "ethos" of the family. The first was a story of a love affair between a married nobleman and a shopkeeper's wife (double adultery!), and it has little beside erotic piquancy to recommend it. In the second tale a wife discovered her husband and his mistress together but acted with forbearance. The mistress, in turn, broke off the relationship, leaving her lover three gifts for his legitimate daughters, gifts which then become prized symbols of happiness within the family.

This aroused Fritz to start his second tale about a tradition in his own famliy, only, after having barely begun, to stop in confusion and run from the room. The *Unterhaltungen* is a fragment and the incident is never explained. Was it accidental that both the stories told by Karl, who was in favor of the revolution, concern adultery, and hence are inimical to the deepest family ideals, while the stories of Fritz, who opposed the revolution, show a well developed family sense? Fritz was the only one, later, who thought that he understood the abbé's story of the soprano Antonelli (J. A. v. 16, 203:25-28).

Before considering the tales of the abbé, we should mention the mysterious incident involving a writing desk cover splitting with a loud report at the precise moment when a duplicate in the French castle of the family was being consumed in flames. What did Goethe intend to symbolize here? The realm of the family might well furnish an explanation. The two desks had been made exactly alike, of wood from the same tree, at the same time, by the same artisan, at the order of a lady who wanted one for herself, one for her sister. Hence the desks may well be meant to symbolize the family. When one, in France, was destroyed by fire, as the revolution destroyed families there, the other, in Germany, suffered a serious split, even as the family of the story did in Germany, over arguments about the revolution.

In the four anecdotes told by the abbé, the men, at least insofar as the desire to form a family is concerned, are the central figures. In the first (J. A. v. 16, 191:15-203:22), the soprano Antonelli, who had been accustomed to a rapidly changing series of lovers, longed for a platonic friend whom she found in a young Genoan merchant. The friendship, however, soon became a love affair, which then degenerated and ended in separation. Embittered because he desired marriage, a state which the childishly selfish and hedonistic "Philine" refused to consider, the of lovers, longed for a platonic friend whom she found in a young terrifying noises. These grew less frightening in time and were eventually replaced by pleasant sounds as if to indicate that the departed one understood at last that he, in his intense desire to found a family, had chosen the wrong woman to be his partner, but had finally come to be thankful for what happiness she had given him.

In the story of the old merchant with a young wife (J. A. v. 16, 215:32-237:6) a family is founded and kept intact in the face of difficulties. Despite his advanced middle age, the merchant, at the sight of happy children, took a young wife. When he found that the unaccustomed sedentary married life was undermining his health, the old seafarer went back to sea for another voyage, fully aware of the risks involved in leaving a beautiful young wife unguarded. In parting, he advised his wife that if she should find a lover desirable in his absence, she should take a discreet one. Outraged at the suggestion at first, she did eventually wish for a lover, and chose the "Prokurator," who proved to be the hero of the story. Cleverly, he induced her to undergo first a period of chastity and abstinance. The pious and abstemious life helped her overcome her desires. Glad to have been saved from committing a serious wrong, she bid farewell to the "Prokurator" with thanks for having taught her to master her inclinations, and with the prophecy that he would one day enjoy the honor of being titled "der Vater des Vaterlands (J. A. v. 16, 237:6)."

The abbé concludes that the only possible moral story should show that man had power to act against his inclinations. No desire was good in itself but only insofar as it accomplished something good. Self-control, or "Entsagung," is again presented as necessary in any true family relationship.

The following account of the love of Ferdinand and Ottilie (J. A. v. 16, 240:12-264:5) also centers around a man who wanted to found a family but represents an advance over the preceding stories in several respects. Ferdinand was first attracted by Ottilie, who was as unworthy as the soprano Antonelli. He saw his error and shifted his affection to the much more suitable country girl. The "Volk" idea revealed in the closing words of the last story, "Vater seines Vaterlands," is here even more apparent. Ferdinand, as Hermann did later, rejected in Ottilie the world of fashion and chose a simpler girl from the "Volk." Furthermore, while Ferdinand's business naturally benefited him, it also enriched and raised the status of the artisans of his area. Thus in the wife he selected, in his place of residence, and in his economic activity Ferdinand chose a natural, organic union with his local "Volk." What is more, the development that led him to this happy solution shows him as a strong character. He had stolen from his father. Determined to rectify his error he had practiced rigid economy in money matters, that is, self-control or "Entsagung" in Goethe's sense. The self-correction culminated in his prayer, which, in terms of Goethe's scientific language, meant that he was subjecting himself, with proper humility, to eternal divine laws; to the laws of nature.

The last of the abbé's stories, the *Märchen*, while clearly meant to be the climax of the work, has thus far eluded a satisfactory and generally acceptable explanation for all its mystifying symbolism. This is not the place to recount all the efforts at interpretation or weigh their individual merits. From the standpoint of the family as "Urform und Metamorphose," certain things are clear, no matter how the symbolism is interpreted in detail. The fairy-tale realm was split by an unbridged river; it was threatened by a mysterious giant; it lacked its great temple now below the ground. Both the youth from one side of the river and Lilie from the other were under certain serious handicaps. The youth was trying to re-found the realm of his ancestors, while Lilie, under a curse, turned all living things that she touched into precious metals or jewels and all dead things she touched into a peculiar, half-alive state.

All of these difficulties and troubles were happily solved by the marriage of the youth and Lilie. Love is the healing element; the old man with the lamp says "Die Liebe herrscht nicht, aber sie bildet, und das ist mehr (J. A. v. 16, 300:22-23)" and later, "Von heute an ist keine Ehe mehr gültig, die nicht aufs neue geschlossen wird (J. A. v. 16, 301:33-34)." The youth found his realm to rule over, Lilie was freed of her curses, the temple rose to its proper place beside the river which was spanned by a fine bridge, and the dangerous giant turned into a useful fountain. Most important was the fact that at this marriage the entire land on both sides of the river, now no longer a dividing line, was peopled with a healthy, happy and prosperous "Volk."

Although the *Unterhaltungen* is a fragment, the extant portions are enough to show clearly Goethe's basic purpose, namely to hold up to his fellow-countrymen the ideal of the family, not only as a force with which to meet successfully the forces of war and revolution, but also as the only natural, organic source from which the principles of proper social organization are derived. As Jockers said, marriage is " . . . die erste und wichtigste 'pädagogische Provinz,' die ewige Grundlage von Gesellschaft und Staat."[48] This means that Goethe considered that the family embodied the principles which are necessary for the attainment of "Volkheit," which, when accomplished, would render Germany immune to the siren song (abstract ideas!) of "Liberté, Égalité, Fraternité."

In the next work which Goethe mentioned, *Die Aufgeregten*, which dates from 1793, the family as such, although it is present in many ways, relinquished the central position to its metamorphosis, the "Volk."

The evidences of the family that do occur are relatively minor, as for instance the fact that the good-hearted but comical Breme von Bremefeld was led into his dangerously amateurish political meddling by his zeal to equal or surpass the record of his grandfather, the "Bürgermeister (J. A. v. 15, 78:9-15 and 85:11 f)." The family of the countess was endangered by the fall of the young count, which is also symbolic, for both the injury and the threatened uprising could only have occurred in the absence of the countess who was leader of her own family and of the "Volk" as well. With her away, careless or ill-willed people could act unchecked. The only love affair contained in the play was totally unsuited to end in the founding of a family, as it was between the lascivious Baron and the deluded Karoline.

The revolution was also shown as destructive of families. Breme's continued absence from home at political meetings allowed the baron an opportunity to turn Karoline's head. The same political meeting caused the servants of the countess to become careless, which in turn resulted in the injury to the young count. Furthermore, the imitation of the French Revolutionary assembly, which occurred in the incompleted third act, was directly responsible for bringing the evil, revolutionary influences to a head.

The countess, as representative of the nobility, was shocked by what she saw on her visit to Paris to the extent of resolving to her utmost to right any and all social wrongs, " . . . und wenn ich auch unter dem verhassten Namen einer Demokratin verschrien werden sollte (J. A. v. 15, 99:4-5) ;" while the "Hofrat," finest exponent of the middle class, was determined to retain his respect for the position and capacities of the nobility, ". . . und wenn man mir auch den verhassten Namen eines Aristokraten zueignete (J. A. v. 15, 99:33-34)." Thus each rose above his respective social class for the good of the "Volk" as a whole.[49] These two acting in concert attempted to remedy the local injustices, which they did although the direct and energetic young huntress Friederike accelerated the solution by acting on her own initiative (J. A. v. 15, 116:5-20).

The fifth act, also only sketched in, showed the countess and the "Hofrat" dispersing the assembled rebels in newly regained mutual harmony. How important Goethe considered this dramatic fragment is evident from his statement to Eckermann that it was his ". . . politisches Glaubensbekenntnis jener Zeit."[50]

Hermann und Dorothea, written in 1796 and printed the following year, is a reversal of *Die Aufgeregten* inasmuch as the family is almost the sole center of interest, with the "Volk" playing a very much smaller role. We need to select only a few threads from this familiar epic which has been properly referred to as "das hohe Lied der Familie."

Hermann showed himself willing to form a family when he sharply rejected the apothecary's statement that bachelors were better off than married men in unsettled times as they could flee more quickly without encumbrances (Terpsichore 95-96).

Hermann's mother quickly agreed, telling how she and his father had married after the disaster of the fire which had destroyed the city. She praised her son " . . . dass du . . . es wagtest, zu frein im Kriege und über den Trümmern (Terpsichore 155-157)." This is the common human reaction of trying to set up something firm and relatively permanent, a marriage, in the face of, and as a positive response to, the negative challenge of catastrophe.

Like Ferdinand in the *Unterhaltungen,* Hermann did not take a fashionable girl as a fiancée. His father's unjust criticism caused him, momentarily at least, to consider going off to war (Euterpe, 89-90). Also involved in Hermann's angry reaction was his respect for his father shown by his pride in having defended him from ridicule among the children. But the largest part of his emotion is naturally caused by his love for the girl from the refugee train, Dorothea.

Dorothea also showed unusual aptitude for family life: she was attending a mother and a new-born babe when Hermann first saw her; she was adored by the children of her group; she had already been engaged, only to have her fiancé killed in the revolution, and she had personally taken effective action in protecting weaker sisters from lawless elements of that revolution. Finally, she was the possessor of a beautiful and healthy body.

In numerous ways Goethe showed in this work how the family instinct works to establish and benefit the "Volk" as a whole. After the fire, Hermann's father had shouldered public responsibility in addition to his own private cares to help rebuild the city. Six times he had been "Bauherr" in the city council (Thalia 33). The judge among the refugees, speaking of the progress of the revolution, noted:

> Losgebunden erscheint, sobald die Schranken hinweg sind,
> Alles Böse, das tief das Gesetz in die Winkel zurücktrieb (Klio 79-80).

Dorothea was almost alone in her group in realizing what the revolution portended. She did not share the illusory hope that the refugees would soon be able to return home,

> Denn gelöst sind die Bande der Welt, wer knüpfet sie wieder
> Als allein nur die Not, die höchste, die uns bevorsteht (Erato, 89-90).

In her fiancé's farewell, she recalled, he had clearly shown his understanding of "Volk." He saw dislocations in his native land on three ascending levels, ownership, friendship, and love.

"Liebe den Liebenden rein," he told her, "und halte dem Guten dich dankbar (Urania 285)."

In the famous concluding lines, Hermann, confident in his own impending marriage, and having come to a new understanding of the spiritual and material values it secured for his new family, at once and instinctively understood how these values applied to his "Volk" as well:

> Nicht dem Deutschen geziemt es, die fürchterliche Bewegung
> Fortzuleiten, und auch zu wanken hierhin und dorthin.
> Dies ist unser! so lass uns sagen und so es behaupten!
> Denn es werden noch stets die entschlossenen Völker gepriesen,
> Die für Gott und Gesetz, für Eltern, Weiber und Kinder
> Stritten und gegen den Feind zusammenstehend erlagen.
> Du bist mein; und nun ist das Meine meiner als jemals.
> (Urania 305-311).

How important the "Revolutionsdichtungen" were to Goethe, and what a vital role the family plays in them, has been conclusively summed up by Jockers:

> Das sittliche Fundament, aber, auf das alles ankommt und das alle miteinander gemeinsam haben, ist die Familie, d.h. die Liebe als verpflichtendes Gesetz. Mit einer vorbildlichen, bäuerlichen Ehe beginnt der 'Bürgergeneral,' mit der Aussicht auf eine Ehe schliesst 'Der Gross-Kophta.' Die Ehe zwischen einem Adligen und einem einfachen Mädchen aus dem Volk ist das Zentralproblem im 'Mädchen von Oberkirch.' Sie ist Mittelpunkt der Erziehungsgespräche in den 'Unterhaltungen deutscher Ausgewanderten,' und sie ist die Krönung des symbolischen Geschehens im 'Märchen.' Vor ihrem Lichte fliehen die Irrlichter und der Schatten der Revolution. Durch sie werden alle schlafenden Volkskräfte geweckt. Aus ihrem Geist baut sich der Tempel der Kultur wieder auf, 'und dieser Tempel ist der besuchteste auf der ganzen Erde.' Die Volkwerdung aller Stände, die das Thema der 'Aufgeregten' ist, wird im *'Märchen'* gleichnishaft vollzogen. Von Liebe und Ehe werden Worte gesagt, die dem Geist des Neuen Testaments verwandt sind: 'Die Liebe herrscht nicht, sie bildet, und keine Ehe ist fortan mehr gültig, die nicht aufs neue geschlossen,' d.h. die nicht mit dem Willen zur Dauer, also aus dem sittlichen Motiv der Gesetzesbefolgung, eingegangen wird. Hier liegt der Anfang zur Heiligsprechung der Ehe, die bei 'Hermann und Dorothea' vom Pfarrherrn, bei Wilhelm und Eugenie vom eigenen Gewissen vollzogen und in den 'Wahlverwandtschaften' vom Dichter selbst geradezu als christliches Sakrament verkündet wird. In diesem Licht betrachtet, gewinnen, wie Franz Schulz längst richtig bemerkt hat, alle Revolutionsdichtungen erhöhte Bedeutung. Sie predigen die eine grosse Lehre, dass soziale und

politische Übel letztlich nur durch reine sittliche Tätigkeit der Menschen selbst, nicht durch Zwangsverordnungen von oben oder Drohungen von unten beseitigt werden können.[51]

In the *Campagne* Goethe mentioned the émigrés who had settled near Weimar, recalling all of them in highly favorable tones for good reasons: they had accepted their fate, and, fitting themselves into their surroundings, tried to live useful lives. In short: they successfully faced reality (212:4-8).

The role of the poet in great political controversies then occupied Goethe. He, as a German man of letters, had understood the trends of the day and knew that they threatened his own people. Furthermore, he had tried to take action in his own sphere, namely poetry, only to be misunderstood and blamed. He said:

> ... dass in allen wichtigen politischen Fällen immer diejenigen Zuschauer am besten dran sind, welche Partei nehmen: ... Der Dichter aber, der seiner Natur nach unparteiisch sein und bleiben muss, sucht sich von den Zuständen beider kämpfenden Teile zu durchdringen, wo er denn, wenn Vermittelung unmöglich wird, sich entschliessen muss, tragisch zu endigen (212:17-27).

Thus Goethe refused to join either party. He was deeply suspicious of the "status-quo" party, as we have seen, because of the disunity of Germany, the cynical, Machiavellian dynastic policies, and, most importantly, because this party was decaying at the top in many places, as its inability to provide competent leadership in the campaign against the revolution had shown him. What is more, it ignored or stifled the principle of "Volkheit" which Goethe considered a necessary basis of a truly united nation. This party not only was not a product of proper, organic principles of family growth, it was frequently in conflict with those principles.

He also refused to join the pro-revolutionary party, repelled by its sanguinary excesses, by its immoderate devotion to abstract principles ("Liberté, Égalité, Fraternité"); and he deeply suspected the motives of the revolutionists. Above all, here, too, he did not see the principle of the family at work, the necessary "Volkheit." He had found a "Volk" in France, to be sure. But this had nothing to do with the decrees of the revolutionary government. It was, rather, the culmination of a long historical process which ran counter to the ideals of the revolution although Napoleon later used the "Volk" ideas consciously. The application of the revolutionary principles in Germany would be far worse for the hoped-for "Volkheit," would stifle it completely under foreign (French) influence.

In the presentation of his position outlined above, however, Goethe has been slightly misleading. He was not an impartial or inactive observer. He did in fact take sides as the "Revolutionsdichtungen" and the *Campagne* prove; he did become a fighter in this struggle, but the side that he chose to fight for, unfortunately, numbered only one individual among its adherents, namely himself. This is what he meant by saying that the poet must end in tragedy.

Goethe now returned to the contemporary events, speaking of his shock at the trial and execution of the French king, and of the changing military situation in the Rhineland. He received a summons from the duke to rejoin him for the siege of Mainz.

Goethe cherished all the more the short time still left with his family. Thus the work ends clearly and strongly with *the family*, the central theme and unifying factor underlying the *Campagne*. Now the poet's own family is in the foreground, martial exertions are in the background, a reversal of the situation of most of the *Campagne* where war and revolution formed the harsh and real present, his own family an inspiring though distant dream of the future. But the work as a whole portrays war *versus* the family — social insanity on a large scale *versus* social constructiveness in its basic unit.

The account of the winter in Weimar forms the meaningful core to the entire *Campagne-Belagerung*. It shows Goethe's efforts to organize his social activities in accordance with proper "family" principles and, implicitly by his own good example, to exhort his fellow countrymen to do the same. In the first two of these "families," namely in his own family and in that of the Weimar theater group, his efforts were successful. In the third, that of the "Weimarischen Kunstfreunde," they succeeded only in part. He failed in the fourth, consisting of all Germans. Indeed, his efforts were disapproved and disowned. His "Revolutionsdichtungen," intended to lead the German people toward a "Volkheit," failed lamentably to arouse the desired response. So Goethe, bitterly musing on the tragic role of the unbiased, impartial, and far-sighted poet, took refuge in his own family for the short time that remained to him before returning to war.

At the very end of his work Goethe referred to a contemporary sketch that he had made, showing Christiane and his son in the garden against the background of the house. The verse accompanying the sketch cannot be numbered among Goethe's great lyric expressions. It is constructed around a cliché, which seems surprising from one of the greatest lyric talents of modern times, if not the greatest. Or did Goethe strike this tone intentionally? We cannot avoid the conclusion that Goethe, in his closing words, purposefully suited ideas, figures, and language to the good-hearted, normal, average small-town family life:

> Hier sind wir denn vorerst ganz still zu Haus,
> Von Tür zu Türe sieht es lieblich aus;
> Der Künstler froh die stillen Blicke hegt,
> Wo Leben sich zum Leben freundlich regt.
> Und wie wir auch durch ferne Lande ziehn,
> Da kommt es her, da kehrt es wieder hin;
> Wir wenden uns, wie auch die Welt entzücke,
> Der Enge zu, die uns allein beglücke.

C. BELAGERUNG VON MAINZ

I. MILITARY OPERATIONS

Goethe's participation in the siege of Mainz covered the period from the twenty-sixth of May to the twenty-second of August, 1793. The parallels between Goethe's literary account of it and that of the *Campagne* are obvious; but there are also differences. One must not take too literally Goethe's remark that this time he was going: " . . . um, wie früher an einem beweglichen Übel, so nun an einem stationären teilzunehmen (213:29-30)." Since the *Belagerung* forms the finale to the *Campagne-Belagerung* considered as a whole, it is to be expected that many of the themes of the *Campagne* will be encountered again. But the *Belagerung* is also a summation, in Goethe's language, a "Steigerung." Hence the similarities and differences will have to be traced in detail.

Again Goethe depended heavily on other written sources. The importance of such "borrowings" in the *Campagne* was discussed above. The paucity of his own sketches and diaries made this dependence necessary in both cases. Here in the *Belagerung* Wagner's diary was again indispensable.

In this work, too, most of the incidents are related in very compressed form, while relatively few are described at length. Two factors bring this about. Goethe would naturally recount only briefly the incidents he found described elsewhere, while first-hand experiences would be treated in considerably more detail. But the more important factor is the tendency, discernible in the *Campagne* as well, to develop broadly the incidents that are important to Goethe for the purposes of establishing his point, and, on the other hand, to condense others needed only to maintain the thread of the narrative.

After many delays Goethe left Weimar on the twelfth of May, 1793, and proceeded in a leisurely fashion towards Mainz. The slowness of the journey evinces the same mood of reluctance he had shown when he joined the army for the *Campagne*. He stayed for a week with his mother in Frankfurt, and did not arrive in the allied camp until the twenty-seventh.

On the evening of the twenty-eighth Goethe dined with the officers of the Weimar regiment. He skillfully used the topic of their conversation to set the tone for the entire *Belagerung*.

The officers recalled his Valmy remark of the preceding year, which Goethe then quoted verbatim, thus again underlining the importance of the subject: "Von hier und heute geht eine neue Epoche der Weltgeschichte aus, und ihr könnt sagen, ihr seid dabei gewesen (219:19-21)." Goethe then went on:

> Wunderbar genug sah man diese Prophezeiung nicht etwa nur dem allgemeinen Sinn, sondern dem besonderen Buchstaben nach genau erfüllt, indem die Franzosen ihren Kalender von diesen Tagen an datierten (219:22-25).

We know from our discussion of the *Campagne* that Goethe understood the Valmy cannonade as a dividing point in the history of Europe inasmuch as it marked, on the one hand, the decline and eventual fall of the old dynastic, monarchical order, divorced from the "Volk," and, on the other hand, the rise of the new, nationalistic state, based on the concept of "Volk" in Goethe's sense. This was the note Goethe wished to emphasize again in the *Belagerung*. It was another incident in the conflict between the disintegrating old order and the rising new order.

a) Inefficiency of Command

One of the first persons on whom Goethe called after his arrival in Mainz was General Kalckreuth with whom he dined the same evening. Upon his first arrival in Mainz the year before Goethe had called on Herr vom Stein. The ensuing conversation had given him points that remained important throughout the *Campagne*. A similar situation is evident in the *Belagerung*. Goethe and the general discussed the rumor that General von Schönfeld, an unpopular officer, had deserted to the French. The unfounded rumor is worth mentioning only as evidence of the widespread lack of respect for or confidence in the general. The rumor was so generally believed that as a matter of precaution the pass-word was changed. "Feldgeschrei," the term that Goethe used when "pass-word" was meant, was the current one at the time and is important for later consideration.

The discussion of the rest of the conversation contains this veiled remark:

> Viel ward gesprochen über Persönlichkeiten und deren Verhältnisse, die gar mancherlei wirken, ohne dass sie zur Sprache kommen (218:15-17).

Stripped of the protective language screen that Goethe knew how to use so well, this means that Kalckreuth was complaining of his great responsibilities, without having a commensurate voice in the decisions that he had to execute. As if to underline the importance of this concealed comment, Goethe added, generalizing, that it is often impossible to know how and why certain events occurred as the full story is often not recorded (218:17-19).

The next day Goethe visited Freiherr vom Stein again. Dissatisfaction with the leadership of the army must have been discussed although Goethe does not mention it in his account. Vom Stein had warned the allied command that Mainz was endangered by the French forces. But his warnings had been ignored and the city subsequently occupied by the French. Reinforcements or fortification, in accordance with vom Stein's timely warning, could have saved it (Dove 300). That evening Goethe dined in the headquarters, where Kalckreuth, "... seiner Laune gegen die Theoristen freien Lauf (liess) (218:31-32)." Coming from the responsible commanding general, the term "Theoristen" can only refer to the critics of the operations.

Thus on the second page of the work criticism of the command is hinted at three times and an additional occasion is passed over in silence. The allied army had learned nothing then from its recent failure, and we may expect to hear many of the items of the previous indictment repeated.

The quarters occupied by the high-ranking officers were now subjected to some acid comment. The magnificence of the quarters of vom Stein were referred to (218:20-25), then the extravagant pains taken to render the quarters of the Landgraf von Darmstadt "bequem und prächtig (220:13-17)." The theme was continued, after a second reference without derogatory comment to the magnificent quarters of Herr vom Stein (226:6-8) in connection with a banquet given by Karl August: "... in einem grossen, von Zimmerwerk zu solchen Festen auferbauten Saale (226:15-16)." As climax, Goethe devoted nineteen lines to the splendid quarters built for the King of Prussia. Landscape architects and skilled gardeners were imported to transform the area into a beautiful park with a splendid view. It can hardly be considered an accident, that, inserted between these descriptions, one finds the note: "... (ich) ... setzte ... meine Arbeit an *Reineke Fuchs* fleissig fort (227:5-6)."

As if to cap his account of such incongruities, Goethe described the arrival of the beautiful princesses of Mecklenburg in the camp. They had come to call on their fiancés, the princes, at the Prussian headquarters. Goethe speaks highly of the beauty of the charming princesses, to be sure. But his picture of a camp, supposedly military, where such events occurred speaks for itself.

Then follows proof of the incompetence of the command, the story of the near-success of the surprise French attack on Marienborn, the village in which both Kalckreuth and Prince Louis Ferdinand had their headquarters. Goethe had written an account, at the time of the events, for Karl August, an account that has been preserved (W.A. I, 33, p. 335). Here in the *Belagerung* he simply quotes it (221:5-222:11) with very few stylistic alterations. This account is interesting because it contains veiled criticism of the command written at the time of the events. There were, "unfortunately," he reported, gaps between the Prussian and the Austrian sentry posts "Wegen geringen Wechsels von Höhen und Tiefen (223:17)." Furthermore, the French had been able to penetrate the allied lines by following peasants, who had, under cover of darkness, been mowing the fields lying between the lines, and some sentries had been "dadurch irre gemacht (223:25)." So much for Goethe's contemporary account. Actually, between 4,000 and 6,000 Frenchmen were involved in the affair (Roethe 136). Chuquet[52] called attention to a fact that Goethe omitted: the Prussian custom of having the sentries repeat the password in a loud tone on being relieved, thus enabling the enemy to overhear it. The irony in the general use of the term "Feldgeschrei" ("war whoop") for "password" and the implicit criticism of the command are apparent. The Prussian command itself, according to Chuquet, admitted its stupidity by, on the next day, forbidding further loud exchange of passwords. The French reached the village, were nearly successful in their attempts to capture the commanders, and set fire to the village. During the French retreat, the Prussians distinguished themselves by firing at their own troops in the confusion, "ein unglücklicher Zufall (224:20)."

On the following day Goethe visited the mortally wounded Rittmeister von Voss (225:17-20). On leaving the sickroom, an acquaintance reminded Goethe that, only a few days before, a heated argument had arisen in the same room. The officers had maintained that Marienborn was much too exposed to be a headquarters and that preparations should be made at once to prevent a possible surprise attack from the French. Goethe then continued with a comment that pointed up sharply the relationship of the officers to the higher command:

> Weil aber überhaupt eine heftige Widerrede gegen alles, was von oben herein befohlen und veranstaltet war, zur Tagesordnung gehörte, so ging man drüber hinaus und liess diese Warnung, wie so manche andere, verhallen (225:21-24).

In other words, criticism of the command had become so commonplace that it exerted a paralyzing effect. Nothing was done in the matter.

Goethe now turned to the description of the siege operations proper, "das offenbare Geheimnis (227:12)." An obstructing French fortification had been overrun and destroyed, and on the night of the sixteenth, with greatest secrecy, Austrians marched out to begin the operations. Some allied outposts had not been alerted to what was planned, and the attempt resulted in spectacular failure as one ally shot up another (229:34-230:11). This constituted, of course, a culpable failure of command. It is interesting that Goethe devoted a full page to the failure of the first attempt while the next, successful one is reported in only one line (230:21).

Goethe turned then with bitter irony to the plight of the city of Mainz, for it had become a popular spectacle:

> Und so war nach und nach das innere, grenzenlose Unglück einer Stadt aussen und in der Umgegend Anlass zu einer Lustpartie geworden (234:27-29).

Country people in their Sunday best came after church to view the attraction from a fortification near Weisenau. It is not difficult to imagine Goethe's emotions in observing the sightseers, to avoid an oncoming cannonball, throwing themselves headlong into the dust at the sentry's warning shout (235:12-27). The better society of Frankfurt also appeared in their coaches to see the entertaining show. The account ends in a cynical comment on the effectiveness of the military arrangements:

> Auch wurde bei einiger Aufmerksamkeit des Militärs der Eintritt einer solchen Menge gar bald verboten, und die Frankfurter nahmen einen Umweg, auf welchem sie unbemerkt und unerreicht in das Hauptquartier gelangten (235:35-236:4).

Also the story of the floating battery belongs in this account of allied waste and incompetence (232:1-233:34). Apparently this contraption was a large, armored barge (Goethe called it "ein Lokal"), constructed at great effort and expense and carrying a large crew manning the cannon. It was intended to bombard Mainz from the river; but it proved so unmanageable that it drifted helplessly in circles until it grounded on the French side where it and the entire crew were captured before it had fired a shot. It would be difficult to find a better illustration of Goethe's views on the subject than when he complained in his letter to Jacobi that the means employed were disproportionate to the ends attained (2 July, 1793. W. A. IV, 10, p. 83).

Later Goethe described a night attack to eliminate one of the outer French fortifications. He accepted the prospective losses as necessary, except for "ein bedenklicher Umstand," namely the circumstance that cavalry was to be used in the attack. The plan was stupid. The men would have to lead their horses single file through a trench to the place of attack, then leave the trench and get into formation under the very muzzles of the enemy guns (241:17-28). Goethe was worried for the safety of his friend von Oppen who was to lead the cavalry attack; fortunately he escaped unscathed, however.

On the twenty-fourth of July, while he was at the headquarters of the duke on the highway, Goethe noted a number of carriages escaping from the city that had just capitulated. Everyone suspected that they contained escaping "Mainzer Klubisten:" those who had accepted the ideas of the revolution and collaborated with the French forces. But nothing was done to stop them. The laxity of the allied command is again criticized:

> ... wieder andere wollten sich verwundern, dass auf dem ganzen Weg keine Spur von Wache, noch Piquett, noch Aufsicht erschiene, woraus erhelle, sagten sie, dass man von oben herein durch die Finger zu sehen, und alles, was sich ereignen könnte, dem Zufall zu überlassen geneigt sei (245:16-21).

In this finale to the *Campagne-Belagerung* then, the *Campagne* criticism of command is repeated. This time, however, the material is presented more openly and forcefully, a "Steigerung" typical of Goethe and quite fitting for a finale.

b) Anti-War Comment

On the twenty-fourth of June the French, to conserve food,

tried to expel all the women, children, old people and invalids from the city. The allies, naturally, would not let them through the lines, but tried to make them return into the city in order to shorten the siege. As a result, the poor unfortunates spent two days of heart-rending misery in no-man's land until the French finally re-admitted them. What Goethe's reaction to this treatment of families was needs no elaboration. This condemnation of war is all the more interesting because all the events Goethe described occurred on the opposite (northern) side of the city. He could not possibly have observed the misery himself.

Similar bitterness becomes apparent in Goethe's description of the scenes regarding the night bombardment of the city. Goethe noted that his friends, Herr Gorr and Rat Kraus, made drawings and, later, even a transparency to show this lurid scene:

> Und wie deutete nicht ein solcher Anblick auf die traurigste Lage, indem wir, uns zu retten, uns einigermassen herzustellen, zu solchen Mitteln greifen mussten! (231:31-35).

One is reminded, as Goethe must have been, of the contrast between the burning Mainz and the city of Cassel, as he saw it in the *Campagne*, which seemed to be lighted from within by the warmth of family living.

c) Lücke

Another type of anti-war comment is represented by the *Lücke*, which Goethe inserted at this juncture. Various commentators have pointed to the internal and external parallels that exist between the *Zwischenrede* of the *Campagne* and the *Lücke* of the *Belagerung*. Such parallels are obvious, but the differences are more illuminating; for one thing, the *Zwischenrede* was inserted at the end of the military parts of the *Campagne* and formed a transition to the remainder of the work, while the *Lücke* falls in the middle of the military description, and tells something of vital importance about that military portion.

In both interpolations Goethe described his own inner condition. But the similarity ceases there. Here, as will be shown, Goethe indicates that even he is affected by the peculiar, wildly venturesome and yet mentally benumbed mood that overcomes men in daily danger of violent death. The *Zwischenrede* serves the important function of preparing for the Pempelfort, Duisburg, and Münster visits while the *Lücke* is not a preparation for anything. Instead it stands independently as a monument, proving that Goethe had participated fully in the psychological experience of war although his war-experiences had all been short and apparently superficial. The part he had played was that of a favored observer without duties (referred to several times, *i.e.* "unberufen" [236:31]; "ohne Ordre und Beruf" [237:15]). This passage was written entirely in the 1820's. But it also represented his contemporary mood as we know from a letter to Voigt of the third of July, 1793:

> Mich wandelt in meiner jetzigen Lage eine Art Stupor an, und ich finde den trivialen Ausdruck: *der Verstand steht mir still* trefflich um die Lage meines Geistes auszudrücken (W. A. IV. 10, p. 85).

The note of wild daring is struck at the very beginning of the *Lücke*.

> Von der wilden, wüsten Gefahr angezogen wie von dem Blick einer Klapperschlange, stürzte man sich unberufen in die tödlichen Räume ... (236:29-31).

Goethe's use of "man" as a convenient screen to hide the "ich" has been noted. Then we read the remarkable statement:

> ... manchem Schwerblessierten wünschte man baldige Erlösung vom grimmigen Leiden, und die Toten hätte man nicht ins Leben zurückgerufen (237:2-4).

Here the two levels of meaning must be carefully examined. It has been noted above that on occasion Goethe himself warned the perceptive, the "assimilating," reader to read with care. In the *Lücke* he again sounded a warning that justifies a very careful reading of the material:

> Bedenkt man nun, dass ein solcher Zustand, wo man sich, die Angst zu übertäuben, jeder Vernichtung aussetzte, bei drei Wochen dauerte, so wird man uns verzeihen, wenn wir über diese schrecklichen Tage wie über einen glühenden Boden hinüberzueilen trachten (238:26-30).

It is well to re-examine in this light the statement to the effect that he wished a quick release from terrible suffering for many a severely wounded man. On the surface, it seems to contain nothing but a becoming pity for the suffering. But it is to be noted that he wished release for the severely wounded ("Schwerblessierten"), not the mortally wounded, that he wished release for them ("Erlösung"), *i.e.* death, *not* recovery. And he went on to say "Die Toten hätte man nicht ins Leben zurückgerufen." This is the mood of desperation. Thus Goethe was saying that he too had experienced the terrible war mood in which emotions silence reason, in which there is an undertone of exulting in death and destruction. Goethe too had shared this sobering experience, common to all soldiers at all times when the most powerful of all psychological stimuli, that of imminent death, is received at too frequent intervals. The mood arises out of the powerful stimulus caused by risk of death, is colored with an exultant sense of the power of destruction, and contains also a completely selfish element, the animal exultation in surviving, in remaining alive while others die. This war mood is all the more terrible because all men, even the mature and morally firm, are subject to it. Anyone can see the corrosive effect of war on societies, but only those who experience it, as Goethe did here, can fully appreciate its brutalizing effect on human character, even on the best individuals. These elements gleaming through the pages of the *Belagerung* explain Goethe's remark that he wanted to hurry silently over those days "wie über einen glühenden Boden."

The remainder of the *Lücke* is in essence a series of anecdotes of Goethe's wild escapades under fire. They underline the war mood just discussed. To afford Goethe a superb view of the city, a sentry let him enter a half ruined building still under fire (237:21-238:6). In a destroyed village, also still under fire, he sought malformed bones in a charnel house (237:18-20). He drank wine in the cellar of a former nunnery as the shot rained into the upper stories (238:7-10). Then he went forward and crouched behind low earthworks as close to the enemy guns as possible (238:12-19). Finally he recalled the "Kanonenfieber" of the *Campagne* as well as his frequent willful exposure to enemy fire before Mainz.

The bearing of this material on the family is two-fold. First, the entire *Campagne-Belagerung* paints the two great opposing forces, family, or social constructiveness in its basic unit on the one hand, and war and revolution, or social insanity on the grand scale, on the other. Goethe proves here that his experience of war was just as thorough as his experience of the family. Secondly, the *Lücke* demonstrates that the psychological effect of war on the individual is diametrically opposed to that of the family.

In these scenes, as in the *Campagne*, art and science formed a diversion and an escape from, as well as a constructive antidote to, war. The artistic activities of Herr Gore and Rat Kraus have been mentioned. Goethe sketched the men and their activities in some detail (239:29-240:8). In addition to his work on *Reineke*, noted above, Goethe was occupied with scientific and literary projects (letters to: Herder, 15th June; Knebel, 2nd July; Voigt, 3rd; Jacobi, 7th; Meyer, 10th).

The diary entries were resumed on the first of July. They are much shorter than formerly, consisting frequently of only a line for a day's entry. Actually, Goethe had stopped keeping a diary early in June, after the Marienborn affair (Roethe 254). He had been urged, apparently, to keep a running record. But he had become disgusted even as he had during the *Campagne*; he didn't want to write what he was allowed to, and he could not write what he wanted to. To Jacobi he wrote quite specifically:

> Ich hatte die ersten Tage meines Hierseyns manches aufzuzeichnen angefangen, ich hörte aber bald auf; meine natürliche Faulheit fand gar manche Entschuldigung. Es gehört dazu mehr *Commerage* und Kannegiesserei als ich aufbringen kann, und was ist's zu letzt? alles, was man weiss, und gerade das worauf alles ankommt darf man nicht sagen *und da bleibt's eine Art Advokatenarbeit die sehr gut bezahlt werden müsste, wenn man sie mit einigem Humor unternehmen sollte* (July 7, W. A. IV. 10, p. 88; italics added).

Thus in the first portion of the *Belagerung* the same criticism of the command is to be noted that was found in the *Campagne* though here it is couched in sharper, less veiled language. But the *Lücke* brings something new: the portrayal of some of the eroding effects of warfare on the human individuality which contrast with the constructive effects of the family, both as ideal and as concrete reality.

II. THE CONQUERED CITY

The armistice went into effect on the twenty-second of July. On the next day Goethe met an exiled Mainz wig-maker. The latter was foaming with rage at the French and particularly the "Klubisten." This gave Goethe a chance to preach his doctrine of civic order:

> ... dass die Rückkehr in einen friedlichen und *häuslichen* Zustand nicht mit neuem bürgerlichen Krieg, Hass und Rache müsse verunreinigt werden, weil sich das Unglück ja sonst verewige (244:25-29; italics added).

He added that punishment must be left to the rightful rulers and the allied commanders.

On the next day, from the headquarters on the highway, Goethe's party noted the "Klubisten" escaping singly in fast carriages as there were no guards to halt them.

When the French cavalry rode out of the surrendered city in formation, Goethe found them impressive: " . . . einzeln hätte man sie dem Don Quixote vergleichen können, in Masse erschienen sie höchst ehrwürdig (246:11)." Likewise the dwarf-like, motley infantry from Marseille impressed him in spite of himself, particularly the slow, dignified march to the tune of the Marseillaise. Despite the ridiculous exterior appearance of the troops, Goethe was struck by their spirit, the spirit of unity. He recognized the fact that most of the French were united into a "Volk" as he had observed earlier in the French peasants of the *Campagne*.

By the next day, the twenty-fifth, the danger of mob violence had become acute because of the continued failure of the allied authorities to maintain order:

> Am Morgen dieses Tages bemerk' ich, dass leider abermals keine Anstalten auf der Chaussee und in deren Nähe gemacht waren, um Unordnungen zu verhüten. Sie schienen heute um so nötiger, als die armen, ausgewanderten, grenzenlos unglücklichen Mainzer, von entfernteren Orten her nunmehr angekommen, scharenweis die Chaussee umlagerten, mit Fluch- und Racheworten das gequälte und geängstigte Herz erleichternd (246:29-247:2).

The inevitable soon happened. One of the "Klubisten" was discovered in a coach, dragged out and beaten half to death. The French, however, were allowed to pass unmolested! (247:8-10). We are reminded of the French peasants of the *Campagne* who

THE CONQUERED CITY

attacked the émigrés, but let the allies go unharmed. The citizens of Mainz were showing by their actions that the "Klubisten" were excluded from the "Volk" of the city of Mainz. However, they were not, by Goethe's standards, a real "Volk" in the fullest sense of the word as the following scene shows.

As the mob was about to get out of hand, Goethe personally intervened in behalf of someone he had never seen before (249:10-20). His orders were disputed by a member of the mob, the same wig-maker Goethe had befriended previously. Goethe reminded the man (and he uses direct quotation in his account):

> ". . . dass man durch Selbstrache sich schuldig macht, das man Gott und seinen Oberen die Strafe der Verbrecher überlassen soll, wie man ihnen das Ende dieses Elends zu bewirken auch überlassen müsste" (250:3-8).

Gore was later amazed at Goethe's daring action which the latter explains thus: "Es liegt nun einmal in meiner Natur; ich will lieber eine Ungerechtigkeit begehen, als Unordnung ertragen (251:21-23)." Here we see Goethe stepping out of his role as observer and acting fast to uphold order since the proper authorities had failed to do so. One is reminded of Goethe's assertion in the *Campagne* that he recalled Prince Louis Ferdinand out of danger. In both cases there is serious doubt that Goethe actually took this action. In a letter to Jacobi of the twenty-seventh of July he sketched a very different picture: "Am Chausseehause (the headquarters) schrie das Volk sein *kreuzige* . . . (W. A. IV, 10, pp. 100, 101)," he wrote, noting that only the presence of the Prussian officers kept the mob from executing lynch justice on the spot. He reported that several "Klubisten" were maltreated, and that other citizens were sending from the city lists to the loyal Mainzers of persons to be captured on the highway. The latter then arrested the traitors "durch ein Kommando" although they did not molest the French. Furthermore, the people inside the city had organized to prevent looting, and Goethe ended with the important statement: "Der Modus, dass man die Sache gleichsam dem Zufall überliess und die Gefangennehmung von unten herauf bewirckte, deucht mir gut (W.A. IV 10, pp. 100, 101)."

Actually then there *had* been Prussian officers along the road, Goethe *had not* intervened to maintain order. There *was* evidence of a respectable spontaneous organization among the citizens of Mainz. But Goethe did not mention these facts in the *Belagerung*. He might have used them as evidence of their united group feeling, of the fact that they were a "Volk." But to Goethe they were not. It will be recalled that they had accepted the French with open arms, in contrast to the people of Frankfurt, a matter which had been discussed at the Jacobis (160:24-29). Furthermore the Mainzers had indulged in mob violence, a cardinal sin in Goethe's view. Hence he could not present them as exemplary.

On the twenty-sixth Goethe entered the ruined city. Most of the sketches of the misery and destruction that follow involve the family in some way. Civil order and the police had ceased to function, he says (252:3), and plundering had been prevalent. This contrasts sharply with the contemporary letter to Jacobi quoted above. Many houses, family dwellings, were destroyed, to be sure. But many others were wantonly besmirched.

While Goethe's party was in the city, the first proclamation of the new governor was made public, of which Goethe says: "... ich fand sie in eben dem Sinne, ja fast mit den gleichen Worten meiner Anmahnung an jenen ausgewanderten Perückenmacher ... (253:25-27)." This proclamation had been reprinted in one of the main sources that Goethe used[53] and was doubtless the inspiration for the invented incident on the highway.

The behavior of the citizens of the city in defending their families and homes during the siege had been in part heroic. Many had learned to extinguish "bombs" by quickly pouring water on them, a dangerous procedure that had claimed a number of lives (257:16-30); they had shown readiness for heroic self-sacrifice for family and "Volk."

But all the members of the Mainz "family" agreed that those who had been expelled from the city to spend two days in no-man's land had suffered most.

> Denn nicht der Krieg allein, sondern der durch Unsinn aufgelöste bürgerliche Zustand hatte ein solches Unglück bereitet und herbeigeführt (257:13-15).

The divisive tendencies of the revolution must share blame with the war.

Everyone was amazed that Mainz had not held out longer, for great stores of food and wine were found. Goethe speculated (correctly) that the French political leaders, having heard of a political re-alignment in Paris, were anxious to return, be on the spot, and profit from the new conditions. This was, of course, in line with Goethe's conviction that most of the revolutionary leaders were unmitigated scoundrels. The overly hasty surrender of the city by the French had still another effect: it shows the achievement of the allied armies in capturing the city in a very poor light. Goethe thus has shown, in effect, in the *Campagne-Belagerung*, that the army was badly beaten in the *Campagne* by its own incompetence, not by the enemy, and that it was successful in the *Belagerung* only because the French wanted to surrender the city!

In these sketches of Mainz and its population, then, Goethe again changed, suppressed, or invented material to bend the final account to his basic purpose. He suppressed evidences of a spontaneous and responsible organization among the citizens; he changed his original approval of independent action by the citizens to disapproval, and apparently invented the incident with the wig-maker before the "Chausseehaus" of whole cloth.

III. MANNHEIM AND HEIDELBERG

Goethe left Mainz on August second and proceeded to Mannheim, where, while at an inn, he was approached by von Rietz of the staff of the King of Prussia (259:1-28). Von Rietz expressed pleasure and amazement at finding in Goethe a man of genius with a good physique and of pleasant appearance. Goethe contrasted this encounter with an unsuccessful attempt to form a friendship on the part of an officer who had shown an interest in Goethe previously. The man had turned out to be very cool and distant on closer approach, saying that he could see from Goethe's exterior that he, Goethe, was not the man he had imagined him to be (226:15-20 and 226:24-227:11). These contrasting contacts described by Goethe are interesting, for they reflect again Lavater's physiognomical theories. The first officer had expected to find this genius to be a bookworm, an abstract thinker, and impractical, "eine vermüffte Person (259:27)," in Goethe's words. He had expected a Plessing, apparently in the belief that such an exterior went hand in hand with genius. Finding an individual of normal appearance, he had apparently concluded that Goethe could not have been a real genius after all! Thus by means of two meetings with strangers, thirty pages apart, Goethe managed to recall in this finale the Plessing episode, with all the opinions and warnings that it contained.

The last and the most important parallel to the *Campagne* is to be found in the description of the meeting with Schlosser, Goethe's brother-in-law, which forms the conclusion of the work. Though in more condensed form, it is strikingly similar to the accounts of the visits at Pempelfort, Duisburg, and Münster and forms a final "Steigerung."

From the fourth to the seventh of August the two men were guests at the home of an old friend, the Demoiselle Delph in Heidelberg. Goethe was fully preoccupied with his optical theories on which he had been working during the siege (see also Jacobi ltr. 2 July, W.A. IV v. 10, p. 84). Schlosser inquired how these were related to those of Euler, a disciple of Newton. Goethe admitted the latter had little in common with his (260:2 ff). In the absence of equipment to show Schlosser what he meant, Goethe then began to read to him an essay on the subject that he had written during the siege. This essay is still extant,

Einige allgemeine Sätze über die Eintheilung der Farben, usw (W. A. II, v. 5, pt. 1, pp. 83-98).
The essay outlines how a widely diversified group or family of scientists and professional men, physicists, mathematicians, painters, mechanics, etc., should contribute, each in his specialty, to the advancement of knowledge on optics. But Schlosser became impatient:

> ... als ich ihm aber die Abhandlung im einzelnen vorlesen wollte, verbat er sich's und lachte mich aus: ich sei, meinte er, in meinen alten Tagen noch immer ein Kind und ein Neuling, dass ich mir einbilde, es werde jemand an demjenigen teilnehmen, wofür ich Interesse zeige, es werde jemand ein fremdes Verfahren billigen und es zu dem seinigen machen, es könne in Deutschland irgend eine gemeinsame Wirkung und Mitwirkung stattfinden! (260:20-30).

Schlosser had spoken in a similar manner on other subjects. But Goethe had always tried to explain them away with references to the harsh life that Schlosser had had (260:31-261:2). This time Schlosser had gone too far. He not only had ridiculed the idea of a "family" of scientists and experts, united in a common task, but he had immensely broadened his scorn by ridiculing Goethe's belief that cooperation of any kind could take place *in Germany*. This, of course, struck at the heart of Goethe's whole social thinking in which the family was the "Urform" of the German "Volk" of the future, making cooperation necessary in every endeavor. All this Schlosser was casting aside with cynical pessimism and, at the same time, laughing at Goethe's deeply patriotic feeling that such a "Volk" could and should be founded without delay in Germany.

How seriously Goethe took this denial of his dearest convictions and aims can be seen from his reaction to it, " . . . (es) regte sich abermals der alte Adam . . . (261:9)" as had "das böse Prinzip" at Pempelfort. Of course, Schlosser became angry and, although their hostess was able to restore surface harmony, Goethe was not reconciled. He departed from the house as soon as he decently could (261:15-17).

Goethe, in his search for a real "Volk" in Germany, in search of life organized in accordance with true family principles, had been bitterly disappointed at Pempelfort, Duisburg, and Münster, and again at the failure of his "Revolutionsdichtung." This meeting with Schlosser represents the climax to all these disappointments. Goethe was harshly told that it was naive to expect his fellow countrymen to be guided by anything but narrowly selfish and individualistic motives.

Throughout, Goethe has revealed his feeling by his reactions. The unpleasant political attitude of his friends in Mainz at the beginning of the *Campagne* made Goethe "unwohl." After the Pempelfort disappointments, Goethe came down with an illness that had suspiciously psychological overtones. When it became evident to him that his "Revolutionsdichtungen" were not only misunderstood but also ridiculed, Goethe reacted by turning to the robust and cynical irony of *Reineke Fuchs*. And here in Heidelberg Goethe reacted by leaving the house as soon as possible.

In this connection it is interesting to note Roethe's comment concerning Goethe's aversion to disputes and polemics. Oddly enough, Roethe did not connect it with either Schlosser or the *Campagne-Belagerung*:

> Je älter er (Goethe) wird, um so zürnender rechnet er es den Deutschen zur Kardinal- und Erbsünde an, dass sie sich igelhaft vereinzeln, dass sie sich gegenseitig nicht dankbar und verständnisvoll anzuerkennen vermögen, sondern jeder am Andern mäkelt und zerrt (Roethe 304-305).

The Schlosser incident as described by Goethe becomes even more meaningful when the contemporary letters are examined. They not only fail to show such disagreement with Schlosser, but on the contrary indicate a hearty understanding. To Jacobi, on the eleventh of August, he wrote of spending "a few happy days" with Schlosser, and said: ". . . es freut mich sehr und ist ein grosser Gewinnst für mich, dass wir uns einmal wieder genähert haben (W. A. IV, v. 10, p. 103)." Again to Jacobi, on the eighteenth of November, Goethe wrote: ". . . auch mir hat seine (Schlossers) Gegenwart sehr wohl getan, denn man fühlt bald dass seine Strenge einen sehr zarten Grund bedeckt (W. A. IV, 10, p. 128)." There is reason to believe, then, that the account of the meeting with Schlosser as it stands in the *Belagerung* represents a considerable distortion of the actual facts, possibly even a complete fabrication.

The Schlosser incident represents another highly significant parallel to the *Campagne*. We saw that at the beginning of that work Goethe did not develop the disagreement with the Sömmering-Huber circle in as much detail as he might have. He barely hinted at it. On the other hand, he exaggerated the Jacobi disagreement, exaggerated the poor stage reception of one of the "Revolutionsdichtungen," the *Bürgergeneral.* Now he described disagreements with his brother-in-law which were either exaggerated or invented. He wished to establish a rising line of intensity in these meetings with contemporaries, transforming them into symbols of the various shortcomings of the society of his time in Germany. In all these meetings Goethe has pointed to ways in which the groups failed to live up to his theories of the family as the origin and the guiding model of human society.

It is on this melancholy and seemingly hopeless note that the *Campagne-Belagerung,* to all intents and purposes, comes to an end. Goethe made no reference to his joy at the impending reunion with his own family evident in his contemporary letters:

> Mein herumschweifendes Leben und die politische Stimmung aller Menschen treibt mich nach Hause, wo ich einen Kreis um mich ziehen kann, in welchen ausser Lieb' und Freundschaft, Kunst und Wissenschaft, nichts herein kann (W. A. IV, v. 10, p. 105:19 August).

Unlike the *Campagne,* he meant to have a negative tone prevail at the end of the *Belagerung.* The Schlosser statement denied, in the harshest terms, Goethe's hopes of finding somewhere in Germany a kernel, or at least a readiness to form a kernel of a future German "Volk." Goethe did not restrict himself to omitting all reference to his own family, he closed with the gloomy prospect of the political collapse of 1806, rather than with that of the national rebirth of 1815.

Goethe then referred to the fact that the duke was leaving the Prussian service, which, though Goethe did not mention it, he did in some disgust. Goethe presented it as a sad severing of personal friendships with the officers. Actually, of course, it was something of a personal triumph for Goethe, who had always advised the duke against the Prussian alliance.

The *Belagerung* ends on a note of foreboding:

> Und so wollen wir schliessen, um nicht in Betrachtung der Weltschicksale zu geraten, die uns noch zwölf Jahre (1806!) bedrohten, bis wir von eben denselben Fluten uns überschwemmt, wo nicht verschlungen gesehen (262:4-7).

Roethe could not understand this reference to 1806 rather than to 1815, but as our reading of the *Campagne-Belagerung* has shown, Goethe was too well aware of the internal sickness of the Prussian state—whose army he had watched at close range "im beweglichen wie im stationären Übel"—not to realize that the destruction of 1806 would have to precede any rebirth, such as that of 1815.

D. CONCLUSION

From the foregoing analyses it is clear that the *Campagne-Belagerung* is not merely a series of rather inaccurate autobiographical sketches, but rather a deeply significant statement on Goethe's social philosophy developed in reaction to the French Revolution. Goethe was opposed to and deeply fearful of that revolution as a political movement because it was not founded on the organic principles of the family as he understood them, but rather on abstract ideas ("Liberté, Égalité, Fraternité") which, he was convinced, were false. Most of all he feared the French Revolution for the threat it represented to his beloved country.

The fact that the revolution had been possible was evidence of a French "Volkheit," which of course aroused Goethe's interest. The French people had long since developed a feeling of belonging together, of mutual dependence and assistance and, although the revolution did great harm in France, it never dented the monolithic French "Volkheit." Thus in Goethe's view the French could afford even such a harmful aberration as the revolution, while it would have meant in Germany, which had as yet not achieved a "Volkheit," irrevocable disaster inasmuch as it would have prevented the formation of one.

Goethe was opposed to the revolution, to be sure. But this did not by any means indicate that he aligned himself with its political enemies, namely the émigrés or the dynastic states of Austria and Prussia and their allies. The *Campagne-Belagerung* clearly shows that his condemnation of the *ancien régime* was, if anything, more definite, more explicit, and harsher than his judgment of the revolution. Long passages with scores of incidents constitute devastating criticism of the Austro-Prussian allies and the system they symbolized. Here, too, Goethe not only missed the proper principles of family organization, he also saw the absolutist and dynastic system as an inhibitor of development toward a German "Volkheit."

Seen in this light, his seemingly conflicting statements and acts of later years are understandable and not at all contradictory. His admiration for Napoleon, for instance, was not a lack of sympathy or understanding for German aspirations, it was simply an expression of Goethe's recognition of Napoleon's genius as an instrumentality of fate destined to reorganize and preserve the French "Volkheit." Similar processes of thought observable in the *Campagne-Belagerung* indicate that Goethe's observations on the revolution were not subjective concerns but the fundamentals of his social philosophy, thus lifting the work from the biographical to the sociological sphere.

Altough Goethe nowhere gave a systematic exposition of his social thinking, the *Campagne-Belagerung* is a veiled literary statement of the results of his preoccupations with the forms of human association. Nowhere did he define a group or family; there is no precise formulation of what he meant by "Volk." Nowhere did he explicitly list the proper family principles or goals, nor did he state precisely what the qualities of a good family leader are. Nevertheless, the *Campagne-Belagerung* reveals to the perceptive eye not one but dozens of judgments on each of the sociological elements mentioned above. It is thus possible, as has been demonstrated in the foregoing chapters, to deduce Goethe's social philosophy from the work. As a piece of literature it presents truth in the symbols of poetry rather than in the definitions of a science such as sociology. This characteristic of the work should not blind one to the fact that it is essentially scientific in nature. Goethe has consciously applied scientific principles and methods to his examination of the forms of human association. The chapter on *The Family Concept an Outgrowth of Goethe's Scientific Studies* demonstrates the morphological origin of his social thinking and the rest of the present study attempts to show how Goethe applied the principles so derived to all elements of contemporary society as he found them and how he reached his conclusions. The entire *Campagne-Belagerung* from the *Zwischenrede* onward thus represents Goethe's questing journey through contemporary German society in search of a "Volk," or at least the seeds from which one could some day arise; a search that ended in bitter disappointment. Consequently Goethe deserves serious attention as a forerunner of the modern science of sociology which did not have its formal beginning until some time later.

The *Campagne-Belagerung* is a work of art in the finest sense. It has been demonstrated that the artistic unity of the two works flows from the central concept of the family as "Urform" and "Metamorphose." The preceding chapters have also shown how ruthlessly Goethe could transform, suppress, and even invent "historical" material to make it fit his artistic purposes. The two most striking examples of this, among dozens of others, are his treatment of the Igel monument and his visit to the Jacobis in Pempelfort. Dove, without realizing the full implications of his remark, has aptly summed it up by characterizing the *Campagne-Belagerung* as "Eine Poesie der Geschichte."

Finally, the *Campagne-Belagerung* is a deeply patriotic work. Due largely to the ambiguity of the few surviving statements of the older Goethe on political subjects, he has been variously accused of being a servile lackey to the princes, an immoderate admirer of Napoleon without proper German feelings, of being a cynical opportunist or an apathetic indifferentist. The *Campagne-Belagerung* shows conclusively that these accusations are at least gross distortions of the facts. Goethe was a patriotic German to the depths of his being. When aroused by the threat of the revolution to turn his attention to social matters, his whole thinking centered around Germany. He deplored the evils of the many small German states of his day with their petty intrigues and enmities, and a sense of responsibility for a future German "Volk" was always the core of his social concern. The whole *Campagne-Belagerung* can be termed a futile quest for the germs of a future "Volkheit" in Germany. Not only did he search there for such a patriotic sense of unity and cohesion, he also exerted his not inconsiderable influence with rare foresight and creative wisdom toward fostering the foundations for such a "Volk." In addition to the *Campagne-Belagerung*, all of the "Revolutionsdichtungen" show that Goethe was a dedicated soldier of the pen in his fight to help found German national life on what in his view were the only true, stable, and lasting principles: family and "Volk." His bitter disappointment at being completely misunderstood is detailed repeatedly in the work, and so it was inevitable that eventually he should have resigned himself to being ahead of his time, that in later years he should have come to practice "Entsagung" and watch the political contortions of his contemporaries with a weary sense of impotence.

In this connection it has been noted how Goethe consistently betrayed his personal feelings and beliefs by his reactions to events, people, and situations. It was the French Revolution which first impelled him to seek and attempt to apply a social principle for the main purpose of protecting his beloved Germany from that revolution. In the *Campagne-Belagerung* itself Goethe reacted to the pro-revolutionary talk of the Sömmerings and Hubers by becoming ill. At the Jacobis his disappointment showed itself by arousing sarcasm and irony to the point where, he said, he played "das böse Prinzip." In addition, he got sick there also and then fled. Flight likewise ended his visit with the "vermüffte Person" Plessing, as it also cut short his contact with "das ewig Künftige" at the Princess Gallitzin's. When, during the winter in Weimar, his "Revolutionsdichtungen" were completely misunderstood, he turned with sardonic relish to pillorying the human race in *Reineke Fuchs*, and, lastly, when Schlosser in harsh and sweeping terms denied the possibility of a "Volkheit" in Germany, "der alte Adam" was aroused in Goethe, and then he fled again. There can be no doubt of the depth of his patriotic emotions.

Goethe's apparent aloofness from German national life from the Napoleonic era onwards is thus neither indifference nor Olympian detachment, but rather the resignation of a fighter who has bloodied his head in vain battle for goals which, as he had come to understand, could only be achieved in a distant future, beyond the end of his own life-time. But this aloofness is only apparent, not real, for the writing of the *Campagne-Belagerung* after all falls in this period, in 1820-22, thus constituting evidence of Goethe's continuing sense of responsibility for the national life of his own people. That Goethe did not choose to reveal himself bluntly here, but rather veiled the record of his thinking, his actions and beliefs behind the poetic façade that one finds in the *Campagne-Belagerung* was unavoidable, for his fellow-countrymen had proved by their reception of his "Revolutionsdichtungen" that they were incapable of understanding his position, unable even to recognize, to say nothing of accepting and working toward, the goal of German "Volkheit" which he prophetically envisioned.

ANNOTATIONS

1. Chuquet, A.: *Campagne de France*, Paris, 1884. School edition of *Campagne* up to return to Trier. Introduction and notes. Also *Goethe en Champagne*, in *Études de litérature allemande*, 2. série, Paris, 1902, pp. 73-130, and untitled comment in *Revue Critique*, Paris, 1883 p. 322 ff and 1884 p. 308 ff.
2. Roethe, Gustav, *Goethes Kampagne in Frankreich, 1792*, Berlin, 1919. The numerous references to this centrally important work will be made by simply giving the name and the page number in parentheses, thus: (Roethe 212).
3. Dove, Alfred: introduction and annotations to volume 28 (*Campagne* and *Belagerung*) of *Jubiläumsausgabe* (*Goethes Sämtliche Werke*, 40 vols., Berlin and Stuttgart, 1902-1906). From here on references to this work will be given as name and page number in parentheses. Roman numeral indicates introduction, arabic, annotations, thus: (Dove xi) or (Dove 330).
4. References to the works of Goethe will use the *Jubiläumsausgabe* (J.A.), then numerals for volume and line. If line designation is used, it will be separated from page numeral by colon, thus: (J.A. v. 26, 157:19).
    References to the text of the *Campagne-Belagerung* will be to volume 28 of the *Jubiläumsausgabe*, and will consist in simple numerals separated by a colon, the first indicating page, the second line, thus: (158:14-28).
    References to *Weimar Ausgabe* will have roman numeral for part, thus: (W. A. IV v. 10, 130).
5. Never published. Roethe cited important bits from it, as did Bergemann (see bibliography). Was in the Goethe-Schiller Archiv in Weimar, where it presumably still exists, although inquiry concerning it has gone unanswered. See Roethe *op. cit.* p. 57.
6. *Gedenkausgabe der Werke, Briefe und Gespräche*, ed. Ernst Beutler, Zürich, 1949. Vol. 12 Joseph Kunz, hereinafter referred to with name and page number, thus: (Kunz 791).
7. Bergemann, Fritz, ed., vol. 18, *Goethes Werke: Festausgabe*, Leipzig, 1926.
8. Buchwald, Reinhard, *Goethe und das deutsche Schicksal*, München, 1948, p. 146.
9. For instance:
    Haecker, Valentin: *Goethes morphologische Arbeiten*, Jena, 1927.
    Hansen, A.: *Die sachlichen und philosophischen Grundlagen von Goethes Morphologie*, Giessen, 1919.
    Loesche, M.: *Goethes geistige Welt*, Stuttgart, 1948.
    Magnus, Rudolf: *Goethe as a Scientist*, N.Y. 1949.
    Trapp, Marianne: *Goethes naturphilosophische Denkweise*, Stuttgart, 1949.
    Walther, J.: *Goethe als Seher und Erforscher der Natur*, Halle, 1930.
10. Jockers, Ernst: *Morphologie und Klassik Goethes*, in *Goethe und die Wissenschaften, Vorträge gehalten anlässlich des Gelehrtenkongresses in Frankfurt a/M. im August, 1949*, Frankfurt a/M., 1951, p. 76.
11. To Kanzler von Müller, 31 Oct. 1819. Biedermann, F. von: *Goethes Gespräche ohne die Gespräche mit Eckermann*, 10 vols. Leipzig n.d., vol IV, p. 17.
12, 13, 14. See bibliography.
15. Such notes as "Das Nächste durchgedacht" appear 26 and 30 January; 10, 13, 23, and 26 February and 12 March.
16. As developed by Weniger, E.: *Goethe und die Generale*, Leipzig, 1942, p. 17 ff.
17. Dove 269. Also Coudenhoven in *Deutsche Allgemeine Biographie*, Leipzig, 1876, vol. 4, p. 533.
18. Magnus, Rudolf: *Goethe as a Scientist*, N.Y. 1949, p. 60 ff.
19. Chuquet, A.: *Campagne de France*, Paris 1884, p. 4.

20. Jockers, E.: *Morphologie und Klassik Goethes*, pp. 76-77.
21. Plates I and III and the modern interpretation of the monument are from Dragendorff and Krüger, *Das Grabmal von Igel*.
22. Jaro Springer, in *Goethe-Jahrbuch*, v. xiii, pp. 231-233, reported the existence in the Imperial Prussian collection of drawings of one by Goethe, showing an ancient monument "in dem trotz starker Abweichungen das römische Denkmal von Igel bei Trier erkannt werden muss . . . Das Denkmal ist offenbar bald darauf aus der *Errinnerung von ihm gezeichnet* worden." Later he reported that the drawing was "in der ungefähren Gestalt" of the Igel monument. Catalogue no. 3971, size 335x195mm. No reproduction or other description of the drawing is available; its present location uncertain. Springer noted that the name "Goethe" at the bottom was a later addition, thus raising doubts as to authenticity. The points of interest for this investigation of the date and how it differs from the original are treated vaguely in Springer's description.
23. Not in W.A. v. 33, but obtained by Roethe from the Goethearchiv and reprinted in his work, p. 362.
24. Dragendorff and Krüger, *op. cit.* pp. 27-28.
25. Wyttenbach, J. H.: *Strangers' Guide to the Roman Antiquities at Treves*, London, 1839. Translated by D. Turner from an unindicated, undated original, although a footnote, p. 126, refers to "my" (Wyttenbach's?) essay in the Treves Chronicle (Trierische Chronik?) for 1821, p. 44, *Einige Worte über die vorzüglichsten bildlichen Darstellungen auf dem Monument zu Igel*.
26. Quednow, C. F.: *Beschreibung der Alterthümer in Trier und dessen Umgebungen aus der gallisch-belgischen und römischen Periode*, 2 vols., Trier, 1820.
27. Quednow, C. F.: *op. cit.*, v. ii, p. 122.
28. Massenbach, C. K. A. L.: *Memoiren zur Geschichte des Preussischen Staates unter den Regierungen*, etc., 2 vols., Amsterdam, 1809, vol. 1, p. 49.
29. As quoted by Dove 276, also in Chuquet's *Campagne de France*, p. 66. The officer was a Lt. Puttkammer.
30. Mommsen, W.: *Die politischen Anschauungen Goethes*, Stuttgart, 1948, p. 96.
31. Massenbach, *op. cit.* I, p. 49.
32. Chuquet, *Campagne de France*, p. 104.
33. Chuquet, *op. cit.*, p. 118.
34. *La vie et les mémoires du général Dumouriez*, in Barrière's *Collection des mémoires relatifs à la révolution française*, Paris, 1822, v. 23, p. 322.
35. Chuquet, A.: *Revue Critique*, p. 304, f.
36. Massenbach, *op. cit.* v. 1, p. 105.
37. *Collection universelle des mémoires particuliers relatifs à l'histoire de France*, Paris, 1785. I, p. 110 f.
38. Massenbach, *op. cit.* p. 166.
39. von Müller, J.: *Attila, der Held des 5. Jahrhunderts*, Berlin, 1806 (anti-Napoleon).
40. Lauckhard, *Briefe* . . ., p. 39.
41. Lauckhard, *Briefe* . . ., p. 149 ff.
42. Lauckhard, *Leben* . . ., p. 11 ff.
43. Brion, Marcel: *Génie et destinée de Goethe*, Paris, 1949, p. 295.
44. Zeiller, Martin: *Topographia archiepiscopatum moguntinensis, trevirensis et coloniensis*, Frankfurt a/M., 1646.
45. Bode, Wilhelm: *Goethes Leben*, 9 vols., Berlin, 1922-27. Quoted Chapter VII, 191, without indication of source or date.
46. Baumgartner, A. and Stockmann, A.: *Goethe, sein Leben und seine Werke*, 2 vols., Freiburg i/B., 1911-13; vol. 2, p. 103.
47. Mommsen, W.: *Die politischen Anschauungen Goethes*, Stuttgart, 1948, p. 92.

48. Jockers, E.: *Soziale Polarität in Goethes Klassik*, Philadelphia, 1942, p. 29.
49. Jockers, *Soziale Polarität*, pp. 24, 25.
50. To Eckermann, 4 Jan., 1824. Biedermann, W.: *Goethes Gespräche*, v. V, p. 10.
51. Jockers, *Morphologie und Klassik Goethes*, pp. 78-79.
52. Chuquet, A.: *Revue Critique*, p. 308 f.
53. Anonymous: *Darstellung der Mainzer Revolution*, Mainz, 1794.

BIBLIOGRAPHY

No attempt is made here to give a complete Goethe bibliography. The works listed are the most important of those used in this study.

Angelloz, F. J.: *Goethe*, Paris, 1949.
Baumgartner, A. and Stockmann, A.: *Goethe, sein Leben und seine Werke*, 2 vols. Freiburg i/B. 1911-13.
Baumgartner, O. G.: *Goethe und der Sozialismus, Literarisches Echo*, vol. 12, p. 1012.
Bergemann, Fritz: ed., vol. 18, *Goethes Werke: Festausgabe*, Leipzig, 1926.
Biedermann, F. von: *Goethes Gespräche ohne die Gespräche mit Eckermann*, Leipzig, 10 vols., n.d.
Bock, A.: *Zur Campagne in Frankreich, Goethe-Jahrbuch*, vol. 21, 1900, p. 276.
Bode, Wilhelm: *Goethes Leben*, 9 vols., Berlin, 1922-27.
Boucke, Ewald Augustus: *Goethes Epen*, introduction to vol. 4 of the "Festausgabe" of Goethe's works, Leipzig, 1926.
Boucke, Ewald Augustus: *Goethes Weltanschauung auf historischer Grundlage*, Stuttgart, 1907.
Brion, Marcel: *Génie et destinée de Goethe*, Paris, 1949.
Buchwald, Reinhard: *Goethe und das deutsche Schicksal*, München, 1948.
Buchwald, Reinhard: *Das Vermächtnis der deutschen Klassiker*, Leipzig, 1944.
Campe, Rudolf: *Der liberale Gedanke in Goethes Weltanschauung*, Leipzig, 1931.
Chamberlain, Houston Stewart: *Goethe*, München, 1912.
Chuquet, A.: *Campagne de France*, Paris, 1884.
Chuquet, A.: *Goethe en Champagne*, in *Études de littérature allemande*, 2. série, Paris, 1902, pp. 73-130.
Chuquet, A.: Untitled comment in *Revue Critique*, Paris, 1883, p. 322 ff. and 1884, pp. 308 ff.
Cysarz, H.: *Goethe und das geschichtliche Weltbild*, in *Sieben Wesensbildnisse*, Brünn, 1943.
Danckert, Werner: *Goethe: der mythische Urgrund seiner Weltschau*, Berlin, 1951.
Darstellung der Mainzer Revolution, (anonymous), Mainz, 1794.
Dragendorff, H. und Krüger, E.: *Das Grabmal von Igel*, Trier, 1924.
Dumouriez, C. F. D.: *La vie du général Dumouriez*, 4 vol. in Barrière's *Collection des mémoires relatifs à la révolution française*, Paris, 1822, vols. 22-25.
Eck, Samuel: *Goethes Lebensanschauung*, Tübingen und Leipzig, 1902.
Fairley, Barker: *A Study of Goethe*, Oxford, 1947.
Fischer, Andreas: *Goethe und Napoleon*, Frauenfeld, 1900.
Franz, A.: *Goethe als religiöser Denker*, Tübingen, 1932.
Fuchs, Albert: *Goethe, un homme face à la vie*, Paris, 1946.
Gerhardt, Melitta: *Goethes Erleben der französischen Revolution im Spiegel der Natürlichen Tochter, Deutsche Vierteljahrsschrift*, 1923, vol. 1, p. 281.

Gespräche Goethes in den letzten Jahren seines Lebens mit Johann Peter Eckermann, ed. H. H. Houben, Leipzig, 1925.
Goethe and the Modern Age, International Goethe Bicentennial Convocation and Music Festival, ed. Bergsträsser, A., Chicago, 1950.
Goethe und die Wissenschaften, Vorträge gehalten anlässlich des Gelehrtenkongresses in Frankfurt a/M. in August, 1949, Frankfurt a/M., 1951.
Goethes Unterhaltungen mit dem Kanzler von Müller, Stuttgart, 1870.
Grabowski, Adolf: *Die Natürliche Tochter als politisches Bekenntnis*, Zeitschrift für Politik, 1933, vol. 22, p. 93.
Gräf, Hans Gerhard: *Goethe über seine Dichtungen*, 9 vols., Frankfurt a/M., 1901.
Haecker, Valentin: *Goethes morphologische Arbeiten*, Jena, 1927.
Hankamer, Paul: *Spiel der Mächte*, Tübingen, 1943.
Hansen, A.: *Die sachlichen und philosophischen Grundlagen von Goethes Morphologie*, Giessen, 1919.
Harnack, Otto: *Goethe in der Epoche seiner Vollendung*, Leipzig, 1887.
Härtel, Emmy: *Einiges aus Alexander Herzens Memoiren über Goethe*, Goethe-Jahrbuch, vol. 33, 1912, pp. 158-173.
Hartung, Fritz: *Goethe als Staatsmann*. Jahrbuch der Goethe Gesellschaft, vol. 9., 1922, pp. 297-314.
Hellersberg-Wendriner, Anna: *Soziologischer Wandel im Weltbild Goethes*, in *PMLA*, vol. LVI, June, 1941, pp. 447-465.
Hettner, Hermann: *Goethe und der Sozialismus*, Deutsche Literaturzeitung, 1884, #36.
Hildebrandt, Kurt: *Goethe, seine Weisheit im Gesamtwerk*, Leipzig, 1942.
Huffer, H.: *Zu Goethes Campagne in Frankreich*, Goethe-Jahrbuch, vol. 4, 1883, pp. 79-106.
Jalouz, E.: *Goethe*, Paris, 1949.
Jockers, Ernst: *Morphologie und Klassik Goethes*, in *Goethe und die Wissenschaften*, Vorträge gehalten anlässlich des Gelehrtenkongresses in Frankfurt a/M. in August, 1949, Frankfurt a/M., 1951.
Jockers, Ernst: *Soziale Polarität in Goethes Klassik*, Philadelphia, 1942.
Joinville, Sire de: *Mémoires*, in *Collection universelle des Memoires particuliers relatifs à l'histoire de France*, Paris, 1785.
Keferstein, G.: *Goethes Verhältnis zur Politik*, Deutsche Vierteljahrsschrift für Literatur- und Geistesgeschichte, vol. 15.
Klassen, Peter: *Justus Möser*, Frankfurt a/M., 1936.
Korff, August Hermann: *Geist der Goethezeit*, 3 vols., Leipzig, 1923-40.
Korff, H. R.: *Goethe. Zur Betrachtung über sein Verhältnis zu Freiheit und Gesetz*, Zeitschrift für Deutschkunde vol. 46, 1932, pp. 129-67.
Kosegarten, W.: *Goethes politische Anschauung und Richtung*, Goethe-Jahrbuch, vol. 7, 1886, p. 115.
Knickenberger, Fritz: *Zu Goethes Aufsatz: 'Das altrömische Denkmal bei Igel,'* Goethe-Jahrbuch, vol. 26, 1905, pp. 93-98.
Kramer, U.: *Unbekanntes aus Goethes politischer Tätigkeit*, Euphorion, vol. 33, p. 299.
Lauckhard, C. F.: *Briefe eines preussischen Augenzeugen über den Feldzug des Herzogs von Braunschweig gegen die Neufranken im Jahre 1792*, Hamburg, 1793.

Lauckhard, C. F.: *Magister C. F. Lauckhards Leben und Schicksale, von ihm selbst beschrieben,* in Petersens *Memoirenbibliothek,* Series II, vol. 15, Stuttgart, n.d.
van der Leeuw, Gerardus: *Goethe and the Crisis of Civilization,* in *Goethe and the Modern Age,* ed. Bergsträsser, A., Chicago, 1950.
Loerke, O.: *Goethes Kampagne in Frankreich, Die neue Rundschau* Berlin, 1940, pp. 123-126.
Loesche, Martin: *Goethes geistige Welt,* Stuttgart, 1948.
Loiseau, H.: *L'évolution morale du Goethe,* Paris, 1911.
Magnus, Rudolf: *Goethe as a Scientist,* N.Y. 1949.
Mann, Thomas: *Goethe als Repräsentant des bürgerlichen Zeitalters,* Berlin, 1932.
Mann, Thomas: *Goethe und die Demokratie, Die neue Rundschau,* Berlin, 1949, Heft, 15, pp. 295-318.
Massenbach, C. K. A. L.: *Memoiren zur Geschichte des preussischen Staates unter den Regierungen Friedrich Wilhelm II und Friedrich Wilhelm III,* 2 vols., Amsterdam, 1809.
Meinecke, Friedrich: *Entstehung des Historismus,* 2 vols., Berlin and München, 1836.
Meinecke, Friedrich: *Weltbürgertum und Nationalstaat,* München und Berlin, 1928.
Meyer, Eva Alexander: *Politische Symbolik bei Goethe,* Heidelberg, 1949.
Meyer, Hans Heinrich: *Kleine Schriften zur Kunst von Heinrich Meyer,* Heilbronn, 1886.
Meyer, Heinrich: *Goethe. Das Leben im Werk,* Hamburg, 1949.
Meyer, Richard Moritz: *Goethe,* Berlin, 1905.
Mézières, A.: *L'invasion prussienne en 1792-1870. Goethe et les Allemands d'aujourdhui. Goethe au siège de Mayence. Revue des deux mondes,* 1871, 1 and 12 January.
Mommsen, Wilhelm: *Die politischen Anschauungen Goethes,* Stuttgart, 1948.
Müllensiefern, Paul: *Die französische Revolution und Napoleon in Goethes Weltanschauung. Jahrbuch der Goethe Gesellschaft,* vol. 16, 1930, pp. 73-108.
Müller, Georg: *Goethe und die deutsche Gegenwart,* Gütersloh, 1946.
Müller, Günther: *Kleine Goethe Biographie,* 2nd ed. Bonn, 1948.
Müller, J. von: *Attila, der Held des 5. Jahrhunderts,* Berlin, 1806.
Originalbriefwechsel der Emigrierten. I. Theil, aus dem Französischen übersetzt, Frankfurt und Leipzig, 1793.
Peters, Ilse: *Das Napoleonbild Goethes in seiner Spätzeit, Goethe,* vol. 9, 1943, pp. 140, 171.
Pollack, V.: *Zur Belagerung von Mainz, Goethe-Jahrbuch,* vol. 19, 1898, pp. 261 f.
Quednow, Carl Friedrich: *Beschreibung der Alterthümer in Trier und dessen Umgebungen aus der gallisch-belgischen und römischen Periode,* Trier, 1820.
Raabe, August: *Der Begriff des Ungeheuren in den 'Unterhaltungen Deutscher Ausgewanderten.' Goethe,* vol. 4, 1939, p. 23 f.
Reitz, Gertrud: *Die Gestalt des Mittlers in Goethes Dichtungen,* Frankfurt a/M., 1932.

Resch, Johannes: *Goethe, Vermächtnis und Aufruf*, Berlin, 1949.
Richter, W.: *Goethe und der Staat*, Jena, 1932.
Roethe, Gustav: *Goethes Kampagne in Frankreich, 1792*, Berlin, 1919.
Ruland, C.: zu "*Goethe als Politiker*," *Goethe-Jahrbuch*. vol. 15, 1894, p. 276.
Schaber, Will: *Goethe und das Soziale*, in *Goethe, On Human Creativeness*, University of Georgia Press, 1950.
Schaginjan, M.: *Goethe*, Berlin, 1952.
Schmidt, Richard: *Politischer Lehrgehalt in Goethes Lebenswerk*, *Zeitschrift für Politik*, vol. 22, 1933, p. 85.
Schröer, K. J.: *Goethes Stellung zur Politik, zur Nation und zur Gegenwart*, *Chronik des Wiener Goethe-Vereins*, vol. 4, pp. 41,47,53.
Spielhagen, F.: *Die epische Piesie und Goethe*, *Goethe-Jahrbuch*, vol. 16, 1895, Anhang, pp. 1-29.
Schultz, Franz: *Klassik und Romantik der Deutschen*, 2 vols., 2nd. ed., Stuttgart, 1952.
Schweizer, Albert: *Goethe, Four Studies*, Boston, 1949.
Sethur, Fr.: *Goethe und die Politik*, *PMLA*, vols. 51/52, 1937/38.
Spohr, Wilhelm: *Goethe, sein Leben und Wirken*, Berlin, 1949.
Springer, Jaro: *Goethe's Handzeichnungen im K. Kupferstichkabinet in Berlin*, *Goethe-Jahrbuch*, vol. 13, 1892, pp. 231 ff.
Srbik, M. von: *Goethe und das Reich*, *Goethe*, vol. 4, 1939, pp. 211-232.
Strecker, Reinhard: *Religion und Politik bei Goethe*, Giessen, 1908.
Suphan, B., ed.: *Gedanken Goethes über Freiheit und Gleichheit*, *Goethe-Jahrbuch*, vol. 22, 1901.
Trapp, Marianne: *Goethes naturphilosophische Denkweise*, Stuttgart, 1949.
Dem Tüchtigen ist diese Welt nicht stumm. Beiträge zum Goethebild, Preisker, H., Vincent, E., etc., Jena, 1949.
Vermeil, Edmond: *Revolutionäre Hintergründe in Goethes Faust II*, in *Spiegelungen Goethes in unserer Zeit*, Wiesbaden, 1949.
Viëtor, Karl: *Goethe — Dichtung, Wissenschaft, Weltbild*, Bern, 1949.
Wais, Kurt: *Goethe und Frankreich*, *Deutsche Vierteljahrsschrift für Literatur- und Geisteswissenschaft*, vol. 23, 1949, pp. 472-500.
Weniger, E.: *Goethe und die Generale*, Leipzig, 1942.
Willige, W.: *Verantwortung und Gemeinschaftsgesinnung in Goethes Mannesjahren*, *Zeitschrift für Deutschkunde*, Leipzig, vol. 49, 1933, pp. 111-119.
Witkop, Philipp: *Goethe, Leben und Werk*, Stuttgart, 1931.
Witkowski, G.: *Das Leben Goethes*, Berlin, 1932.
Witkowski, G.: *Goethe*, Leipzig, 1899.
Wittich, W.: *Goethe et la guerre*, in *Goethe, Études publiées pour le centenaire de sa mort par l'université de Strasbourg*, Strasbourg, 1932.
Wolff, Hans M.: *Goethes Weg zur Humanität*, Bern, 1951.
Wundt, Max: *Goethes Wilhelm Meister und die Entwicklung des modernen Lebensideals*, Berlin, 2nd ed., 1932.
Wyttenbach, J. H.: *Stranger's Guide to Roman Antiquities at Treves*, London, Trans. D. Turner, 1839.
Zeiller, Martin: *Topographia archiepiscopatum moguntinensis, trevirensis et coloniensis*, Frankfurt a/M, M. Merian, 1646.

INDEX

A.
Aisne (river), 77.
Alexander I of Russia, 23.
American Revolution, 37, 39.
Amor, 122.
Anna Amalia, 29, 46, 68, 79, 90f.
Arlon, 49, 81ff., 86.
"Assignats," 33, 34, 40, 62, 81f.
Attila anecdote, 93f.
Augustus, Emperor, 51, 52, 53.
Austria, 22, 38, 39, 40, 76, 149, 165.

B.
Babo, Joseph Marius, 129.
"Baumannshöhle," 115, 116f., 125.
Baumgartner, A., & Stockmann, A. (see bibliog.), 123.
Beaurepaire, Nicole Joseph, 64ff.
Beck, Joseph Christoph, 133.
Bellomo, 128.
Bergemann, Fritz (see bibliog.), 7.
Berry, Charles Ferdinand, Duc de, 24.
Böhmer (later: Schlegel), Caroline, 36.
Böttiger, Karl August, 63.
Bouillée, François Claude Amour, Marquis de, 67.
Breteuil, Louis Auguste le Tonnelier, Baron de, 80, 83f.
Brion, Marcel (see bibliog.), 97.
Brunswick, Karl Wilhelm Ferdinand, Duke of, 25, 29, 49, 58, 59ff., 72f., 76-80.
    Manifestos of (1. Marquis de Limon; 2. Comte Moustier), 62f., 76-80, 93.
Buchwald, Reinhard (see bibliog.), 7.

C.
Caligula, Emperor, 51.
Carved gem collection, 4, 92f., 120f., 128, 130-131.
Cassel, 126f., 152.
Catholicism, 120-125.
Chantilly, 33.
Chuquet, Artur (see bibliog.), 2, 74, 93, 149.
Coblenz, 79, 82, 88-94.
Color experiments, 4, 10, 17, 131ff.
Condé, Louis Joseph, Prince de, 33.
Constantine, Emperor, 51.
Corsican Revolt, 37, 39.
Coudenhoven, Sophie, Freifrau von, 32, 108f.

D.
Darmstadt, Ludwix X, Landgraf von, 148.
Diderot, Denis, 105.
Delph, Helene Dorothea, Demoiselle, 160.
Dove, Alfred (see bibliog.), 2, 3-4, 42, 54, 57, 72, 92, 99, 111, 114ff., 127f., 130, 167.
Dragendorff, H., & Krüger E. (see bibliog.), 50ff.
Duisburg, 26, 113-118, 153, 161.
Dumouriez, Charles François, 24, 77, 92f., 131.
Düsseldorf, 10, 36, 111.

E.
Eckermann, J. P., 140.
Emigrés, 25, 34, 38, 40, 41, 62, 66-69, 80-83, 85, 86, 93, 108f., 113, 119, 126ff., 143, 157, 165.
Etain, 49, 85f.
Euler, Leonhard, 160.

F.
Family concept, 9-20, and *passim*.
Fischer, Franz (actor), 128.
Fischer, Johann Karl (Gehler, Johann Samuel Traugott), *Physikalisches Lexikon*, 78.
Florian, Jean Pierre Claris de, 133.
Forster, Georg, 9, 34, 36.
Frankfurt a/M., 31, 88ff., 90, 98, 108f., 146, 150, 158.
"Frankfurter Graduierten," 90f.
French Assembly, 74.
    Convention, 74, 77.
French grenadier, 64f.
French Revolution, 3, 5, 6, 12, 19, 21, 22, 30, 31, 35, 37f., 65, 80f., 83, 90f., 94, 98, 103, 104f., 107, 132-145, 165f.
Fritsch, Leutnant Ludwig von, 48.
Fürstenberg, Franz Friedrich Wilhelm, Freiherr von, 119ff.

G.
Gallitzin, Amalie, Fürstin von, 2, 9, 27, 36, 119-125, 130, 168.
Glorieux, 59, 67.
Goethe, Katharina Elisabeth, Frau Rat, 31, 34, 48, 146.
    Letter from, 88-90, 94.
Goethe, Johann Wolfgang von, *passim*.
    Relatives: Textor, Johann Jost (uncle), 88.
    Textor, Johann Wolfgang, Schultheiss (grandfather), 88.
    Works:
      Annalen, 23, 36.
      Die Aufgeregten, 134, 139ff.
      Belagerung von Mainz, *passim*.
        Lücke, 152-155.
      Der Bürgergeneral, 133ff., 142, 163.
      Campagne in Frankreich, *passim*.
      Dichtung und Wahrheit, 1, 112.
      Einfache Nachahmung der Natur, Manier, Stil (1789), 18, 30.
      Faust II, 33.
      Geschichte meines botanischen Studiums, 17, 30, 95.
        Verfolg, 17, 30, 95.
      Götz von Berlichingen, 132.
      Der Gross-Kophta, 105, 132-133, 142.
      Harzreise im Winter, 115f.
      Hermann und Dorothea, 20, 118, 134, 138, 140-142.
      Iphigenia, 103, 105, 124, 132.
      Das Mädchen von Oberkirch, 142.

INDEX

Die natürliche Tochter, 20, 131.
Prometheus, 24.
Reineke Fuchs, 134, 148, 155, 162, 168.
Reise der Söhne Megaprazons, 103, 105.
Revolutionsdichtung(en), 104, 128, 132-142, 162, 163, 168.
Die Römischen Elegien, 101.
Das Römische Karneval, 18, 19, 30, 95, 124.
Tages- und Jahreshefte, 1821, 29.
Über die Gesetze der Organisation überhaupt, 17.
Unterhaltungen Deutscher Ausgewanderten, 134-139, 142.
Das Märchen, 137f., 142f.
Venetianische Epigramme, 30, 101.
Versuch, die Metamorphose der Pflanzen zu erklären, 13f., 106.
Versuch einer allgemeinen Vergleichungslehre, 12, 15.
Versuch über die Gestalt der Tiere, 12
Von den Vorteilen der vergleichenden Anatomie, 16.
Die Wahlverwandtschaften, 142.
Werther, 113, 118.
Wilhelm Meister, 20, 142.
  Lehrjahre, 127f., 135.
  Theatralische Sendung, 124.
  Wanderjahre, 5.
Götze, Paul, 31, 41, 49, 69, 93, 133.
Gore, Charles, 152, 155, 157.
Gozzi, Carlo, Count, 130.
Gräf, Hans Gerhard, 9.
Grevenmachern, 42, 43, 48, 66, 69.
Grimm, Friedrich Melchior, Baron von, 109.

H.

Hagemann, Friedrich Gustav, 129.
Hagemeister, Johann Gottlob Lukas, 129.
Hamann, Johann Georg, 119.
Harz, 115f.
Heidelberg, 10, 37, 160-164.
Hemsterhuis, Franz, 105, 119ff.
Herder, Johann Gottfried, 11, 80, 90, 155.
Huber, Ferdinand, 34ff., 118, 168.
Humboldt, Alexander von, & Wilhelm, Freiherr von, 16.
Hubertusburger Frieden, 37.

I.

Iffland, August Wilhelm, 129.
Igel Monument, 7, 42-57, 89, 90, 127, 167.
Ilmenau, 114.
Intermaxillary bone, 11, 12, 125.
Italy, 6, 13, 17, 18, 30, 35, 52, 53, 95, 101, 106, 107, 124, 132.

J.

Jacobi, Friedrich Heinrich, 2, 6, 9, 27, 31, 36, 54, 97f., 103-112, 117, 119f., 121, 123f., 151, 155, 157, 160, 162, 167, 168.
Jena, University of, 23.
Jenaische Allgemeine Literatur-Zeitung, 131.

Jockers, Ernst (*see* bibliog.), 19, 47, 129, 142-143.
Joinville, Jean, Sieur de, 93.

K.

Kalckreuth, General Friedrich Adolf, Graf von, 147.
Kant, Immanuel, *Kritik der Urteilskraft*, 97.
Karl August, Duke of Sachsen-Weimar, 22, 29, 30, 31, 32, 48, 59, 72f., 88, 89, 94, 144, 148, 163.
Karlsbad, 23.
Kaufmann, Angelica, 52.
Kellermann, François Christophe, General, 25.
Knebel, Karl Ludwig von, 73, 155.
Körner, Christoph Gottfried, 35, 111.
Kotzebue, August von, 23, 129.
Kraus, Georg Melchior, Rat, 152, 155.
Kunz, Joseph, 6f.

L.

Lafayette, Marie Joseph de Motier, Marquis de, 107.
Lauckhard, C. F. (*see* bibliog.), 24, 65, 93f.
Lavater, Johann Kaspar, 11, 113f., 123, 160.
Liseur, 49, 81f., 85.
Loder, Justus Christian, Professor, 11.
Longwy, 25, 48, 58, 67, 69.
Louis XVI, 62, 74, 77, 144.
Lucchesini, Girolamo, Marchese de, 88.
Lux, Adam, 35.
Luxembourg, 42, 80, 81, 88-94.

M.

Magnus, Rudolf (*see* bibliog.), 34.
Mainz, 10, 28, 32, 37, 40, 66, 74, 90, 96, 108, 109, 112, 113, 134f., 144, 146-155, 160.
Malkomi, Pius Alexander (Wolff), 129, 133.
Mann, Thomas, 110.
Mannheim, 160-174.
Marienborn, 140f., 155.
Marseilles, 156.
Massenbach, C. K. A. L. (*see* bibliog.), 59, 73, 93.
Massiges, 58.
Massmann, Hans Ferdinand, 22.
Mecklenburg, Luise & Friederike, Princesses of, 149.
Merrem, Blasius, 10, 117.
Metternich, Clemens Wenzel Lothar, Fürst von, 22, 23.
Meulen, Adam Franz van der, 62.
Meyer, Heinrich, 23, 90, 92, 127, 131, 155.
Mirabeau, Honoré Gabriel de Riqueti, Comte de, 107.
Mommsen, Wilhelm (*see* bibliog.), 73.
Monaco, Catharina, Princess of, 33.
"Moniteur," *Journal Officiel ou Moniteur Universelle*, 93.
Mosel (river), 27, 42, 82, 91.
Mozart, Wolfgang Amadeus, 130.
Müller, Kanzler Friedrich von, 23.

Münster, 2, 6, 27, 36, 96, 111, 119-125, 153, 160, 161.

N.
Napoleon I, 143, 165, 167, 168.
Newton, Sir Isaac, 106, 131, 160.
Nordhausen, 115.

O.
Originalbriefwechsel der Emigrierten, 25.
Oedipus Coloneus (Sophocles), 103.

P.
Duc d'Orleans (Philip Egalité), 33.
Padua, 13.
Paris, 70, 72, 74f., 83, 85, 93, 140.
Pars, William, 55f.
de Pauw, Cornelius 105.
Pempelfort, 2, 4, 6, 26, 96ff., 103-112, 119, 121, 122, 125, 134, 153, 161f., 168.
Physiognomy, *see* Lavater.
Pillon, 62.
Plessing, Friedrich, 2, 97, 113-118, 121, 125, 160, 168.
Poland, Partition of, 37f., 39, 73.
Potocki, Stanislaus Kostka, 35.
Prussia, 22, 23, 29, 31, 32, 37ff., 64, 73, 165.
  Prussian Army, 49, 58ff., 67, 72f., 74, 76-87, 91, 96, 146-155.
  Prussian King Friedrich Wilhelm II, 49, 59f., 67, 72, 109, 148f., 160.
  Prussian King Frederick the Great, 75.
  Prussian Princes, 149.

Q.
Quednow, Carl Friedrich (*see bibliog.*), 54f.

R.
Rabelais, François, 103.
Regret, 59, 67.
Reiffenstein, Johann Friedrich, 52.
Reuss-Greiz, Heinrich XIV, Prinz von, 9, 96, 112, 118, 123.
Rhine (river), 98f., 107, 144.
Riemer, Friedrich Wilhelm, 26.
von Rietz (Geheimkämmerer Ritz von Preussen), 160.
Roethe, Gustav (*see* bibliog), *passim*.
Rousseau, Jean-Jacques, 105, 119.
Rubens, Peter Paul, 107.

S.
Saar (river), 42.
Sachsen-Weimar, 22, 31, 49.
St. Louis anecdote, 89, 93.
Samogneux, 63.
Sand, Carl, 23.
Schiller, Friedrich, 130.
Schlegel (formerly Böhmer, née Michaelis), Caroline, 36.
Schlosser (Goethes' brother-in-law), 10, 37, 160-164.
Schnaps (dramatic character), 133.

Schönfeld, General von, 147.
Schröder, Friedrich Ludwig, 129.
Schulz, Franz (*see* bibliog.), 142.
Shakespeare, 130.
Sicily, 13.
Silesian Campaign (1790), 17, 101.
Sivry, 49, 82, 83ff., 87, 106, 120.
Somme-Tourbe, 61.
Sömmering, Samuel Thomas, 9, 34f., 36, 95, 97, 109, 112, 118, 162, 167.
Spincourt, 49, 85.
Spinoza, Baruch de, 10.
Stein, Freiherr Johann vom, 32, 148.
Stein, Frau Charlotte von, 79.
Stolberg, Sophie Gräfin von, 111.
Storck, Professor, 55.
Strassburg, 11.

T.
Tischbein, Johann Heinrich Wilhelm, 52.
Tourbe (river), 61.
Trarbach, 92.
Trier, 9, 26, 40, 41f., 43, 45, 52, 81f., 88-94, 96f.

U.
"Urpflanze," 13, 125.

V.
Valmy, 2, 43, 45, 70, 72-75, 76, 83.
"Valmyspruch," 72ff., 93, 147.
Venice, 68.
Venus Urania, 122.
Verdun, 48, 60, 64f., 66, 69, 82f., 86, 113.
Voigt, Johann Karl Wilhelm, 155.
Voltaire, François Marie Arouet, 105.
Voss' *Luise*, 124.
Vulpius, Christiane, 31, 33, 90f., 101, 111, 145.

W.
Wagner, J. C. ("Kämmerier"), 5, 25, 42, 51, 52, 54, 92f., 146.
Wall, Anton, *Stammbaum*, 133.
Wartburg Festival, 1817, 22.
Weimar, 2, 30, 46, 47, 90, 114, 123, 132, 143, 146.
  Weimar Regiment, 70, 74, 76, 91, 94, 146.
  "Weimarische Kunstfreunde," 127f., 129-131.
  Winter in Weimar, 2, 4, 6, 10, 27, 126-145, 168.
Weisenau, 150.
Wernigerode, 116.
Winckelmann, Johann Joachim, 52.
Wyttenbach, Johann Hugo, 9, 53f., 96f., 112, 118, 123.

Z.
Zeiller, Martin (Zeiller-Merian, *see* bibliog.), 98.
Zelter, Karl Friedrich, 24, 28.
Zumpft, H., 56.

www.ingramcontent.com/pod-product-compliance
Lightning Source LLC
Chambersburg PA
CBHW031313150426
43191CB00005B/210